# EDUCATIONAL MANAGEMENT: REDEFINING THEORY, POLICY AND PRACTICE

# Educational Management: Redefining Theory, Policy and Practice

*edited by*

Tony Bush, Les Bell, Ray Bolam, Ron Glatter
and Peter Ribbins

**Published in association with The Standing Conference
for Research in Educational Leadership and Management**

**P·C·P**

**Paul Chapman
Publishing Ltd**

Paul Chapman Publishing Ltd
A SAGE Publications Company
6 Bonhill Street
London EC2A 4PU

SAGE Publications Inc
2455 Teller Road
Thousand Oaks, California 91320

SAGE Publications India Pvt Ltd
32, M-Block Market
Greater Kailash-I
New Delhi 110 048

**British Library Cataloguing in Publication data**
A catalogue record for this book is available from the British Library

ISBN 0 7619 6554 8
ISBN 0 7619 6555 6 (pbk)

**Library of Congress catalog card number available**

Typeset by Anneset, Weston-super-Mare, Somerset
Printed and bound in Great Britain

A B C D E F G H   9

# Contents

# Preface

This book is one of the major outcomes of the Seminar Series funded by the Economic and Social Research Council (ESRC) from 1997 to 1999. The Series proposal arose from discussions between two of the editors (Tony Bush and Ray Bolam) about the need for a review of the academic discipline of educational management in the light of the significant changes in policy and practice during the 1980s and 1990s. The aim of the Series was to redefine the subject to take account of the many developments in policy, practice, theory and research since educational management first became established in the United Kingdom in the 1970s.

This aim was pursued through academic papers and discussion at four two-day seminars as follows:

- June 1997 in Leicester
- October 1997 in Cardiff
- June 1998 in Milton Keynes
- October 1998 in Liverpool.

A group of leading UK academics and commentators was identified who provided continuity between meetings by attending all or most seminars. These core members were:

| | | |
|---|---|---|
| Les Bell | Ray Bolam | Mike Bottery |
| Tony Bush | Brent Davies | Bob Doe |
| John Fitz | Ron Glatter | Helen Gunter |
| Valerie Hall | Rosalind Levačić | Alex McEwen |
| Agnes McMahon | Janet Ouston | Peter Ribbins |
| Kathryn Riley | Tim Simkins | Geoff Southworth |
| Mike Wallace | Dick Weindling | |

Most of these core participants contributed papers for one or more seminars. At each seminar, local academics and practitioners augmented the core group and many of these also presented papers. A total of 44 papers was delivered at the four seminars and 17 of the best appear as chapters in this volume. Eight papers also appear in the special edition of *Educational Management and Administration* (Vol. 27, No. 3) which is another major outcome of the Series.

The main themes emerging from the Series relate closely to many of the policy issues being debated in England and Wales and elsewhere:

- Has self-management achieved the success predicted for it?
- What should be the nature of professional development for educational leaders?
- How, and to what extent, can education benefit by drawing from practice in business and industry?
- What is the value of theory in informing management practice in education?
- How can research contribute to educational improvement?
- In what ways can leaders help to improve classroom practice?

These issues are all addressed in this volume by experienced academics and practitioners who provide thoughtful comments, often based on empirical research, about the current status of educational management as an academic subject as well as about these wider themes.

The third major outcome of the Seminar Series was the establishment of a new body to enhance the profile of research in educational management and leadership. The Standing Conference for Research in Educational Leadership and Management (SCRELM) was setup in May 1999 at an inaugural seminar in Birmingham. All the core members of the ESRC Series were invited to provide continuity while several other leading academics also took part in the Birmingham seminar. The initial co-ordinating group for SCRELM comprises three of the ESRC co-ordinators and four additional members. The full Group is:

| | | |
|---|---|---|
| Les Bell | Ray Bolam | Jack Lumby |
| Janet Ouston | Peter Ribbins | Tim Simkins |
| Geoff Southworth | | |

This volume is published in association with SCRELM.

The editors are grateful to all the contributors to this volume, and to the other participants in the Series, for their wisdom, commitment and friendship during and between the four seminars. We are also indebted to the administrators in the four universities which hosted the seminars. Finally, we wish to express our appreciation to Joyce Palmer of Leicester University who managed the production of the manuscript to a very tight deadline while maintaining a sense of humour.

*Tony Bush,*
*Les Bell,*
*Ray Bolam,*
*Ron Glatter,*
*Peter Ribbins*
*June 1999*

# 1

## Introduction: Setting the Scene

### TONY BUSH

### THE GENESIS OF THIS VOLUME

This book is one of the major outcomes of the Seminar Series funded by the Economic and Social Research Council (ESRC) from 1997 to 1999 (R45126449596). The other main publishing venture arising from the Series is a special edition (Vol. 27, No. 3) of *Educational Management and Administration*, the leading UK-based journal in this field. The Series proposal arose from discussions between two of the editors (Tony Bush and Ray Bolam) about the need for a review of the academic discipline of educational management in the light of the momentous changes in policy and practice during the 1980s and 1990s. The main policy developments affecting England and Wales were as follows:

1. The implementation of the **1988 Education Reform Act** which located significant management responsibilities with principals, senior staff and governing bodies of self-managing schools and colleges.
2. The introduction of the **OFSTED inspection regime** for schools, and similar arrangements for further and higher education, which explicitly assess the quality of institutional leadership and management.
3. The *Teacher Training Agency's* (TTA's) agenda for competence based training of senior and middle managers in schools, including the Headlamp programme for new headteachers and the National Professional Qualification for Headship, introduced throughout England and Wales in 1997.

These developments were matched by similar initiatives in many other countries. The shift to self-management is an international development (Caldwell and Spinks, 1992), involving Australia, Hong Kong, New Zealand, the United Kingdom and the United States, among others, although the extent and nature of autonomy varies according to local needs and traditions. The motivation for decentralisation is the belief that professionals and lay governors within schools and colleges are more likely to be able to assess the specific needs of their students and pupils, and to deliver high quality programmes to meet those needs, than politicians and officials in national, regional or local government, however well intentioned.

The enhanced autonomy enjoyed (?) by school and college leaders has been matched by an increased emphasis on accountability; freedom has its price. Governments were prepared to allow greater discretion over the management of schools but the inspection regime has been used to ensure adherence to national norms. Autonomy relates much more to how reform should be implemented than to the nature of that reform which, in practice, has been largely determined by the centre.

These policy issues have been accompanied by important academic and theoretical developments. The main themes addressed by the Seminar Series were as follows:

1. The rapid growth of the academic subject of educational management which is often the most significant course in education departments, in terms of numbers of students following masters' or other postgraduate programmes. This growth led to questions about the nature of the subject and the extent to which there is a clear epistemological underpinning for the discipline.

   There are differences of view about whether educational management should be regarded as a 'field' or a 'discipline'. Bolam (in Chapter 15) argues that it is a field of study 'which draws upon several forms of knowledge and a range of disciplines' (p. 194). The alternative view, supported by the present author (Bush, 1995), is that educational management is an applied discipline, drawing on longer established disciplines but with its own body of knowledge.
2. The related issue of the nature of educational management theory. There is no single widely-accepted theory of educational management; rather the discipline is characterised by conceptual pluralism. Bureaucracy was the dominant model in the 1960s but it has been increasingly challenged by new theories (micropolitics, subjective models, ambiguity, organisational culture and collegiality) during the 1970s, 1980s and 1990s.
3. The lack of clarity about the nature of the relationship between general management theory and practice, and management specific to the educational context. The TTA, for example, urges the use of best practice inside and outside education in training and developing headteachers.

The aim of the Seminar Series was to redefine the discipline of educational management in the light of the seismic changes in practice during the 1990s. The specific objectives were:

1. To assess the impact of the 1988 Education Reform Act, and other subsequent, major policy initiatives, on the management role of headteachers, principals and senior management teams in schools and colleges.
2. To consider the implications of recent national changes in the training of headteachers, particularly the TTA initiatives, for headteachers' training and learning.
3. To develop a forum for the exchange of views of leading academics, policy-

makers and practitioners about the discipline of educational management in the changing policy climate of the late 1990s.

4. To clarify and redefine educational management theory and assess its applicability to self-managing schools and colleges.
5. To assess and redefine the contribution of general management theory to practice in educational contexts.
6. To review recent research in educational management and to consider priorities for any future programmes of research in this field.

Most of these issues are addressed in subsequent chapters of this volume.

## THE ORIGINS AND GROWTH OF EDUCATIONAL MANAGEMENT

Educational management is a relatively new academic discipline in the United Kingdom. The first specialist courses were offered at the University of London Institute of Education in the 1960s. Chairs were established at the Open and Birmingham universities in the 1970s. George Baron, Ron Glatter and Meredydd Hughes, who briefly held chairs at the same time in the late 1970s, may be fairly regarded as the founders of the subject in the UK.

The first educational management courses were characterised by a heavy reliance on concepts and practice derived from industrial settings and from the United States, where programmes (in educational administration) had developed strongly in the 1950s and 1960s. This approach was very much that of a fledgling subject seeking to justify its place in the academic world.

During the 1970s and 1980s there was a parallel growth in the discipline in Europe and the Commonwealth. The Commonwealth Council for Educational Administration, now the Commonwealth Council for Educational Administration and Management (CCEAM), was founded in 1970 and now has some 40 countries as affiliates. The European Forum on Educational Administration (EFEA) was established in 1976 and now has 20 members. It is increasingly evident that, despite significant contextual differences, many of the issues facing the subject in Britain are also apparent in other countries.

Educational management as a field of study and practice was derived from management principles first applied to industry and commerce, mainly in the United States, as noted earlier. The former infant prodigy has progressed from being dependent upon ideas developed in other settings to become an established discipline with its own theories and some empirical data to test their validity in education. This transition has been accompanied by lively argument about the extent to which education should be regarded as simply another field for the application of general principles of management or be seen as a separate discipline with its own body of knowledge.

The debate about the most appropriate relationship between general management and that specific to education has been rekindled since 1995 with the Teacher Training Agency's (TTA's) clear emphasis on the need to take account of 'best practice outside education' in devising professional development programmes for headteachers. This stance is partly driven by political imperatives; satisfying the ideologically-driven view that the private sector has much to teach, and little to learn, from education. However, it also rests on the valid assumption that management in education should be able to benefit from good practice wherever it occurs.

The TTA's focus on leadership and management outside education has been further emphasised by the design of the training programme for serving headteachers (TTA, 1998). The training includes a business mentor scheme where heads are paired with leaders from industry and commerce. The latter are expected to help heads to improve in the following aspects of management:

- strategic development, action planning and performance measurement;
- financial budgeting and expenditure;
- leadership;
- human resource management, including recruitment and professional development; and
- institutional and cultural change, marketing and public relations (TTA, 1998).

The focus on business mentoring, and the wider emphasis on drawing on good practice from the private sector, is puzzling because it is evident that the core issue of managing learning and teaching is specifically educational and cannot be derived from business.


## SCHOOLS AND SELF-MANAGEMENT

The Education Reform Act has transformed the context within which educational leaders have to operate and its main features remain intact more than a decade later. While there has been significant centralisation, there is also greater scope for schools and colleges to determine their own policies within that national framework.

The research on self-management in England and Wales (Bush *et al.*, 1993; Levačić, 1995; Thomas and Martin, 1996) largely supports the hypothesis that the (partial) shift towards school autonomy has been beneficial. These UK perspectives are consistent with much of the international evidence on self-management. An OECD synthesis of studies in nine countries gives a cautious welcome to self-management and concludes that it is likely to be beneficial:

> Greater autonomy in schools ... [leads] to greater effectiveness through greater flexibility in and therefore better use of resources; to professional development selected at school level; to more knowledgeable teachers and parents, so to better financial decisions; to whole school planning and implementation with priorities set

on the basis of data about student [outcomes] and needs.

(Quoted in Thomas and Martin 1996, 28)

Despite the widespread support for self-management, and the research evidence suggesting that it is welcomed in schools, there are sceptics who argue that it is a way of deflecting criticism from governments for policies emanating from the centre but implemented, in their detail, by school governors and managers (Ball, 1994; Smyth, 1996).

Ball (1994, p.78) argues that the presence of the National Curriculum means that there is no real autonomy. 'Self-management is a mechanism for delivering reform rather than a vehicle for institutional initiative and innovation.' Ball expresses concern about the changes in the working conditions of staff and concludes with a stinging attack on 'the textual apologists of self-management. . . .' These texts are firmly imbricated in the construction of new forms of control. (Ball, 1994, p.83).

The first section of this volume, edited by Ron Glatter, provides further significant evidence relevant to this debate. Chapter 2, by Rosalind Levačić, Derek Glover, Nigel Bennett and Megan Crawford, points out that decentralisation to school leaders is based on a rational-technicist model. Heads are expected to adopt rational approaches to budgeting and development planning, for example, and this is reinforced by OFSTED's inspection criteria and by the TTA's National Standards for headteachers. However, the authors point to 'the tension between the rhetoric of rationality and the reality of practice' (p. 26) in their case study schools, which were sometimes effective without rational planning.

The third chapter, by Peter Karstanje, illustrates the international dimension of self-management in two ways. The author is based in Amsterdam and his paper proposes a model for the analysis of different modes of decentralisation. The model links five major task areas in school management to the extent of decentralisation. He illustrates and supports his model through examples from several Eastern and Western European countries.

Geoff Southworth's paper constitutes Chapter 4. It focuses on the impact of legislation and related policy initiatives, including the National Curriculum, Local Management of Schools and the enhanced role of school governors, on the work of primary headteachers. The author concludes, along with others (e.g. Campbell and Neill, 1997), that heads have responded to change by increasing their workload and may be reaching saturation point, a factor which may limit their ability to develop their schools.

Chapter 5, by Les Bell, completes the opening section, and also examines the impact of self-management on primary schools. He reports the outcomes of a large-scale ESRC-funded project on how far management practice varies amongst three types of primary schools: local education authority (LEA), grant-maintained and private. Bell concludes that 'marketing the school and competing aggressively within a market environment is not part of the ethos of heads in primary schools' (p. 72).

## PROFESSIONAL DEVELOPMENT

Self-management may not have produced all the intended outcomes but there is evidence that it has produced significant changes in the professional lives of principals, headteachers and senior staff. The responsibilities of school and college leaders at the end of the twentieth century are very different from those of the mid-1980s, for example. Financial management is now primarily the task of heads, working with their governing bodies. Despite the cautions expressed by Bell, they also operate in a market environment, knowing that school income depends on its continuing popularity with parents and potential parents. They also face unprecedented accountability requirements, notably through the OFSTED inspection regime. 'The job of being a headteacher and managing a school in England and Wales has changed dramatically in the past decade' (Bolam, 1997, p.266).

Until the establishment of the TTA, there was no sustained professional development programme for headteachers. The School Management Task Force (SMTF), which operated from 1989 until 1992, produced an important report and sponsored the mentoring programme for new heads (Bolam *et al.*, 1995; Southworth, 1995; Bush *et al.*, 1996) which constituted the main professional development opportunity for heads until the Headlamp programme was introduced in 1995. Mentoring was grounded in notions of peer support and was widely welcomed by participants despite the evidence that it was too cosy and undemanding (Bush and Coleman, 1995). This was the high point of 'professional' development and headteacher training has now been taken over by those who favour a competence model with clear summative assessment. The TTA's chief executive, Anthea Millett (1996), illustrates this tough approach with her insistence that NPQH will 'provide a demanding and objective assessment that will sort out those who are ready to be leaders of schools from those who only give the appearance of being ready.'

The second section of this book, edited by Ray Bolam, addresses many of these issues. Chapter 6, by Peter Ribbins, provides a wide-ranging review of leadership and the concept of career, and also expresses several reservations about the NPQH. Drawing on what he admits is 'unsystematic' feedback, he questions whether NPQH will succeed in developing 'higher order' skills such as judgement, intuition, political acumen, integrity and commitment. He expresses incredulity at the notion, set out in the evaluation report (TTA, 1997), that NPQH was perceived as too theoretical by some candidates, and also expresses concern about aspects of the assessment process.

In Chapter 7, Dick Weindling draws on research about new headteachers, particularly his own longitudinal studies, to examine the stages of headship transition. He claims that 'becoming a school leader is an ongoing process of socialisation' which has two dimensions; professional and organisational, where the latter relates to the requirements of a particular school. He concludes with a model suggesting seven stages of transition through headship.

Agnes McMahon's focus, in Chapter 8, is on the continuing professional development (CPD) of all teachers, and on the leader's role in promoting CPD. Drawing on findings from a Leverhulme funded study, she presents teacher perceptions of CPD in secondary schools. She points out that CPD has been skewed by the need to implement centrally imposed innovations and concludes that more flexible and diverse approaches will be required if teachers are to grow and develop as professionals.

Chapter 9, by Michael Eraut, draws on his experience outside education, to assess headteachers' knowledge and practice. He concludes by suggesting that training for new heads should focus on nine aspects, including situational analysis of their new schools and leadership of the senior management team, a dimension greatly under-valued by the current emphasis on leadership as headship. The demands of school management in the next century are unlikely to be easier than they are at the end of the 1990s and can only be accommodated, or even contemplated, within a team model.

## THEORY DEVELOPMENT

Educational theory is unfashionable in the late 1990s. It is often used by policy-makers and government agencies, such as OFSTED and the TTA, as a term of derision or an indicator of failure. Teacher training programmes are deemed to be too 'theoretical' and remote from the realities of the classroom while the new National Professional Qualification for Headship (NPQH) is a 'professional' qualification which the TTA (1997) wishes to distance from 'over theoretical' academic courses.

The implementation of the Education Reform Act, and the development of the TTA agenda for CPD, have led to an emphasis on the *practice* of educational management. Heads and principals, in particular, have been inundated with advice from politicians, officials, officers of quangos, academics and consultants, about how to manage their schools and colleges. Many of these prescriptions are not underpinned by explicit values or concepts.

The absence of theory from much of the discourse of educational management contributes to allegations of 'managerialism', a stress on procedures at the expense of educational purpose and values. The argument, for example by Ball (1994), Hargreaves (1994) and Gunter (1997), is that implementation of externally imposed agendas reduces the scope for practitioners to debate what should be taught, and why. The ideologies of central government drive the agenda, replacing the values of practitioners, individually and collectively, and limiting internal debate to implementation of a prescribed curriculum.

This argument is valid but it can be shown that the educational reforms, in the UK and other countries, are underpinned by a *de facto* rational model.

> The model of good management practice . . . is essentially a rational one. It advocates a system for allocating resources which is directed at the explicit achievement of institutional objectives. This requires clarity in the specification of objectives, gathering and analysing information on alternative ways of attaining objectives,

evaluating alternatives and selecting those actions most likely to maximise the achievement of the objectives.

(Levačić 1995, 62)

Levačić's argument illustrates the pervasiveness of theory; it remains a significant influence on practice even when it is disavowed. Perhaps the resistance to theory relates in part to the reluctance of policy-makers to consider alternatives to the normatively preferred rational model, overlaid with a limited version of collegiality, linked to implementation of centrally-determined policy (Hargreaves, 1994). The acceptance of the notion of 'conceptual pluralism' (see page 2) might be perceived as threatening to the hegemony of the rational model and lead to unwelcome questioning of the nature of government reforms.

Section 3 of the book, edited by Peter Ribbins, addresses these important theoretical issues and relates them to educational management practice. Chapter 10, by Mike Wallace, combines two important alternatives to the rational-collegial model and illustrates them from research with LEAs. He questions the value of relying on a single approach, 'any quest for one best super-theory...is probably futile', indirectly debunking policy-makers' reliance on rationality, and advocating the merits of cultural and political perspectives. The latter, described by the American writers Bolman and Deal (1984, p.144), as 'the only realistic portrayal of organisations', certainly appears valid given the heightened power accorded to principals and heads within self-managing schools and colleges. The former has become increasingly influential in the 1990s and its stress on the informal aspects of organisations is a welcome counter to the rational model's emphasis on formal structures.

Chris James, in Chapter 11, discusses the rarely acknowledged psychodynamic perspective on educational management. He begins by outlining some key concepts of this approach and sets out several features which make educational institutions centres for anxiety. These include the level and extent of imposed change and the related issue of changes in the external environment, factors which would be well understood by teachers in many countries. Teacher anxiety is exacerbated because it 'remains hidden and is never explicitly asserted for a variety of reasons', notably the understandable desire to maintain others' confidence in their professional competence. This hidden anxiety surely contributes to the record level of stress-related retirements in England and Wales (Crawford, 1997).

In Chapter 12, Valerie Hall extends and develops her analysis of gender issues in education. She argues that an understanding of educational management is enhanced by a focus on gender issues that goes beyond the established theme of women's under-representation in promoted posts in education. She acknowledges the continuing importance of that theme, citing Coleman's (1998) recent work showing the extent of disadvantage experienced by women. At the same time, she stresses the need to turn the spotlight on men as well as women in educational management; and to integrate gender, race and class into a social justice framework for understanding the field.

Janet Ouston questions some of the received wisdom of the school effectiveness and school improvement 'movements' in Chapter 13. She points to the significance of school and national cultures to suggest caution in transporting theories and findings from one context to another. She questions the appropriateness of rational planning models and expresses concern about the dominance of examination and test results as the major performance indicators for schools. Ouston also provides, as a member of the research team, some fascinating insights into the legendary Rutter *et al.* (1979) project which still influences the school effectiveness debate.

In Chapter 14, the leading American researchers Philip Hallinger and Ronald Heck provide a critical perspective on the policy assumption that there is a causal relationship between the quality of school leadership, the quality of schools and levels of pupil achievement. They answer the question 'can leadership enhance school effectiveness?' in the affirmative but suggest that they do so indirectly via their influence on school and classroom processes. They also emphasise, like Ouston, the significance of cultural variables on the effectiveness of leaders.

## RESEARCH IN EDUCATIONAL MANAGEMENT

Educational research has been the subject of severe criticism in the late 1990s (Hargreaves, 1996; Tooley and Darby, 1998). It stands accused of superficiality, irrelevance and methodological weakness. While these strictures are not addressed specifically to educational management, it is important to take account of them in developing a research agenda for the discipline. Because it is a relatively new field, research is vital to establish its theoretical base and to link theory to the practice of management. It is also valuable in evaluating policy changes to provide an independent assessment of whether the intended benefits of reform have materialised. This will always be uncomfortable for politicians who do not want to learn about policy failure and are reluctant to sponsor research which may produce the 'wrong' answer.

The final section of the book, edited by Les Bell, surveys the field and suggests certain priorities for educational management research in the next decade. Chapter 15, by Ray Bolam, links research priorities to the process of redefinition. He proposes a four-part typology of research in educational management and argues that future research should relate to both 'knowledge for understanding' and 'knowledge for action'. As an applied discipline, educational management research should be responsive to central policy and research initiatives but also be proactive in setting out its own priorities independent of the current policy climate.

Mike Wallace and Dick Weindling, in Chapter 16, review ESRC-funded projects related to school management between 1990 and 1995. The authors demonstrate that most research relates to aspects of government reform rather than being directly concerned with the tasks and processes of management. They also point to areas of school management not included in the research, notably the management of nursery and special schools. There is considerable diversity in the extent and nature of the theoretical aspects of the research, leading Wallace and Weindling to be pessimistic about the prospect of developing a coherent theory of educational management.

In Chapter 17 Philippa Cordingley explains the TTA's research agenda. She states that the TTA's main focus is on pedagogy and addresses its relationship with school management. She stresses the need for research to be seen as a means of improving teaching and raising standards and not just as an end in itself. Cordingley concludes by urging that priorities for educational management research should take pedagogy as a starting point and contribute to the improvement of teaching and learning.

The final chapter, by Helen Gunter, examines the development of the field of educational management in England and Wales through the professional biographies of 16 people working in higher education and scrutiny of documentation held by the British Educational Management and Administration Society (BEMAS). She stresses the value of personal histories as a research approach and examines the dilemma for educational management specialists who need to develop academic careers while remaining credible professional practitioners.

## CONCLUSION: THE PROCESS OF REDEFINITION

This book surveys several important aspects of educational management which are all significant for the process of redefinition. Self-management has become an international movement predicated on the assumption that school-based leaders must be able to make better decisions for their pupils than national or local politicians or officials. The rhetoric is even being used in those educational systems, for example in South Africa (Bush *et al.*, forthcoming), where it is evident that most principals and governing bodies, because of the legacy of apartheid, are not yet prepared to take the main responsibility for school management. While greater autonomy has been welcomed by headteachers (Bush *et al.*, 1993; Levačić, 1995), more research is required to establish whether there is a causal relationship between autonomy and school improvement (Bush, 1996). It is also important for educational management specialists, who have hitherto focused mainly on the organisational level, to address issues of classroom practice and their links with whole-school management.

Until the establishment of the TTA, university educational management centres in England and Wales were the major providers of professional development programmes for school and college managers. The TTA's CPD agenda now provides a serious challenge to the dominance of universities. While some departments benefit from the TTA's INSET funding, this is only partial and still leaves fee-paying masters' and doctoral programmes to compete against free government sponsored programmes which have the additional cachet of leading directly to advancement, notably in respect of NPQH. Many universities have now linked their provision to NPQH and allowed partial exemptions from modular programmes, but ultimately courses will survive only if they are perceived as relevant to the concerns of busy practitioners. The process of redefinition thus involves scrutiny of the educational management curriculum to assess its relevance to practice.

Educational management must be focused on contemporary practice, or it will risk the decline experienced by certain other educational specialisms, but it must continue to develop its own theoretical base. While it will continue to draw on other more established disciplines, including the general management field so popular with policy-makers, the development of a specifically *educational* management discipline requires a distinctive body of theory 'grounded' (Glaser and Strauss, 1967) in educational practice. This inevitably leads to the need for a coherent programme of research in all types of school and college which test theoretical constructs, preferably in several different national contexts. Strengthening existing national and international networks is an essential part of such a strategy.

Educational management has become an important academic subject which is very popular with practitioners who, unlike many policy-makers, sense that practice without theory is shallow. However, it needs a period of review to take account of the agendas of governments and national agencies. Educational management requires a new sense of direction to enable it to meet the needs of teachers and educational institutions in the new millennium. If this book contributes to the process of renewal, the editors will be well satisfied.

## REFERENCES

Ball, S. (1994) *Education Reform: A critical and post-structural approach*, Buckingham: Open University Press.

Blackmore, J. (1993) In the shadow of men, the historical construction of educational administration as a 'masculine' enterprise, in J. Blackmore and J. Kenny (eds.) *Gender Matters in Educational Administration and Policy: A feminist introduction*, London: The Falmer Press.

Bolam, R. (1997) Management development for headteachers, *Educational Management and Administration*, Vol. 25, No. 3, pp. 265–284.

Bolam, R., McMahon, A., Pocklington, K. and Weindling, D. (1995) Mentoring for new headteachers: recent British experience, *Journal of Educational Administration*, Vol. 33, No. 5, pp. 29–44.

Bolman, L. and Deal, T. (1984) *Modern Approaches to Understanding and Managing Organisations*, San Francisco: Jossey Bass.

Bush, T. (1995) *Theories of Educational Management: Second edition*, London: Paul Chapman.

Bush, T. (1996) School autonomy and school improvement, in J. Gray, D. Reynolds, C. Fitz-Gibbon, and D. Jesson (eds.) *Merging Traditions: The future of research on school effectiveness and school improvement*, London: Cassell.

Bush, T. and Coleman, M. (1995) Professional development for heads: the role of mentoring, *Journal of Educational Administration*, Vol. 33, No. 5, pp. 60–73.

Bush, T., Coleman, M. and Glover, D. (1993) *Managing Autonomous Schools: The grant-maintained experience*, London: Paul Chapman.

Bush, T., Coleman, M., Wall, D. and West-Burnham, J. (1996) Mentoring and continuing professional development, in D. McIntyre and H. Haggar (eds.) *Mentors in Schools: Developing the Profession of Teaching*, London: David Fulton.

Bush, T., Coleman, M. and Thurlow, M. (forthcoming) *Leadership and Strategic Management in South African Schools*, Durban: Kasigo.

Caldwell, B. and Spinks, J. (1992) *Leading the Self-Managing School*, London: The Falmer Press.

Campbell, J. and Neill, S. (1997) Managing teachers' time under systemic reform, in T. Bush and D. Middlewood (eds.) *Managing People in Education*, London: Paul Chapman.

Coleman, M. (1998) *Women in Educational Management: The career progress and leadership styles of female secondary headteachers in England and Wales*, unpublished Ph.D. thesis: University of Leicester.

Crawford, M. (1997) Managing stress in education, in T. Bush and D. Middlewood (eds.) *Managing People in Education*, London: Paul Chapman.

Glaser, B. and Strauss, A. (1967) *The Discovery of Grounded Theory*, London: Weidenfeld and Nicholson.

Gunter, H. (1997) *Rethinking Education: The consequences of Jurassic management*, London: Cassell.

Hargreaves, A. (1994) *Changing Teachers, Changing Times: Teachers' work and culture in the postmodern age*, London: Cassell.

Hargreaves, D. (1996) *Teaching as a Research-Based Profession: Possibilities and prospects*, London: Teacher Training Agency.

Levačić R. (1995) *Local Management of Schools: Analysis and practice*, Buckingham: Open University Press.

Millett, A. (1996) A head is more than a manager, *Times Educational Supplement*, 15 July.

Rutter, M., Maugham, B., Mortimore, P. and Ouston, J. (1979) *Fifteen Thousand Hours*, London: Open Books.

Smyth, J. (1996) The socially just alternative to the self-managing school, in J. Leithwood, J. Chapman, D. Corson, P. Hallinger and A. Hart (eds.) *International Handbook of Educational Leadership and Administration*, Boston: Kluwer.

Southworth, G. (1995) Reflections on mentoring for school leaders, *Journal of Educational Administration*, Vol. 33, No. 5, pp. 17–28.

Teacher Training Agency (1997) *National Professional Qualification for Headship: Report of evaluation of trials*, London: Teacher Training Agency.

Teacher Training Agency (1998) *TTA National Leadership Programme for Serving Headteachers*, London: Teacher Training Agency.

Thomas, H. and Martin, J. (1996) *Managing Resources for School Improvement*, London: Routledge.

Tooley, J. and Darby, D. (1998) *Education Research: An OFSTED critique*, London: OFSTED.

# SECTION 1

# SCHOOLS AND SELF-MANAGEMENT

## Edited by Ron Glatter

# 2

# Modern Headship for the Rationally Managed School: Combining Cerebral and Insightful Approaches

ROSALIND LEVAČIĆ, DEREK GLOVER, NIGEL BENNETT
AND MEGAN CRAWFORD

## INTRODUCTION

This chapter is concerned with the increased range and complexity of the management skills required of the headteachers of locally managed schools operating within an increasingly tight accountability framework set by central government. In particular, the chapter focuses on the external pressures for schools to be managed rationally, as effective and efficient organisations which achieve a tight coupling between inputs, processes and outputs, while at the same time being underpinned by values and a common educational purpose reflected in a shared organisational culture. In examining how schools combine both approaches, the chapter draws in particular upon a set of studies done at the Open University within a project on Managing for Effectiveness and Efficiency in Schools.

## CEREBRAL AND INSIGHTFUL APPROACHES TO MANAGEMENT

A major development in educational management in the last decade has been much greater emphasis on defining effective leadership by individuals in management posts in terms of the effectiveness of their organisation, which is increasingly judged in relation to measurable learning outcomes for students. In the UK both major political parties have pursued educational policies which seek to diminish the traditional ambiguity and lack of coupling (Weick, 1976) between inputs, processes and outcomes in educational organisations. This is argued to require a rational-technicist approach to the structuring of decision-making.

At the same time, increased emphasis is also being given to the importance in educational leadership of values and institutional vision. The OFSTED inspection framework, with its emphasis on effective leadership based upon a vision for the school translated into a school ethos focused on pupil behaviour and learning and continuous improvement, attempts to weld the two management traditions. Despite the rationality of official guidance, there is strong emphasis in training programmes for headteachers on the need for leadership and management styles which enhance the human side of headship, as in Section 5 of Teacher Training Agency *National Standards for Headteachers* (Teacher Training Agency, 1997). From this perspective, the prime role of educational leadership is to create and maintain an integrated organisational culture (Meyerson and Martin, 1997) of shared values and purpose.

In all of this it is possible to discern a tension between two approaches to management theory (Bennett, 1995). The first approach, often known as scientific management or Taylorism, is steeped in the view that human beings have to be driven to meet objectives and that they will only be efficient in their work if they are managed, controlled and supervised in a way which secures the required output for the organisation. As Bennett, (1997) notes, in modern versions of scientific management, managers can direct and control through the construction of self-regulating organisational systems rather than direct supervision. A key feature of scientific management is rationality. 'From a technical rational perspective, organizations exist to attain specific, predetermined goals: . . . they develop technologies to attain goals . . . and generate structures to enhance efficiency' (Ogawa and Bossert, 1997). The contrasting approach, referred to by Bennett (1997) as non-rational, emphasises the a-rationality of organisations and draws strongly from the humanist approach based on the view that individuals are more strongly motivated to work by affective factors rather than by fear of sanctions and direct monetary reward. This approach stresses the importance of socially constructed meanings in influencing how people work and hence the importance from a management perspective of creating an organisational culture within which people are motivated and enabled to work effectively.

Mintzberg (1990) argues that, rather than there being an irreconcilable tension between these two approaches, the work of organisational leaders draws upon elements of both rationality and culture: some of the work of leaders involves the application of rationality – which he calls the 'cerebral' aspects – and part on the development of vision and encouragement of others – which he refers to as the 'insightful' aspect. In this chapter we use the terms 'cerebral' and 'insightful' as a shorthand way of referring to these two traditions in management theory and practice. Our focus is on how school leaderships blend the cerebral and the insightful in responding to external pressures to manage schools rationally.

## THE RATIONAL-TECHNICIST MODEL

A rationally managed organisation is one which has explicit goals against which it measures performance. It uses a rational planning process. This is sequential. Objectives are agreed, and then information is obtained on all the alternative means by which the objectives might be attained. The selection of the most appropriate course of action then depends upon knowledge of its projected costs balanced against expected benefits. Thus ends and means are clearly linked. The budgetary planning process, because it identifies costs and relates them to anticipated benefits, is an essential part of rational planning. The establishment of cyclic systems of audit, planning, prioritising, implementing and evaluating are advocated by the Audit Commission (1993) and the National Audit Office (1996). For example the Audit Commission (1993) states that:

> The school should have a medium term educational and budget plan (covering at least three years) indicating the intended use of resources in achieving its educational goals. Even though the funding available to each school will change annually, the school development plan should outline which areas are the priority for spending, and why.

> (para 2.2)

The importance of planning to identify organisational development priorities was evident in the 'advisory' literature of the immediate post-1988 Education Reform Act era (Hargreaves *et al.*, 1989; Hargreaves and Hopkins, 1991). Building upon the earlier model to offer a process by which schools can apply rational planning, Hopkins (1994) outlines the detail of action plans with targets and tasks, a time frame and evaluation checks. Later literature has made the link between rational approaches and school improvement more explicit (Stoll and Fink, 1996; Hopkins *et al.*, 1997).

An example of the official view of how cerebral and insightful approaches should be combined is given in OFSTED, 1995:

> strong leadership provides clear educational direction ... the school has aims, values and policies which are reflected through all its work ... the school through its development planning, identifies relevant priorities and targets, takes the necessary action, and monitors and evaluates its progress towards them ... there is a positive ethos, which reflect the school's commitment to high achievement, an effective learning environment, good relationships, and equality of opportunity for all pupils.

> (OFSTED, 1995, p. 100)

The technicist approach has been developed further by the Labour Government with the requirement for schools to set quantitative targets at Key Stages 2 and 4 (DfEE, 1998) and School Standards and Framework Act 1998, under which LEAs must submit to the DfEE educational development plans for actions to meet performance targets.

## THE ADOPTION OF THE RATIONAL-TECHNICIST APPROACH IN SCHOOLS

Our research over the past four years has been concerned with the extent to which schools have adopted the rational-technicist approach to management. We have used OFSTED inspection reports as a main source of evidence, examining four samples of reports: 66 secondary reports done in 1993; 117 secondary reports from 1994; 120 primary reports produced in 1994/95; and a follow up of 30 primary and 20 secondary reports in 1997/98. The schools were from LEA areas which varied in social composition and geography. Content analyses of the inspection report and case studies of four secondary and nine primary schools were undertaken.

The comments made by inspectors which related to management of the school were first categorised in relation to the constituent elements of the rational-technicist model (Glover et al., 1997; Levačić and Glover, 1997; Levačić and Glover, 1998). Examples of these elements include:

**planning processes:**
>   quality of development planning (prioritisation for planned activities, identification and rationale for curriculum planning links);
>   use of development plan objectives as a planning framework;
>   use of staff costing, e.g. INSET related to planned developments;
>   use of resource costing, e.g. new materials for planned development;
>   use of accommodation costing, e.g. re-grouping of rooms;

**monitoring and evaluation:**
>   use of educational outcomes;
>   consistency of practice across departments;
>   involvement of senior and middle management and governors.

Inspectors' comments were then graded by the researchers on a three-point scale: category 3 indicates commendations of good practice; category 2 contains satisfactory comments with suggestions for refinements; category 1 indicates critical comments. Examples of critical and commendatory comments for two primary schools are given on page 19.

Analysis of this material gathered over a period of time must be treated with some caution. During the period under consideration there was a change in the procedures for reporting by OFSTED. We also recognise that our later analysis has been of a smaller sample of schools, and that our method hinges on subjective assessment of comments which themselves have a degree of subjectivity. That said, this analysis offers evidence of progressive improvement in resource management. Overall the tendency in our samples is for the percentage of adverse comments on management to decline over time and for there to be an increase in commended practice. In the primary sector planning, resource allocation, financial management and evaluation processes are

**Critical comment**

*Secondary:* The school development plan is for one year only and does not fully indicate the intentions of the governing body and the senior management in planning for the future. All projects now need to be brought within a comprehensive action plan showing short, medium and long term objectives, the time scale and approximate costs so that progress can be measured and any necessary modifications made in the full knowledge of their effects.

*Primary:* The development plan is also brief and shows little evidence of thought being given to the detail of what needs to be done. It was produced primarily by the headteacher with little input from the governing body. It gives no details of the use of resources, training requirements or financial implications, nor is it checked systematically for its impact on standards of attainment.

**Commendatory comment**

*Secondary:* There are clear procedures for preparing the school budget to reflect and support the targets in the development plan. The approach shows in departmental planning as well as in planning for the whole school and this is achieved with a high level of consistency. Through taking a fresh look at the way funding was previously allocated senior staff have been able to make moneys available for development work.

*Primary:* The global targets have identified sub-targets, resource implications are considered, items are costed, manpower implications are accounted for, monitoring procedures are given together with success criteria. The sub-targets are recorded on further sheets which carry more detailed success criteria and further details of how the target is to be addressed.

judged to have improved over time. Lack of progress has been where headteachers and governors have remained closely tied to historic budgeting processes and have, for example, maintained high-cost staffing levels without investigating alternatives.

In the secondary sector schools have increasingly adopted all aspects of the rational model except in some cases where schools:

- have been slow to develop refined management information systems;
- do not plan the teaching force and its deployment in relation to curriculum, but are excessively constrained by staff's existing expertise;
- have inadequate accommodation as a result of a priority being given to funding staff during a period of declining real resources.

Further evidence of the extent to which heads have developed the rationalist model is given in the annual reports of the Chief Inspector for OFSTED. These provide a general summary of the progress of schools inspected in any one year towards the official model. Consideration of comments on aspects of development planning as the basis for financial management shows progress towards more sophisticated expectations of headteachers as illustrated in this comparison of comments in the Annual Reports for 1992/3 and 1996/7 (OFSTED, 1993; OFSTED, 1998).

**1992/3**

*Primary sector:* ... many administrative tasks were still undertaken inappropriately by senior staff. This limited the time they had available for strategic planning, monitoring and evaluating the quality and standards of work. In over one third of primary schools the links between the identification of aims for curriculum development and budget costing were weak. (para.8)

*Secondary sector:* Schools are just beginning to develop strategies to increase their efficiency, but as yet little systematic analysis of resource patterns and demands has been carried out. Few consider expenditure in terms of finding the most cost-effective ways of achieving the improvements in standards they seek. (para.35)

**1996/7**

*Primary sector:* In about one in six schools, financial planning is insufficiently linked to development planning, and not enough thought is given to establishing procedures for evaluating the cost effectiveness or opportunity costs of spending decisions. Less than one in ten schools provides poor value for money; two in five schools provide good value for money. (para 77)

*Secondary sector:* Financial planning is improving but is weak in about one school in six...some schools have difficulty in costing planned developments, including resource provision and provision of in-service training. (para 149)
Many schools have found difficulties with long term strategic planning. (para 150)
Half provide good value for money.

## MANAGEMENT PRACTICE IN EFFECTIVE SCHOOLS: EVIDENCE FROM CASE STUDIES

A key assumption underlying the official rational-technicist model is that efficient resource management is required for schools to be educationally effective. In order to investigate how links between resource management and educational effectiveness are made in schools, we undertook detailed case studies of four secondary schools and nine primary schools judged by OFSTED to be offering good value for money.

### Conceptual frameworks

Of particular interest for the issues addressed in this chapter is the extent to which management practice relies on rational systems (the cerebral) or school culture (the insightful) as means of securing organisational control. Organisational control in this context refers to 'assuring that desired results are obtained' (Antony and Herzlinger, 1989). The means for securing organisational control do not only include supervision of subordinates by line managers and accounting systems, but also embrace the creation and management of an 'integrated' organisational culture whereby normative power is used to secure organisational members' commitment to organisational goals through the sharing of common norms, values and meanings. The concept of an 'integrated' organisational culture is developed by Meyerson and Martin (1997), who distinguish three concepts of organisational culture:

- integrated:         consistency, consensus and leader centredness;
- differentiated:    diversity, inconsistency and lack of consensus;
- ambiguous:        complexity, dynamism and fluidity.

Only in the case of an integrated organisational culture are there shared and stable norms, values and meanings which relate to the organisation's purposes, how human relationships are conducted and how work is done. Thus the creation and maintenance of an integrated culture as an organisational control device requires the insightful aspect of leadership, while the development and operation of formal systems for planning, implementation and review require 'cerebral' capacities.

Within the rational perspective there has been a long-running debate about how organisations plan and conduct strategy. The main distinction is between what Mintzberg (1994) calls 'deliberate strategic planning' (where the organisation follows predetermined actions designed to secure its goals, which requires high predictability and organisational control) and emergent strategy (where organisations steer a direction in response to unfolding events). These two approaches to 'rational planning' are termed 'synoptic' and 'retroactive' in Scheerens' (1997) development of a theoretical foundation for school effectiveness research which links it to organisational theory. Synoptic planning is characterised by high predictability, proactive statement of goals and objectives, decomposition and sequencing of actions, and monitoring using quantitative data. Retroactive planning is characterised by reacting to unpredicted events with incremental responses based on a cycle of feedback, review and correction which is guided by a vision of a future desired direction and by organisational norms (i.e. reliance on an integrated culture).

## Evidence

Data for the case studies were obtained from school documents, interviews with a wide range of staff and with some governors, and a culture questionnaire administered to all teaching staff which posed ten questions on ideal and actual collegial practice (Bennett, 1998). We summarise key findings below, referring to schools by fictional names.

Two key findings from the secondary case studies (Glover et al., 1996) are:

- There were two distinct approaches to organisational planning and resource management in schools deemed educationally effective. One was the rational-technicist systems approach or synoptic planning. The other was retroactive planning with extensive reliance on an integrated school culture with flexible and loosely defined procedures, much interpersonal communication and pragmatism. All four schools used both approaches but in differing degrees so we were able to range the schools on a continuum from the most systems based school, Runnymede, to Uplands, the most reliant on an integrated culture. Each school's stance was very dependent on the leadership philosophy and style of the headteacher. This in turn both depended upon and affected the organisational culture of the school, its strategic direction and its relationship with its external environment.

* Financial management was driven by the requirements of the school development plan and this in turn was informed by strategic planning. Strategic management depended upon the way the leadership interpreted the needs of the school in relation to the school's external environment. There was a complex coupling of the external environment, school culture and leadership, with the processes of developmental planning and budgeting.

Thus we found effective headteachers combining in different degrees the cerebral and insightful approaches we have distinguished above. Secondary heads relied on their senior management teams, and not just themselves, to provide the full balanced range of the cerebral and insightful approaches.

In the primary study we found that eight of the nine schools had integrated cultures, the ninth being differentiated. Only two of the nine schools, Elms and Thackeray, could be classified as approximating to technicist planning. Elms School was a 330 pupil, ten teacher urban school, whereas Thackeray was a 40 pupil rural school with 2.4 teachers, where the rationality of planning reflected the good personal organisation of the headteacher, who was also successful in securing an integrated culture, which is easier to achieve in a small school. Both these schools were judged to have corporate type school development planning (McGilchrist et al., 1995), i.e. a plan which was characterised by shared ownership and management by all staff with significant positive impact on pupil learning. (Bennett et al., 1999, gives these examples in more detail.)

However, the third school with corporate type development planning, Padingwick, was characterised by retroactive planning which we termed 'guiding plan' approach (Bennett et al., 1999). This was a particularly interesting example of a school in a socially deprived community, with an integrated culture and a clear school improvement agenda led by a highly regarded headteacher. He refused to plan beyond a one-year horizon because of uncertainty and because he gave priority to staff spending time on responding to the immediate needs of pupils and their parents, whose unstable home lives impacted on the daily life of the school. The headteacher had a clear and well communicated educational vision which guided the school and its responses to both opportunities and difficulties. Another of the schools located in a socially deprived community had problems implementing plans because of environmental turbulence, as well as a differentiated culture following the appointment of a new headteacher.

A further finding was that in primary schools not only is the head the chief locus of decision-making, given that governing bodies in practice delegate planning and budgeting to the head, but she/he has to perform many of the support tasks for decision-making (e.g. collecting and analysing data) as well as, in smaller schools, teaching. Unlike secondary heads, primary headteachers do not usually have the support of full-time finance officers or of deputy heads with only half-time teaching responsibilities. The primary head's role is both universal (doing everything) and has become more complex with the demands of local management (Boyle and Woods, 1996).

## A TYPOLOGY OF APPROACHES TO RATIONALITY

The evidence we examined suggests that the main elements of technicism – strategic planning, development planning, efficiency in resource management, monitoring and evaluation for efficiency and effectiveness – are evident to some extent in all the case study schools. Schools closest to the rational-technicist model are those which have stability in both community relationships and staffing, enjoy a marked degree of staff co-operation, and which have a clear understanding and acceptance by staff of the headteacher's leadership style. There is a tendency for primary school development planning to be restricted to the curriculum, while active resource management is restricted to the minor part of the budget left once staffing and building costs have determined on a historic basis. Secondary schools are more likely to take all resources into account in their planning.

The case studies indicated how the adoption of technicism is tempered by context, culture and style. Whilst external judgements of success are made on schools' ability to be cerebral, their capacity to thrive as communities is related to the insightful. There were tensions between official expectations of rationality and headteacher preference for flexibility and interpersonal communication, in particular at Uplands Secondary and Padingwick Primary schools, where senior managers were criticised by OFSTED because of weaknesses in rational planning though the school was judged to be educationally effective.

The case study evidence leads us to suggest a classification of management responses to the external pressures for technicist rationality, when schools are faced with differing degrees of externally generated turbulence, and internally with the need for insightful cultural leadership. In developing this classification we have drawn upon other typologies which have evolved in the analysis of schools as organisations (Hargreaves, 1995; McGilchrist et al., 1995; Barber and Dann, 1996; Tam and Cheng, 1996; Meyerson and Martin, 1997; Scheerens, 1997; Tuohy and Coghlan, 1997).

Whatever the culture, the technicist approach is through planning. Schools are expected to be rational but may be deflected from this by inability or design. This leads to a possible progression through a typology of approaches to rationality which are set out in summary form in Table 2.1:

**Table 2.1**  *A typology of approaches to rationality*

| Aspect of management | Embraced rationality | Accommodated rationality-managed flexibility | Accommodated rationality-value based resistance | Incoherent ambiguity |
|---|---|---|---|---|
| Strategic planning | Long, medium and short term plans related to defined objectives. Governors involved. | Known objectives for two or three years ahead. Governors consulted. | Clear school direction. Planning concerned with immediate needs. Governors consulted. | Absence of planning. Governors peripheral. |
| Development planning | Objectives fully detailed with all costing and criteria listed. No deviation from plans. Staff consultation. | Objectives detailed and priorities guided by plan but interpreted according to immediate need. Staff involvement. | Main objectives articulated. Diffused staff ownership with strong shared values. | Lack of whole-school aims. Limited departmental planning. Lack of ownership. |
| Resource management | Based on tight financial allocation guided by SDP priorities. Sub-units work to development plan. | Looser coupling between budget and SDP. Sub-units work towards whole-school objectives. | Lack of tight systems and documentation linking SDP and budget. Sub-unit compliance achieved through integrated culture. | Budgeting not related to SDP. Historic resource allocation. Sub-units in competition. |
| Efficiency | Explicit links between objectives and inputs to achieve efficiency. Clear targets. Consistent and explicit attention to VFM. | Subjective judgements predominate. Some linkage between outcomes and inputs. Some targets used. Varying interpretation of VFM. | Absence of explicit links between objectives and inputs. Staff concerned to make careful use of resources. VFM not defined clearly. | Low expectations, few targets. Objectives not defined and not related to inputs. Poor VFM. |
| Monitoring/ evaluation | Systematised, formal, objective success criteria, quantitative data, related to SDP at all stages. | Review systems related to outcomes and whole-school aims. Informal, variable. | Informal, on-going. High reliance on qualitative data and interpersonal communications. | Limited or only in crisis situations. Little concern with outcomes. Ambiguous. |

a.  Embraced rationality. This refers to a full adoption of the rational-technicist approach. One example is Runneymede, an 11-16 secondary school, where the headteacher established complex and comprehensive planning and control systems, driven by a whole-school approach to improvement. It is also shown at Thackeray, a very small rural school, where the head maintained that adherence to a comprehensive but simple plan enabled the school to prioritise resource use effectively and to sustain desired developments over time in the face of uncertainty.

b.  Accommodated rationality. This refers to a tempered rational model, where plans are used flexibly as guides rather than blueprints. We distinguish two types of accommodated rationality.

b1. Managed flexibility is seen as a pragmatic response where the headteacher attempts to adhere to the rational model as far as circumstances and capacities permit. This approach embraces most of the schools which had comments at the satisfactory or category 2 level in their OFSTED reports.

b2. Value-based resistance. This is a selective adoption of rationality where headteacher and staff believe they can better attain their objectives by extensive reliance on an integrated school culture and not by rigid adherence to rationality. Uplands Secondary and Padingwick Primary schools are examples of this response.

c.  Incoherent ambiguity – this is not evident in the case study schools because all were chosen for their overall soundness. However, there are OFSTED reports on failing and near-failing schools, which may have superficial rationality but where interpersonal relationships are so unstable that planning is not implemented and interest groups compete for power. The following comment from one report indicates the nature of tensions in one of these schools: 'The management have no clear long-term view of how the school should develop. Therefore financial decision-making is hindered and cannot inform the direction of future financial plans.'

Whilst it is possible to talk in terms of a tendency to one or other of the patterns used in the classification, we recognise that few schools accord with exactly any one model and its descriptors.


## CONCLUSION

In this chapter we have traced the development of an officially advocated rational-technicist approach to management and the expectation that headteachers can combine cerebral and insightful approaches to leadership.

Both OFSTED inspection report and case-study evidence showed that headteachers are increasingly following the rational model in establishing aims for their schools and then endeavouring through planning processes to involve all staff. However, their capacity to do this is affected by the demands of the socio-economic context within which they are working, and the culture of the staff of the school. The divergence between the rational-technicist management model officially advocated and practice in schools, though lessening over time, provides a limited number of examples of embraced rationality in action. Accommodated rationality appears to be the more common model, while a small minority of 8 to 10 per cent of schools (OFSTED, 1998) are failing to put in place such rational processes.

The case-study evidence reflects the tension between the rhetoric of rationality and the reality of practice. Educational effectiveness, as shown with Uplands and Padingwick Schools, is not necessarily dependent upon tightly controlled planning and associated resource management. However, in the course of our investigations we have found a tendency for schools which have sound planning approaches and developed monitoring and evaluation procedures to be more successful in relation to the quality of teaching and learning, student behaviour and attendance (Levačić and Glover, 1997; Levačić and Glover, 1998).

We have also noted that the school context, in particular the degree of turbulence in the external environment – which tends to be more marked for schools in socially deprived communities – influences the extent to which the rational-technicist model can be applied, and what is the appropriate balance between it and reliance on an integrated school culture for securing coupling between educational aims, internal processes and the deployment of resources.

The potential for school improvement hinges upon the ability of headteachers to manage and lead changed attitudes. Rational procedures, we would argue, offer the framework within which this can be facilitated. However, depending on school context, organisational culture and preferred leadership style, *a rational-technicist approach or one which is much more fluid and reliant on interpersonal relations rather than on formal systems can be equally effective.*

The range of qualities now needed for successful headship in a system of locally managed schools within a tight accountability framework has made the role much more complex. Both cerebral and insightful capabilities are required, though they need not, particularly in the secondary context, be possessed in equal amounts by the headteacher, provided any deficiencies are complemented by the strengths of other members of the senior management team.

## REFERENCES

Antony, A. R. and Herzlinger, R. E. (1989) Management control in non-profit organizations, R. Levačić, *Financial Management in Education*, Milton Keynes: Open University Press: 16–31.

Audit Commission (1993) *Adding Up the Sums: Schools' management of their finances*, London: HMSO.

Barber, M. and Dann, R. (1996) *Raising Educational Standards in the Inner Cities: Practical initiatives in action*, London: Cassell.

Bennett, N. (1995) *Managing Professional Teachers: Middle management in primary and secondary schools*, London: Paul Chapman.

Bennett, N. (1997) Analysing management for personal development, L. Kydd, M.

Crawford and C. Riches, *Professional Development for Educational Management*, Buckingham: Open University Press.

Bennett, N. (1998) Culture in the effective primary school, American Education Research Association Annual Meeting, San Diego.

Bennett, N., Levačić, R., Glover, D., Crawford, M. and Earley, P. (1999), *The Reality of School Development Planning in the Effective Primary School: Technicist or guiding plan?* Milton Keynes: Open University.

Boyle, M. and Woods, P. (1996) The composite head: coping with changes in the primary headteacher's role, *British Educational Research Journal* 22(5): 549–568.

DfEE (1998) *Target-setting in schools, circular 11/98*, London: DfEE.

Glover, D., Bennett, N., Crawford, M., and Levačić, R. (1997) Strategic and resource management in primary schools, *School Leadership and Organization*, 17.3.

Glover, D., Levačić, R., Bennett, N. and Earley, P. (1996) Leadership, planning and resource management in four very effective schools, *School Organisation*, 16 (2 and 3).

Hargreaves, D. (1995) School culture, school effectiveness and school improvement, *School Effectiveness and School Improvement* 6(1).

Hargreaves, D. and Hopkins, D. (1991) *The Empowered School*, London: Cassell.

Hargreaves, D., Hopkins, D., Leask, M., Connolly, J. and Robinson, P. (1989) *Planning for School Development*, London: Department for Education.

Hopkins, D. (1994) School improvement in an era of change, P. Ribbins and E. Burridge, *Improving Education*, London: Cassell.

Hopkins, D., Ainscow, M. and West, M. (1997) School improvement: propositions for action, A. Harris, N. Bennett and M. Preedy, *Organizational Effectiveness and Improvement in Education*, Buckingham: Open University Press.

Levačić, R. and Glover, D. (1997) Value for money as a school improvement strategy: evidence from the new inspection system in England, *School Effectiveness and Improvement* 8(2).

Levačić, R. and Glover, D. (1998) The relationship between efficient resource management and school effectiveness: evidence from OFSTED secondary school inspections, *School Effectiveness and School Improvement* 9(1): 95–122.

McGilchrist, B., Mortimer, P., Savage, J. and Beresford, C. (1995) *Planning Matters: The impact of development planning in primary schools*, London: Paul Chapman.

Meyerson, D. and Martin, J. (1997) Cultural change: integration of three different views, A. Harris, N. Bennett and M. Preedy, *Organizational Effectiveness and Improvement in Education,* Buckingham: Open University Press.

Mintzberg, H. (1990) The manager's job: folklore and fact, *Harvard Business Review March/April*: 163–176.

Mintzberg, H. (1994) *The Rise and Fall of Strategic Planning*, Englewood Cliffs, NJ: Prentice Hall.

National Audit Office (1996) *Good Stewardship: NAO examination of value for money at Grant Maintained Schools*, London: HMSO.

OFSTED (1993) *Standards and Quality in Education 1992-93: annual report of Her Majesty's Chief Inspector of Schools*, London: HMSO.

OFSTED (1995) *Guidance on the Inspection of Nursery and Primary Schools*, London: HMSO.

OFSTED (1998) *The Annual Report of Her Majesty's Chief Inspector of Schools*, London: The Stationery Office.

Ogawa, R. T. and Bossert, S. T. (1997) Leadership as an organizational quality, M.

Crawford, L. Kydd and C. Riches, *Leadership and Teams in Educational Management*, Buckingham: Open University Press.

Scheerens, J. (1997) Conceptual models and theory-embedded principles on effective schooling, *School Effectiveness and School Improvement* 8(3): 269–310.

Stoll, L. and Fink, D. (1996) *Changing Our Schools: Linking school effectiveness and school improvement*, Buckingham: Open University Press.

Tam, F. W. M. and Cheng, Y. C. (1996) A typology of primary school environments, *Educational Management and Administration* 24(3): 237–252.

Teacher Training Agency (1997) *National Standards for Headteachers*, London: TTA.

Tuohy, D. and Coghlan, D. (1997) Developments in schools: a systems approach based on organisational levels, *Educational Management and Administration* 25(1): 65–78.

Weick, K. E. (1976) Education Organisations as loosely coupled systems? *Administrative Science Quarterly* 21(1): 1–19.

# 3

# Decentralisation and Deregulation in Europe: Towards a Conceptual Framework

## PETER KARSTANJE

## INTRODUCTION

The developments surrounding increased school autonomy in Western, Central and Eastern Europe are fairly diverse. However, there is a tendency towards increased autonomy in every country. The consequences for the role of educational management are evident. Nevertheless, great differences can be found in the styles of school management in the different countries. This chapter constructs and illustrates a model which makes it possible to trace these differences and might be used for further research into the redefinition of educational management.

## DECENTRALISATION AND DEREGULATION

Many European countries have seen the onset of a trend towards decentralisation and deregulation. In Western Europe, deregulation seems to be a dominant trend; in Central and Eastern Europe the trend leans more towards decentralisation, although both phenomena are detectable in most countries, regardless of whether they are situated in the West or the East.

*Decentralisation* involves the assignment of decision-making tasks to lower levels. In a centralist system, this usually means a shift in decision-making powers from central government to local council level. The motivation behind decentralisation is usually twofold: shortening the distance between the government and the organisation in charge of implementation (school); and shifting the financial risks to a lower level. This does not necessarily mean that schools gain more autonomy. It may just be that the local council dictates as many, if not more rules than central government. In that case, it makes little difference to the school – in terms of independence – where the power of decision-making lies. Shortening the distance from the controlling body may prove favourable or unfavourable to the decision-making process in the school; it all depends on what form the local council's control takes. When decentralisation permeates the institutional level, greater autonomy is the result. The consequences of decentralisation for the autonomy of educational institutions are, therefore, not unequivocal. All the same, schools in highly centralised countries have a fairly low level of autonomy.

*Deregulation* is another trend that has more direct consequences for the autonomy of schools. Deregulation stems from the view that the central authorities, which are situated at some distance from educational institutions, are not capable of taking stock of specific situations at institutions. For this reason, it is often better if the institution itself makes decisions within the parameters set by the government. Deregulation leads to an increase in autonomy if responsibility is transferred to institution level. Deregulation and increased autonomy do not spring entirely from idealistic motives. Van Wieringen (1996), in his arguments supporting increased autonomy, argues that quality can best be improved at school level, and that autonomous schools are closer to parents and clients. At the same time, he also points out that it is easier to process cuts in educational budgets in a more autonomous system. This mix of ideals and pragmatic motives has certainly played a role in England and the Netherlands, where the autonomy of schools is greater than anywhere else in Europe. Throughout Western Europe, the tendency towards increasing the autonomy of schools can be observed practically everywhere, albeit in various degrees.

The developments in Central and Eastern Europe are highly interesting, as little has been published so far about developments there. Although the general tendency towards decentralisation is the same there as in Western Europe, the historical differences are so great that it is important to review separately the developments there over the last ten years.


## INCREASING AUTONOMY IN CENTRAL AND EASTERN EUROPE

Although the Iron Curtain fell in December 1989, it did not result in simultaneous educational reform in all of the countries of the former Soviet bloc. In Hungary, for example, the Education Act of 1985 gave more autonomy to schools and school heads. This was in keeping with a reform of the political system and with a new system for self-managed companies. This autonomy, introduced by the Act, did not mean that school heads were already completely autonomous, as there were insufficient financial resources to release this objective and the political system was too insecure (Balasz, 1994). In Lithuania, educational reforms started in 1988 (Arbatauskas, 1994). However, in most countries, the educational changes came about after the fall of the totalitarian regimes in December 1989. Hereafter, differences in the pace of development were extremely large. These differences could be attributed in part to the history of the countries. One must not forget that Central European countries, and a number of Eastern European countries, were capitalist countries until 1945.

Radelescu (1993, 87 *et seq.*), for example, describes the educational system of Rumania in the decades prior to the Second World War as being moderately centralised. In other words, education was financed predominantly by the central government, but local councils also contributed to it and had a certain amount of control. School heads had a social role and enjoyed a high level of prestige. Collaboration between the school and the local authorities was laid down by law, not just in terms of financial support, but also in terms of cultural relations between school and community.

This decentralised tradition was reorganised under Communism into an absolute form of centralism. In 1948, a law was passed making education exclusively a matter of state. Centralisation and politicisation are characteristics of this process of reorganisation, which left the Communist Party in charge of education. Although education was state financed parents were expected to contribute to the financing of Rumanian education, even though they were allowed no say in matters. The communication was top-down, nontransparent, unmonitorable and extremely bureaucratic. The local authorities had a passive role in this system. Initiative and creativity were – for all intents and purposes – forbidden. Human resource management became politicised; the professional, administrative and political roles of school heads became entangled. Certainly there were training programmes for school heads, but they had one central aim: to preach the prevailing ideology and ensure that school heads acted as efficient instruments of the central regime. There were parents' committees, some of which were compulsory, but they were merely a formality.

The image of the education system under Communism is summarised by Balkanski and Gyoshev (1994) as follows:

- Education was completely controlled by the party.
- Monopolisation of control through party terminology, run by the state and repudiation of signals from parents and public.
- Centralism, hierarchy and bureaucracy in the management of schools.
- Administrative arbitrariness and complete dependency on higher management levels.
- Ideological, distorted content of educational programmes.
- Restriction of freedom for pupil and teacher.
- Authoritarian and formalist repression of creativity and initiative.
- Diminished quality of education and demoralisation of pupils and teachers.
- Constant attempts at educational reform through ideological concepts.
- Teachers were state civil servants, and were treated as such.

Since December 1989, the political control and the monopoly of Communist ideology has disappeared. However, in a number of countries, centralism has continued now for a long time, not only in the sense that there is a state monopoly on educational management, but also that the hierarchy of ministry, inspectorate and school management has remained intact. Information is unilaterally top-down, school heads have no form of training, and communication channels between schools, parents, social partners and other actors in the community are still rare.

For a long time, ex-Communist countries – some more than others – have been faced with the paradox of having rejected totalitarianism while still having to live with a school and education system working in the old tradition. Thus, they are left with an anachronistic system (Radelescu, 1993, 84). For many years, education in some countries continued to be weighed down by socio-political slogans without democracy actually getting underway. A further disadvantage was that governments were not always able, or willing, to give priority to educational reform.

One of the main problems was – and still is – that communication is lacking both within the school system and between schools and the community. For a long time, people carried on working according to the communication principles applied in the Communist regime: atomism, repudiation, paternalism and isolation. This sometimes went hand in hand with a lack of social responsibility, in particular concerning education (Radelescu, 1993, 85).

## REFORMS

In a number of countries, new education acts were introduced fairly soon after the fall of the old regime. In Bulgaria, for example, the new education act was one of the first acts passed by the new house of representatives, the idea being that it would speed up the democratisation process (Gyoshev, 1993). The 28 regional school boards, which had once served as the eyes and ears of the Ministry of Education, were then relieved of their educational management and steering functions; the local councils were given more of a role to play in the area of buildings and the accessibility of schools, and schools now face the task of becoming legal bodies with greater autonomy. This autonomy also extends to the staffing policy. There are school councils within the schools comprised of representatives from the ranks of teachers, parents, pupils and the general public. These councils play an important part in matters such as curriculum development, pupil admission, criteria for passing and much more. Thus, in some respects, they resemble a staff meeting with additional advisory powers.

In many countries democracy in the field of education had not been carried through. In some countries, staff, financial and educational policies are still strongly centralised. Central government determines who teaches at schools and controls the finances for each school. Funds not used up within an academic year are redirected to the state coffers. The school heads still have little control or autonomy over important areas of management. Nevertheless, reforms in most Central and Eastern European countries have been of an exceptional breadth and depth (Kalous, 1996). They extend to the structure of education, the curriculum, legislation, management, administration, finance, the formation of new institutes and much more. The speed at which this has taken place has been extraordinary. In fact, in some cases, as for example in the Czech Republic, the reforms have come from below. It is this spontaneity in particular which has often been to blame for a great deal of educational chaos. Kalous distinguishes three stages in the transformation process. You start by demolishing everything which is a reminder of the past. Then you start to think about what you have actually dispensed with. The third stage involves assembling a new system (which, in Kalous' view, quite often resembles what you demolished in the first stage).

In the Czech Republic it took until 1994 for the government to present an education bill. In it, a number of interesting principles were formulated for the education system:

- The principle of subsidiarity: decision-making is positioned at the lowest possible level.
- The principle of participation: decision-making takes place wherever possible with the participation of those affected by the decision.
- The principle of deregulation: the top level determines and checks the results, while responsibility for implementation is left to the staff carrying out the work.

It is still difficult to determine the extent to which these principles have actually been implemented. Kalous finds that school heads vary greatly in their approach to school management, from authoritarian to co-operative styles of leadership. He also finds that many school heads do not realise how important it is to involve teachers in decisions relating to the school. The fear of having their authority undermined often prevails over their desire to make the school a more democratic institution.

The differences to be found in the various countries, in terms of the development of the education system and educational management after the fall of Communism, can be explained for the most part by the developments in the decades prior to the Fall. The first distinction that should be made here is between countries under Russian rule starting after the Russian Revolution and countries which found themselves on the eastern side of the Iron Curtain after the Second World War. In the latter group, 'Sovietization' was sometimes fairly artificial, and old traditions dating back to before 1948 were left partially intact or, at least, still remembered. The financial distress in these countries was just as great as in the 'old' Soviet states, but the public's outlook was different. It is worth noting that the differences between 'younger' Eastern bloc countries were also considerable.

Karsten and Majoor (1994) sketch the developments in the three 'Visegrad' countries: Poland, Czechoslovakia and Hungary. Of the three, Hungary is clearly the most advanced in its actual reform of the laws, as well as in its decentralisation of administrative tasks to local council level. It also increased the autonomy of schools, granted parents freedom of school choice and created opportunities for opting for an alternative school structure.

In the former Czechoslovakia, new laws were introduced after the Fall, but the fundamental changes were only to be found in the higher education act. They did, however, decentralise, which meant that local authorities gained more control over education. The notion of collective responsibility for education is still strongly supported and there is still much confusion about the relationship between the different governing and administration levels in the field of education. To complicate matters, after the Fall all the school heads were dismissed, and no system has yet been introduced to train new school heads. Some moves towards establishing school management training courses are gradually being made. However, most of these initiatives have originated from a select number of universities and have not been introduced systematically on a large scale. This contrasts with Hungary, where collaboration with Dutch experts has contributed to the ready availability of school management training courses (Karstanje, 1993). In Poland, educational reform was steered by the central government, while the network of independent schools has made great advances at grass-roots level. Responsibility for financing has been fairly swiftly re-assigned to local level, which Karsten and Majoor (1994) describe in terms of the 'decentralisation of poverty'.

All in all, one might argue that the differences between countries in Central and Eastern Europe are no fewer than those between educational developments in Western Europe, especially as compared to developments in the area of decentralisation and deregulation. In the next section, these developments will be discussed in more general terms.


## GENERAL TRENDS IN INCREASED AUTONOMY

The most important motives for decentralisation and deregulation in various Western, Central and Eastern European countries can be characterised as follows.

- Financial reasons, working on the assumption that lower organs (governmental bodies or educational institutions) are more frugal if allotted a fixed budget and given responsibility for the distribution of resources over the different budget categories.
- The opportunity to adjust to local or regional needs and circumstances, particularly since schools are expected to respond flexibly to the demands of parents, the institutions providing and taking clients and the job market. Although greater autonomy does not guarantee flexibility, it does give schools more chance to adjust to the circumstances.
- The fact that it is impossible to govern an educational establishment from a great distance. Problems in schools vary and are determined too much by local circumstances to be solved by government intervention. Subjects,

such as quality monitoring, could be initiated by central government, but cannot be run centrally. Control takes place exclusively by means of stimulating the environment and no longer through direct measures (Van Wieringen, 1996).

## CONTEXT FACTORS AND THE REDEFINITION OF SCHOOL MANAGEMENT

The context of education, here characterised with the concepts decentralisation and deregulation, have far reaching consequences for school management. This can be illustrated by reviewing typical situations in two European countries which differ greatly from one another in this area, namely France and the Netherlands.

In France, the director of a school is known as a *proviseur*, which means a provider. The *proviseur* is someone who channels directives from the ministry to the school, and makes sure that these are carried out properly. These directives are also fairly detailed, and are meant to be followed to the letter. It was not just a wry comment when a school inspector looked at his watch and said: 'At the present moment in every school from Cannes to Lille, they are teaching quadratic equations', it was close to the truth. The head teacher or *proviseur* is a civil servant. Financial matters and personnel fall under the responsibility of the ministry. Employment, promotion and dismissal are tasks assigned to the inspector, who also appraises the quality of the personnel. The inspector serves, therefore, as an important liaison officer between the ministry and the school. A major portion of the inspector's tasks in the country lies in the hands of the heads of schools (usually on behalf of the authorities). It is not surprising that finances are fairly strictly regulated from above. Consequently, heads of schools are not that directly involved in the primary process in the school. This is why school management programmes are so unusual in France. The training institutes which do exist are mostly concerned with rules and how best to implement them. In short: they have a fairly administrative bias. Ministry staff and inspectors play an important role in these training institutes.

This brief sketch of the role assigned to school heads in France contrasts glaringly with the role of their Dutch counterparts. School directors are responsible for the quality of their school. They have their own budget, which is barely adequate and is sometimes supplemented by money from sponsors. However, they are free to spend part of the budget known as the 'lump sum'. If there are necessary building repairs, for which there are no financial reserves, the funds are derived from other budgetary reserves, such as the money allotted for personnel. Directors are in charge of appraisal interviews and are greatly involved in hiring and dismissing staff. In principle, the director acts as the employer, albeit delegated, and negotiates with the unions on working conditions. Usually, however, they allow their organisations to represent them.

A timetable is not prescribed. Within certain parameters (governing the minimum number of hours), schools have the freedom to decide for themselves when, and how often, a certain subject is given. Fifty per cent of the examinations are set by the government and the other half by schools. In contrast to the French *proviseur*, the Dutch director could be called an 'entrepreneur'.

These two examples show how much school management can vary from country to country. Between these two fairly extreme situations, there is a wide range of approaches to organising school management.

The way in which school management is practised depends in part on the relationship between schools and government. This relationship can take on a wide range of outward forms, despite the fact that almost one hundred per cent of the costs of primary and secondary education is state-subsidised in practically every country. However, the existence of these subsidies does not mean that school heads all have the same relationship with the ministry of education; neither does it imply that school heads have the same range of tasks and responsibilities.

## A MODEL FOR SCHOOL AUTONOMY

The increase in the autonomy of schools has an impact on the role of school management. However, the question remains as to what exactly will be affected. In other words, what aspects of school management will change – or should change – due to national decentralisation and deregulation? Table 3.1 represents a model outlining the different possibilities. These have been drawn up to cover two dimensions:

- the extent of decentralisation and deregulation
- the special attention areas in school management.

The degree of decentralisation and deregulation has been drawn up at three levels. Naturally, there is a broad range of intermediate levels. All the same, these three levels indicate the gradations from low to high. The three levels comprise:

1. *A centralised and regulated situation.* This means that the government (usually the central government, or, in countries with a federal structure such as Germany, the regional authorities) regulates almost every aspect of educational institutions, and in so doing, has a central influence on what happens in schools. This is the case in France, Germany's *Länder*, Italy and a few Eastern European countries such as Romania.

2. *A moderate level of centralisation and regulation*, to be found in countries where the national government partially regulates the educational insti-

tutions. Here, one can distinguish different situations. The national government may, for example, strongly emphasise certain fields of interest and be more inclined to designate any other areas as falling under the responsibility of the school. In this system, financial policy and staffing policy may be designated the responsibility of the national government, whereas matters relating to the curriculum, education, school organisation and external relations might be considered as falling under a school's competence. In this 'interim category', one also finds countries with a high degree of decentralisation and a low degree of deregulation. This is the case when local councils or regional authorities have a higher level of authority in regulating the affairs of educational institutions.

3. *A high degree of decentralisation and deregulation*, whereby the national government provides resources and attaches no – or few – rules and conditions as to their use, is rather uncommon. The fact that the government must account for how it spends public funds invested in educational institutions means that a certain degree of regulation is almost a necessity. In the Netherlands, England, and to a lesser extent in Hungary, responsibilities have undergone a partial shift from the government to educational institutions. The national government fulfils its responsibility to carry out quality inspections by requiring schools to combine a solid system of internal quality checks with a quality monitoring system run by government inspectors (the Netherlands) or by private inspectors (England). This system makes high demands on school management. At the same time, it triggers other mechanisms, such as competition between schools.

The second type of approach in Table 3.1 concerns major task areas in school management namely:

- teaching and curriculum
- teaching and non-teaching staff
- organisation
- finances, buildings and facilities
- external relations.

Each sub-area is examined to see what the consequences of the degree of deregulation and decentralisation are.

## CONSEQUENCES FOR DIRECTORS OF EDUCATIONAL INSTITUTIONS

Increased autonomy has consequences for the directors of educational institutions. A look at **teaching and curriculum** in Table 3.1 would show a decline in the number of European countries found in the column on the left. Germany and France have already been mentioned as countries with fairly strict regulations for the range of subjects taught and the contents of teaching materials. School directors in these countries are clearly not set on stimulating curriculum development. Countries in the middle column, with a national core curriculum, such as Norway or Hungary, have a certain measure of freedom in deciding the number of lessons taught as well as the teaching schedule. Thus, they can stimulate curriculum development, although their leeway to do so depends on the extent to which other fields of interest in the figure are distributed to the left and right. Sometimes, school directors also opt to maintain old traditions, even if there is a shift in the degree of educational freedom open to them. This is the case, for example, in many Russian schools, where a considerable portion of the curriculum can now be determined by the board (the local council) and – to a smaller extent – by the school. However, this does not imply that the freedom is automatically put to use. Schools in the Netherlands could best be placed in the middle column. The prescribed final examinations and the core achievement levels mark a clear course for a major portion of the teaching programme. The freedom to develop a school's own timetable, set its own internal examinations and fill in the elective areas in the programme, entails a fair amount of responsibility. This, combined with the fact that Dutch schools are placed somewhat to the right of the diagram in other areas of interest, means that school heads in the Netherlands have their work cut out. Adopting an administrative style of leadership so that they can 'hide away in their offices' is not a viable option.

On a tour of Europe one would not very frequently encounter institutional autonomy in terms of **staff** policy. Spain, Italy, Germany and Eastern European school heads are often amazed to hear that their Dutch counterparts have established an organisation best described as an employers' organisation, and can negotiate with unions about the legal status of their personnel (although this is usually done for them collectively). In most countries, school staff have civil servant or semi-civil servant status. In Sweden, school heads have an office at the town hall, and in Germany an inspector can transfer a teacher from one school to another if the one school has a surplus of staff and the second a shortage. All teachers are employees of the same employer, the central government. This influences the position of school heads, whether their roles are that of 'boss' or 'teacher among teachers'. The latter best describes the position of school heads in Spain, where they are elected by fellow teachers for a period of three years, after which they return to their old teaching posts (if not re-elected). It goes without saying that in this case they do not take on the role of 'employer'.

In most countries, heads are able to determine their own internal **school organisation**. Schools can decide on the decision-making and co-ordination mechanisms themselves. The organisation of pupils into teaching groups, including streaming by general ability and banding by subject ability (also called 'setting') is more determined by the structure of the educational system. The pupil organisation in the classroom is partly related to the external structure as well.

**Table 3.1**  *Major task areas in school management in three different grades of autonomy*

| | *Centralised + regulated* | *Moderately centralised + moderately regulated* | *Decentralised + deregulated* |
|---|---|---|---|
| **Teaching and curriculum** | | | |
| *Subjects* | Prescribed subjects | Compulsory + optional school subjects | Free choice of subjects + groups of subjects |
| *Timetable* | Prescribed timetable | Prescribed for the total number of lessons for the entire school period | Free timetable |
| *Content* | Content of lessons is prescribed | National core curriculum specified | Indications of broad aims |
| *Exams* | National examination | Combined national and school examination | School exams |
| **Staff** | | | |
| *Qualification of staff* | Determined by law | Partly centrally regulated, partly determined by the school board | At the discretion of the school as employer |
| *In-service training* | National obligatory programme | The school chooses from government sponsored courses | Free choice of programme that fits the school's needs |
| *Appointment+ dismissal* | By national government or national inspector | By the school board | By the school director |
| *Appraisal* | By the inspector | By the school board or director | By a co-ordinating teacher |
| **School organisation** | | | |
| *Structure of school* | Regulated by law | Main lines determined by law, details by the school board | Free choice for the school |
| *Differentiation (streaming + setting)* | Regulated by law | Main lines determined by law, details by the school board | Free choice for the school |
| *Decision making structure* | Regulated by law | Main lines determined in an agreement between authorities and school | Free choice for the school |

**Table 3.1** *Cont.*

| | *Centralised +*<br>*regulated* | *Moderately*<br>*centralised +*<br>*moderately regulated* | *Decentralised +*<br>*deregulated* |
|---|---|---|---|
| **Finances, buildings, facilities** | | | |
| *Source of finances* | Financed entirely by government | Partly financed by the government + partly by participants' contributions | Partly financed by government, rest sponsoring, contract activities |
| *Management of finances* | By a governmental organisation | Partly by the school | Entirely by the school management |
| *Responsibility for buildings and facilities* | With the government | Partly by government (for example ownership), partly by the school | Responsibility of the school |
| *Information system* | Information is for external use (e.g. national statistics) | Information is both for statistics and for the management | Information for school improvement |
| *Salary of staff* | Determined and paid by government | Determined centrally, paid by the school board | Determined and paid by the school board as employer |
| *Legal status of staff* | Civil servants | Similar conditions to civil servants (e.g. salary scales and pensions) | Private employee |
| **External relations** | | | |
| *Recruitment of pupils* | From a fixed catchment area | From members of a certain church or denomination | Open admission |
| *Competition between schools* | Non-existent | Slight competition between schools | Strong competition between schools |
| *Relationship with other schools and business* | None | Only with schools | Intensive relationships with organisations outside school |
| *Negotiations with unions* | None | About minor issues | About salaries and legal status |

In most countries, the structure of the system is unequivocally prescribed by law. The law determines which types of schools are possible.

Sometimes there is freedom for schools to choose at what age they begin streaming. Hungary is a good example of a country which offers much room for manoeuvring in this respect. There are schools for primary education for the age groups 6–16, 6–14, 6–12 and even 6–10. Thus, there are secondary schools for the age groups 10–18, 12–18, 14–18 and hybrid forms. This freedom of choice, however, has created a great deal of confusion for schools that have to deal with these different system components.

Naturally, school heads can greatly influence the 'internal organisation' of the school. The head as 'teacher among teachers' in Spain or Switzerland is obviously not going to be strong on this point. Segmental organisation also emerges, however, in countries where the structure of school leadership is highly bureaucratic, either due to limited control over educational matters or to a lack of freedom in financial and/or personnel matters (Marx, 1995).

Decentralisation of **finances, buildings and facilities** can serve to make school directors into small (sometimes even medium-sized) entrepreneurs. This is particularly true where they have to provide additional resources. As far as the latter is concerned, Eastern European school heads are old hands. At times, they have to find ways of supplementing their extremely tight budgets through sponsoring, asking for contributions from parents and earning from contract activities. Understandably, this creates great differences between schools. This is a different sort of freedom, however, than that experienced by schools working with what is known in the Netherlands as a lump sum. This system works with margins of freedom found in no other countries in Europe except England. Thus, the degree of freedom that schools have in the other areas of interest are often considerably curtailed if others (national and local government) decide on the distribution of the finances. School heads who have to negotiate with subsidisers for every penny are not very motivated to be innovative, unless they can obtain extra budgets and the permission to spend them as they see fit.

Good **external relations** are necessary where schools are competing with one another. This is one scenario that could not apply to Germany, as pupils have to go to the school in whose catchment area they live. At most, there might be competition from a *Gesamtschule* – if that type of comprehensive school is allowed to operate in the area concerned. And even then, the numbers are strictly limited and subject to control. In many Eastern European countries, they are beginning to recognise the concept of competition between schools.

A precise, comparative review of the situation in the various Western and Eastern European countries is beyond the scope of this chapter. However, Table 3.1 does present a framework that has been used to illustrate a number of developments and might be used for further research based on the redefinition of educational management.

## REFERENCES

Arbatauskas, A. (1994) Indicators of school managers' activities, K Hämäläinen, F. van Wieringen (eds.), *Reforming Educational Management in Europe*, De Lier:

Academic Book Center, 175–187.

Balázs, E. (1994) School management training needs in Hungary, D. Oldroyd, F. van Wieringen (eds.), *European Issues in Educational Management*, De Lier: Academic Book Center, 69–85.

Balkanski, P., Gyoshev, B. (1994) Social change and teachers, K. Hämäläinen, F. van Wieringen (eds.), *Reforming Educational Management in Europe*, De Lier: Academic Book Center, 13–25.

Ekiert-Grabowska, D. Elsner (1993) Barriers to effective head teacher development and ways of overcoming them, R. Bolam, F. van Wieringen (eds.), *Educational Management Across Europe*, De Lier: Academic Book Center, 295–305.

Gyoshev, B. (1993) Democratic changes in governing Bulgarian education, R. Bolam, F. van Wieringen (eds.), *Educational Management Across Europe*, De Lier: Academic Book Center, 105–117.

Kalous, J. (1996) Transition and transformation of education, J. Kalous, F. van Wieringen (eds.), *Improving Educational Management*, De Lier: Academic Book Center, 5–17.

Karstanje, P.N. (1993) Implementing national infrastructures for school management programmes, R. Bolam, F. van Wieringen (eds.), *Educational Management Across Europe*, De Lier: Academic Book Center, 273–293.

Karstanje, P.N. (1994) The school principal as educational manager, in P. Karstanje, K. Ushakov, *Education Management: Problems and Approaches*, Moscow: September Publishing, 21–40 (English version of original Russian publication).

Karsten, S.D. Majoor (1996) Differences and similarities in Hungary, Czechoslovakia and Poland, S. Karsten, D. Majoor (eds.), *Education in East Central Europe: Educational changes after the fall of Communism*, Münster/New York: Waxmann, 157–164.

Kawecki, M.J. (1993) Schools in Poland – new initiatives, R. Bolam, F. van Wieringen (eds.), *Educational Management Across Europe*, De Lier: Academic Book Center, 139–155.

Marx, E. (1995) Models for school organisation, in P. Karstanje, K. Ushakov, *Education Management: Problems and approaches*, Moscow: September Publishing, 73–90 (English version of Russian publication).

Ouston, J., Early, P., Fidler, B. (eds.) (1996) *OFSTED Inspections, the Early Experience*, London: Fulton.

Quinn, R.E. (1991) *Beyond Rational Management: Mastering the paradoxes and competing demands of high performance*, San Francisco: Jossey Bass.

Radelescu, E. (1993). The decentralisation of educational management, R. Bolam, F. van Wieringen (eds.), *Educational Management Across Europe*, De Lier: Academic Book Center, 83–103.

Wieringen, A.M.L. van (1966) Onderwijsbeleid in Nederland (Educational policy in The Netherlands), Alphen aan den Rijn: Samson HD Tjeenk Willink.

# 4

## Continuities and Changes in Primary Headship

### GEOFF SOUTHWORTH

There are approximately 18,000 primary school headteachers in England (DfEE, 1997), yet we know surprisingly little about them. For example, no national surveys have been conducted to establish a profile of them and no large-scale studies have been attempted to describe exactly what they do. Such research as has been undertaken is now becoming dated since most published work focuses on headship in the 1980s and before the 1988 and 1992 Education Acts took effect. Consequently we know very little about what heads themselves think about their work and the effects of legislated reforms on their role in the 1990s.

Given this lack of knowledge I decided to conduct an enquiry into primary headship in the 1990s which aimed to:

- explore how a sample of ten experienced headteachers viewed the recent past
- investigate what these headteachers had to say about primary headship
- produce a picture of headship grounded in these heads' accounts of headship in the 1990s
- identify emerging themes from these heads' testimonies.

During the 1994–5 school year I interviewed each of the heads (five men, five women) using a common framework of questions. All the interviews were recorded, the transcripts were cleared with the respondents and from the data I developed the main findings which have now been published elsewhere (Southworth, 1995). Details of the heads and their schools are contained in the Tables 4.1 and 4.2.

All had been heads prior to 1988 in order for them compare headship then with now. All were thus mature, experienced heads rather than noviciates. Therefore, I make no claims for these heads being typical of all heads. This was a distinctive set of heads; theirs are the voices of experience. Nevertheless, these heads' views offer insights into primary headship which I will discuss in this chapter.

I shall also include some additional data because since conducting the research a second project has emerged. The research report stimulated interest among headteachers and I have been invited to talk about the project to

**Table 4.1**   *Time in post and time in teaching in 1994–5 academic year*

| Headteacher male/female | Number of years as headteacher | Year first appointed as headteacher | Number of years in present school | Number of headships | How long in teaching |
|---|---|---|---|---|---|
| 1. female | 12 | 1983 | 8+ | 2 | 20 |
| 2. female | 10 | 1984 | 10 | 1 | 24 |
| 3. male | 17 | 1977 | 11 | 2 | 27 |
| 4. female | 11 | 1983 | 11 | 1 | 25 |
| 5. male | 28 | 1966 | 7 | 3 | 40 |
| 6. male | 19 | 1975 | 19 | 1 | 30 |
| 7. female | 7 | 1987 | 7 | 1 | 27 |
| 8. male | 14 | 1980 | 4 | 2 | 25 |
| 9. female | 10 | 1984 | 6 | 2 | 19 |
| 10. male | 20 | 1974 | 14 | 2 | 28 |

**Table 4.2**   *Details of the heads' present schools*

| Headteacher male/female (M/F) | School type | Number of pupils on roll | Number of teachers |
|---|---|---|---|
| Head  1  F | Primary | 240 | 9.7 |
| Head  2  F | Primary (C.E.) | 100 | 4.8 |
| Head  3  M | Primary | 210 | 8.2 |
| Head  4  F | Infant | 275 | 11 |
| Head  5  M | Primary | 400 | 15 |
| Head  6  M | Primary (C.E.) | 210 | 8.9 |
| Head  7  F | Primary | 189 | 8.2 |
| Head  8  M | Primary (C.E.) | 410+26 ft nursery | 16.8 |
| Head  9  F | Primary (C.E.) | 275 | 13 |
| Head 10  M | Primary | 236 | 10.1 |

many groups of them. I estimate I have worked in seminar fashion with over 300 headteachers over the past three years and this has enabled me to carry out further enquiries and analysis. Later in this chapter I will report on these second level analyses.

The chapter is organised in to four sections. First, I set out the main findings from the 'Talking Heads' research. Second, I present five common themes I identified from the experienced heads' comments. Third, I discuss the second level analysis and reflections I have recently undertaken. Fourth, I identify a set of conclusions that include the proposal that the strongest continuity in headship may now need to be the very one which changes.

## MAIN FINDINGS

I invited the ten heads to reflect on the recent past in order to capture their thoughts about the effects of legislation since 1988. All considered the 1988 to 1994 period to have been a time of considerable professional challenge.

They identified positive gains, but most vividly remembered the pains of the reform programme. The key words they used to characterise the 1988–95 period were 'challenge', 'frustration', 'bewilderment', 'pressure'. Some were angry at what the profession had been subjected to in terms of explicit criticisms. In addition to these general remarks, I asked the heads to focus on three specific initiatives: the introduction of the National Curriculum; local management of schools (LMS); increased responsibilities for school governors.

### The introduction of the National Curriculum

The heads' comments about managing the introduction and the implementation of the National Curriculum fall into three contrasting sets. First, the change process had been very problematic. The volume of documentation had often overwhelmed them, because the first drafts of the curriculum were overly detailed and prescriptive.

The introduction of the National Curriculum was seen as a difficult change to manage. There had been no time for consolidation and the incessant amount of curricula revision created confusion. All the heads shared the view that the process of change should have been much better managed by central government and its agencies and they would wholeheartedly agree with Barber's (1996, p. 57) judgement that central government's management of the process of implementation was slipshod.

Second, many of the heads acknowledged that they had been able to use the reforms to move their schools forward. They had sometimes used the curricular reforms as a vehicle for modifying workplace practices in their individual schools. In other words, they had exploited the change process and made the reforms serve their own ends as well as those of central government.

Third, four heads felt the advent of the National Curriculum had impaired their confidence in teaching. None of these four had a time-tabled class teaching commitment and were thus not obliged to teach the National Curriculum in a sustained or regular way. This meant that their previous teaching experience was, in their eyes, largely made redundant. These heads, in common with other research, believed the new curriculum 'reduced their ability to provide curriculum leadership in terms of leading by example' (Webb, 1994, p. 34). In short, their capacity to provide instructional leadership was diminished.

## Local Management of Schools

LMS was recognised to have been a major change in the work of these heads. As one said, it has made headship 'a totally different ballgame'. All were aware that LMS increased their management task load, but most had established systems that kept them free from a day-to-day involvement in the details of LMS. On balance the heads were positive about LMS, although two who had faced budget deficits and teacher redundancies were more muted in their endorsement of it:

> It's fine while the money is going up, it is not so good when the money is coming down.

The finding that heads favour LMS is in line with other studies (Mortimore and Mortimore, 1991; Webb, 1994). Heads appear to enjoy the greater control over their schools which LMS has given them. While it is a mixed blessing in some senses, the evidence suggests that primary heads do not want to return to a time when they did not manage the school's budget because LMS has sustained heads' feelings of being in control of the school.

Indeed, this finding suggests that the increase in financial control acted as a counterbalance to the perceived loss of curricular influence. Prior to the introduction of the National Curriculum it was common for primary heads to feel either in control of the curriculum, or to believe they exerted a powerful influence upon it (Coulson, 1976; Campbell, 1985; Southworth, 1987 and 1995a). The National Curriculum was regarded by some heads as a reduction of their influence over 'their' schools' curriculum. Many heads appeared to feel that they were losing their power over the curriculum. However, the introduction of LMS may have offset these heads' feelings of powerlessness. The perceived loss of control over the curriculum was compensated by an increase in control over the school's finances and resources.

## School Governors

The heads claimed to be on good terms with their schools' governors, yet despite these apparently positive relations many were concerned that their dealings with them were not as productive as the heads wanted.

The heads generally felt they were still assisting their governors and helping them to meet their statutory roles. This meant that the heads were devoting a lot of their time to supporting and developing the governors to implement ways of discharging their responsibilities. In short, these heads were not simply working *with* their governors, they were also working *on them* and both tasks were time consuming. New powers for the governors had not relieved these heads of tasks and responsibilities, if anything their workloads and allotted time with governors had increased.

## EMERGING THEMES

In asking the heads to reflect on the recent reforms I also wanted to use the past to illuminate the present. All had been in post prior to 1988 and I asked them to compare headship then with headship in 1995. This contrast effect proved valuable in helping the heads to say how they felt headship had changed. There are five themes I will focus on here.

### 1. Accountability

Underscoring much that these heads said was their sense of responsibility for 'their' schools. Time and again their comments revealed the assumption that they were the individual who was responsible for the school:

> Ultimately it is all my responsibility, mine with the governors, the buck stops with me.

They saw themselves as personally accountable for the success of the school. While being individually accountable was a weight they had to carry, it was accepted because it was the cost of being the central figure in the school.

Most had wanted to be a head because they perceived it to be the pivotal position in the organisation. They understood that the influence of the head-teacher was paramount in the school. Yet the ambition to become a head was not for self-aggrandisement. These heads did not seek organisational power for its own sake, but as a tool to help them install and develop their educational beliefs and professional values across the school. Although they were aware that they wielded power and influence in their respective schools they wanted to make a difference to their schools' effectiveness. Underneath their sense of being in control lay a particular motive for possessing power – they wanted to develop and improve their schools.

### 2. School Improvers

The heads generally believed they were empowered by their position. Although they were accountable, they were also 'licensed' to lead the school and develop it. At some point each of the heads spoke about 'their' school. All had stories to tell about how they had moved the schools on. Indeed, they seemed fascinated with their schools. Without doubt, each was committed to improving her or his school.

All recognised that they were playing a part in moving their schools forward. Some spoke about what the improvement process was like for them in their respective schools. However it was expressed, it was apparent these heads regarded improving the school as their main priority:

> The most difficult thing in the world is to change classroom practice. A school is a bit like a ship, when it has got its course it is fairly well mapped out; it is like an

oil tanker, it takes a long time to turn it. It has been damned difficult at times, but that is what I wanted to do.

Moreover, the heads were only too aware that the process of improving a school was often impeded by other demands on their time. The range of work pressures too often hindered them in their wish to develop the school. They implied they were juggling competing priorities for their time and attention and often felt they had to relinquish development activities because maintenance tasks were more urgent. Some gave the impression they felt that they were often in the middle of things, but not always at the heart of the school. There was too much management and not enough time for development.

Coupled with the heads' comments about their improvement efforts was a unanimous and deep concern about the Office of Standards in Education's (OFSTED) programme of school inspections.

While in the recent past the arrival of the National Curriculum, LMS and new powers for governors had been major preoccupations for these heads, the OFSTED inspections were now their number one concern. Inspection was and remains *the* contemporary issue. I had by intention not explicitly asked the heads to talk about OFSTED, but all did; not one ignored it. Equally significantly, when they did they spoke at length, with passion, feeling and force.

Undoubtedly one effect of the school inspection programme was that it stimulated in the words of one of the heads *'massive self examination'*. These heads, like others in England (see Coulson, 1976; Southworth, 1987 and 1995), were closely associated with their schools and were sensitive to how the report of the school would reflect on them professionally and, I suspect, personally. For them, the inspection was not only an external audit of the school's strengths or of the quality of its work, it was also, because of the head's strong attachment to the school and identification with it, a professional and personal assessment of the head. At its very core the meaning of school inspection for primary headteachers is that it is they who are being judged. The inspection of the school was tacitly understood by these heads to be an examination of themselves.

### 3. Management and Leadership

It was clear from the accounts of these heads that all had been managing a large number of changes, at a fast pace, under considerable pressure and in a climate of criticism and hostility towards schools and teachers. The heads generally regarded their work as more demanding than it used to be. Managing the mandated changes had been taxing and frustrating. It had also been accomplished in addition to everything else they had been to trying to do in their schools.

The sense of the job being more demanding was evident in a number of ways. Some described the volume of paperwork they now had to deal with. Others spoke about how they were spending more evenings back on site attending a variety of meetings. The heads also believed they were dealing with many 'more players' (Murphy, 1994). Heads today are at the centres of more complex networks of groups, agencies and individuals. The flow of information has expanded and accelerated. Heads, therefore, are processing more pieces of information than in former times. They are also dealing with more professional 'intelligence' than before. Their work has become more intense because they are literally trying to keep so much more in their heads.

While these heads had managed numerous curricular and organisational changes, they had also faced enormous uncertainty because in managing these reforms they had grappled with two other changes. First, they had begun to recognise that the very nature of educational change had altered. All of these heads were, prior to 1988, mainly accustomed to dealing with evolutionary and internally prescribed change. The school's curriculum was *developed* rather than reformed and changes occurred in a serialised form. Since the 1988 Education Reform Act, there had been a switch from dealing with one thing at a time to multiple and simultaneous change. Heads therefore needed to be able to react to this new order. In short, they had to learn to manage the new changes, whilst also coming to terms with a dramatically new process of change.

Second, in responding to this new order heads themselves had to change. They were now managers of change mandated by others. No longer could they manage developments they and their colleagues wanted, suddenly their own agendas were superseded by the priorities of others. The heads therefore felt less ownership of the changes, although they were expected to manage them. And the key term in all of this is *manage*.

The increase in management at the school level created for heads a *tension* between organisational management and professional leadership. Underscoring many of the remarks of these heads was a dilemma. Are they heads or teachers, chief executives or professional leaders (Hughes, 1985), organisational managers or school leaders?

The increase in the scale and scope of the changes in education has led to a commensurate increase in the complexity of school management (Bolam *et al.*, 1993). The deluge of reforms has been accompanied by an upsurge in management activity by heads. As others have explored, this has led heads and senior managers to shift their focus 'from managing education to managing an educational institution' (deputy head cited in Ball, 1993, pp. 71–72).

For some of the headteachers this had been an interesting and relevant part of their professional development, however, several acknowledged that there had been some role displacement. The reform programme diminished the heads' personal influence over the school's curriculum, and substituted in its place increased financial and site responsibilities. However, this trade-off had been made more complicated with the introduction of school inspections which judge the quality of teaching and learning, and which have encouraged heads to re-focus on classroom matters.

These forces have created the situation where heads are now pulled in several directions. They are managers of an organisation, they are expected to provide professional leadership and, in some sense or other, continue to be teachers. As other studies have shown (Coulson, 1986; Southworth, 1995a) the very title *headteacher* is apposite. It accurately frames the admixture of tasks and tensions in the role. Not only is there an in-built role ambiguity, which recent changes have exaggerated, there can now be a strong sense of conflict between the head and teacher components of the role.

Moreover, the day-to-day tasks of managing the school are the cause of heads feeling their teaching has been supplanted, or is in constant danger of being displaced. For example, managerial tasks were time-consuming and reduced opportunities for the heads to work in classrooms. It was also the case that they were not around the school as much as they would have liked because of meetings, case conferences and other demands: they were less visible presences in their schools. Yet several studies have shown that the presence of the head is a key feature in providing cultural leadership (Nias *et al.*, 1989) and instructional leadership (Smith and Andrews, 1989). Heads need to be active and visible participants in 'their' schools; what they attend to and comment on is influential. If heads are taken out of the school, or their presence is lessened, then so too is their influence and professional leadership.

For these reasons then, the heads were discomforted by not always being able to participate in the educational leadership of the school. The school may be managed, but is this at the expense of professional leadership? Urging heads to provide more leadership may fly in the face of the fact that they daily experience the demands of more management tasks. Moreover, asking heads such as these to do more, when they are already working hard and putting in many hours before and after school may be counter-productive. It might well increase feelings of guilt that they cannot do more because they are caught in a management trap of increased bureaucracy – more administration, more people to involve and consult with – yet with very little, if any, additional help. The tension between managing and leading is a source of frustration, if not guilt, for primary headteachers.

### 4. Job Satisfaction and Dissatisfaction

Already certain job satisfiers and dissatisfiers have been mentioned. All of the heads saw themselves as sometimes not wholly in control of their work lives. They saw the work as constantly changing:

> You never know what's going to happen next. There's no predictability to headship . . . it is very draining [but also] very rewarding. You do not know what is going to come through the door.

All felt they needed to be able to think on their feet and to be able to deal with the unexpected. Some spoke about how they were often interrupted in their work and had to switch from one task to another.

These findings are in line with other studies into the work patterns of primary heads. However, what emerged from this study was a slightly different perspective. Although too much task switching is challenging, several of the heads also said how much they enjoyed the variety of the work and derived a sense of job satisfaction from coping with whatever was thrown at them. The work of primary heads may be prone to interruption, reactive in nature and fragmented, but it can also be interestingly varied and rewarding when heads feel they can manage the unexpected.

When asked directly about the least rewarding aspects of their work they complained about the amount of paperwork, or of never having uninterrupted time. One said that going through disciplinary procedures with a failing teacher was the worst thing because it was so 'hurtful' to all concerned. For another 'weak teachers' were a major concern and worry. These comments no doubt reflect individual circumstances, cases and situations and suggest that it is not always possible to generalise about the causes of job dissatisfaction.

By contrast, there was one overwhelming reason for these heads' sense of satisfaction – it was being with the children. I asked each of them what were the most rewarding parts of being a headteacher:

I think working with kids of primary school age is wonderful . . . It's just seeing them grow, their enjoyment.

It's when the children achieve something.

It has to be something to do with children.

Others added it was to do with working with people, colleagues as well as pupils. Several also liked the relative freedom of being a head, of being able, sometimes, to determine what to do and when. For these heads the rewards outweighed the pressures of the job and this state of affairs looked set to continue, providing they could keep in touch with the children and with their respective staff groups. However, it also follows from the above that any severance between the heads and the children in 'their' schools, or any distancing between the two parties, would be an erosion of the heads' job satisfaction and could be a serious blow to their view of the role.

## 5. Effective Headteachers

As part of the interviews I asked the heads to say what they thought an effective headteacher looked like. Their comments raised five sets of ideas.

First, there was a strong correspondence between what the heads said about effective leaders and what others have suggested. These heads believed that effective school leaders need to continue to exhibit similar characteristics to those identified in earlier studies or analyses (e.g. Coulson, 1986; Southworth, 1990; Bolam, 1993).

Second, it is quite clear from what these headteachers said that being a headteacher is not easy. The job is demanding and full of tensions and dilemmas. Moreover, the work appears to have intensified in recent times; more is expected of headteachers. Yet heads have not received very much more in the way of help and support. In the period immediately following the 1988 Education Act heads found themselves managing multiple changes, at an unprecedented pace, and with no clear sense of where they were going. Heads were then very much on their own. Today primary heads feel they have weathered the reforms but are still without significant improvements in their workplace conditions. Budgets are tight, resources are limited and demands from central government continue. It needs to be made plainer than the literature appears to suggest that being an effective head is not an easy task. Some recognition of the trials and challenges of running and leading a school would help counterbalance the seemingly incessant demand for more, while providing no additional means of meeting the demands.

Third, we need to be cautious about offering a view of effective leadership which is untenable. Notions of effectiveness need to provide realistic models of what is possible. Too little attention has been paid to whether effective heads are not actually unusual heads. Maybe effective leaders are sufficiently different from the rest of us that they are models not everyone, or even many, can emulate? Are effective heads really only superwomen and supermen? I tend to think not, but nevertheless there is a real need to take greater account of the circumstances and conditions of headteachers and to be very careful about appearing to offer unrealistic models for others. Indeed, perhaps the greatest benefit of the characteristics of effective headteachers is not their prescriptive impact, but their power to encourage heads to reflect on their own attributes and to use the lists as a stimulus to their own professional development.

Fourth, from my own studies into headship (see Nias et al., 1989 and 1992; Southworth, 1990, 1994, 1995a, 1997, 1997a, 1998) I have formed the view that lists of the characteristics of effectiveness do not by themselves give a very clear view as to what distinguishes a more effective head from a less effective one. Rather, it seems to me that while all the characteristics are probably important some will be more so than others at different times and in different settings. The conundrum of 'effectiveness' is that no one can predict which of the characteristics matters most, because so much depends on the specific circumstances of the school in which the head is working as well as the knowledge and skills of the individual head. For example, in some situations consulting with others may be an inappropriate thing to do, in others it might be vital. It seems to me that one of the characteristics a head needs is the capacity to perceive and understand situations they face and encounter.

However, my main point is to say that lists of effectiveness are only an initial cartoon. We are only at a very early stage in our understanding of effective headteacher behaviour. We need both more detailed pictures and to recognise that there are many ways of being effective or ineffective. Certainly, one strong feature to emerge from interviewing these ten heads was their individuality.

Therefore, in recognising that we are only at an initial understanding of effective school leadership, we also should contemplate the idea that *we may never discover* all there is to know about leader effectiveness. School leadership may be just too complex, too variable, too unpredictable and too contingent upon so many variables that we can never be sure of very much. There may just be 'too many moving parts' (Huberman, 1992), too many factors, contexts and personalities for us ever to develop a definitive understanding. This is not to be defeatist about the need for enquiries, rather, it is to acknowledge that leadership, and school development for that matter, is essentially a dynamic, subtle, varied and complicated set of processes. We cannot be sure of understanding the linkages between the characteristics and I suspect we may never be clear about causal connections.

## FURTHER REFLECTIONS

In sharing much of the foregoing with other headteacher groups I have developed further insights and ideas, particularly in terms of how members of these groups respond to the interpretations developed from the ten talking heads study. In this section I want to focus on these developing ideas and relate them to the theme of change and continuity in school leadership.

The first half of the 1990s was a period when heads and others in schools were involved in assimilating and accommodating all the changes in education. Heads became accustomed to managing imposed reforms. At the same time, headteachers learned through experience that educational change is not what it used to be. The very character of educational change was transformed. It has become systemic and mandated. Heads have had to come to terms with the fact that politicians have created a new orthodoxy of hands-on intervention. Large-scale governmental action has become common and 'structural solutions through top-down regulations' and 'large scale tinkering' (Fullan, 1993, p. 2) have become the norm.

While some were able to combine the external reforms with their internal development plans for the school, by and large the externally driven reforms were associated with imposition and compliance, as well as poor conception, clumsy implementation and unrealistic deadlines. In particular, implementation of the reforms was perceived as muddled and botched. While today the anger that attended the implementation process has receded, it nevertheless remains as something learned by those in schools. In other words, change has developed a bad reputation.

Second, while change is now ever-present in education, it has become discontinuous. Discontinuous change means policy initiatives are unlikely to be 'more of the same only better' (Handy, 1989, p. 6). Rather, heads have become accustomed to policy developments disturbing established structures and creating turbulence in schools (e.g. the introduction of school performance league tables; the advent of school inspections; literacy and numeracy hours). Moreover, such changes powerfully influence, if not shape how teachers' and headteachers' work is organised. Headship, therefore, is less to do with managing a steady-state organisation and more to do with anticipating and responding to new initiatives, challenges and opportunities. The constancy of change in schools, and the acceleration of educational developments, mean that headteachers need to be:

- future oriented;
- capable and sophisticated managers of multiple change;
- able to live with change in proactive and productive ways;
- aware of the professional learning needs of the staff and themselves;
- active in orchestrating development activities which support staff and which advance the school's capacity to improve.

(Hall and Southworth, 1997)

Third, heads have largely responded to the new order by doing *more*. More is a key word when heads talk about the reforms and it is a word used a great deal in this paper. It signals:

- more work – the volume of tasks has increased
- more involvement – there are more players to liaise with
- more haste – deadlines have shortened and pace has accelerated
- more priorities – harder choices have to be made between competing agendas
- more pressure on finite resources
- more initiatives – since the Labour government elected in 1997 has continued the trend set in train by the Conservative administration.

In their own eyes heads feel they are working longer, harder and doing more than they previously did. They frequently articulate the pressures and strains. All, at times, suffer from chronic busyness. If external change has a bad reputation school leaders felt experience of managing it is uncomfortable and arduous.

Fourth, if heads have generally responded to change by doing more are they now approaching a time when they need to change their approach? Most of the heads with whom I have shared the findings voice one enduring concern: the lack of time for a sustained focus on leading the school's improvement efforts to ensure they meet the children's needs and enhance their achievements. It is not that heads cannot do this, rather it is that they often feel distracted from it. Heads undoubtedly want to play a sustained part in improving their schools, but frequently feel prevented from so doing by all their other responsibilities. If this is generally true of headteachers a reappraisal of their task load is overdue and a restructuring of the workplace conditions of primary heads may now be necessary. Without such a reappraisal and revisions the changes and the continuities in headship will combine to limit the degree to which they can do what *they* really want to achieve – the improvement of the school for the children's learning.

This leads to a fifth point. If there are around 18,000 primary heads in England we are not as a profession learning enough from what they have to say. If these men and women are the real world school improvers we need to value and heed the lessons they can teach from their first hand knowledge of improving primary schools. We should listen more than previously to their voices of experience.

## CONCLUSIONS

This chapter explores the relationship between school leadership theory and practice or more accurately the relationship between theory and a group of practitioners. Headteachers' work is theory laden. In much of my work on school leadership I have tried to chart the 'theories' headteachers hold about their work. For many years now I have tried to identify their subjective constructs, their values and explanations of their roles. In short, I am deeply interested in headteachers' 'folk theories' about school leadership.

In this chapter I have outlined the systemic changes that have occurred in education and argued that while structural and organisational changes have taken place, heads have nevertheless continued to do many things, albeit in a more intense manner.

I have suggested that they should be listened to with greater attention than previously. One consistent feature of the dissemination of my talking heads research is that the primary heads who have heard me have taken a crumb of comfort from the idea that at least someone is listening to them. Looked at another way this means they feel undervalued, if not generally ignored. Heads are crucial to the development of their primary schools and many of the feelings reported here do not energise them or sustain them to meet the challenges they face.

Yet, heads have also proved remarkably resilient and most continue to be upbeat about their schools. Their optimism remains intact, but it is probably because day-in and day-out they are in the company of young children who are enthusiastic and excited about their learning. It is from their pupils, as well as their colleagues, that heads derive professional nourishment and satisfaction. By contrast, their wider occupational circumstances look to be less hospitable. Challenge is an important component of the change process, but so too is support. The voices I hear suggest that there is ample of the former and too little of the latter. The morale of headteachers has been sapped by too much external demand and challenge. Furthermore, this is not a novel feature, it has been going on for the best part of a decade, if not longer. Support needs to come in a variety of guises, but whatever form it takes heads need to know it as support because without it the enterprise of primary school improvement may be at risk.

I have also said that these researched heads:

- saw themselves as powerful and controlling
- experience their positional authority as empowering
- believe they can make a difference to 'their' schools and the pupils.

Perhaps these are some of the contemporary myths of headship and form part of the 'romance of leadership' (Gronn, 1996). If they are they have become sedimented into heads' consciousness and into their occupational selves. In a personal and deep sense they believe they can make a difference to pupils' learning and lives. Consequently, when heads are implicitly asked the question what is school management and leadership for, I suspect they would answer to improve the school in order to better meet pupils' needs. Ten years ago they might have said school development, but today it is school improvement. For these heads, educational leadership and management is about improving the outcomes and processes of educational organisations.

Some heads are now involving other senior staff in leading the school's development and have introduced senior management teams or are working in close partnership with the deputy head (Webb, 1994; Southworth, 1998). Such moves are not necessarily intended to empower others, rather, they may only be an acknowledgement of the increased work demands and heads realising they cannot single-handedly deal with everything. Although moves to a shared approach to leadership demonstrate shifts in the distribution of tasks between senior managers, they do not imply the end of the primary headteacher's monopoly on power in the workplace. One constancy in primary school management and leadership is the pre-eminence of the headteacher.

If the pre-eminence of the primary headteacher is *the* continuing feature it may now be the very one which has to change. Revisions to their taskloads and providing greater support may be necessary developments, but they may not be sufficient. A more radical transformation is needed, one which begins to circumscribe the dominance of the headteacher and enables them to be more focused on professional matters rather than on administrative problems, one where leadership is actively developed at all levels in the school, where other staff share in the responsibilities and where there is a more ethical and emancipatory intent. Their power, which heads enjoy and regard as personally empowering, also means they are individually responsible for seemingly everything. Now that everything has expanded they are swamped by the demands and, crucially, less able (some days disabled) to do what they most want to achieve, the improvement of their schools.

The very thing they want to do is slipping – more and more – from their grasp. Consequently, many experience a pervasive sense of guilt that is forging the iron in their souls. Perhaps, then, they should let go of this inherently individualistic and egocentric way of doing headship. Has the time arrived when we invite heads to stop facing the future by looking backwards? Hanging on to all the power just because that is the way headship has always been may only be a recipe for less professional pleasure and more and more pain. If headship has essentially stayed the same, only more so, the context for heads has changed dramatically and it may well be time for a change. Surely we need to open a debate not only about what headship is, but also *what it might be*.

## REFERENCES

Ball, S. (1993) Culture, cost and control: self-management and entrepreneurial schooling in England and Wales, in J. Smyth (ed.), *A Socially Critical View of the Self-Managing School*, London: Falmer Press, 63–82.

Barber, M. (1996) *The Learning Game: Arguments for an education revolution*, London: Victor Gollancz.

Bolam, R., McMahon, A., Pocklington, K. and Weindling, D. (1993) *Effective Management in Schools*, London: DfE/HMSO.

Campbell, R. J. (1985) *Developing the Primary School Curriculum*, London: Holt, Rinehart & Winston.

Coulson, A. (1976) The role of the primary head, in T. Bush *et al.* (eds.), *Approaches to School Management*, London: Harper & Row, 274–292.

Coulson, A. (1986) *The Managerial Work of Primary School Headteachers*, Sheffield: papers in *Education Management, No. 48*, Sheffield City Polytechnic.

DfEE (1997) *Statistics of Education: Schools in England 1997*, London: DfEE.

Fullan, M. (1993) *Change Forces*, London: Falmer Press.

Gronn, P. (1996) From transactions to transformations: a new world order in the study of leadership, *Educational Management and Administration*, 24(1): 7–30.

Hall, V., and Southworth, G. (1997) A review of the literature on headship in England and Wales, *School Leadership and Development*, 17(2): 151–170.

Handy, C. (1989) *The Age of Unreason*, London: Hutchinson.

Huberman, M. (1992) Critical introduction, in M. Fullan, *Successful School Improvement*, Buckingham: Open University Press.

Hughes, M. (1985) Leadership in professionally staffed organisations, in M. Hughes *et al.* (eds.), *Managing Education: The system and the institution*, London: Holt, Rinehart & Winston, 262–290.

Mortimore, P., and Mortimore, J. (1991) *The Primary Head: Roles, responsibilities and reflections*, London: Paul Chapman.

Mortimore, P., Sammons, P., Stoll, L., Lewis, D. and Ecob, R. (1988) *School Matters*, Wells: Open Books.

Murphy, J. (1994) Transformational change and the evolving role of the principal: early empirical evidence, paper presented at AERA Conference, New Orleans, also in Murphy, J. & Louis, K. S. (eds.) *Reshaping the Principalship: Insights from transformational change efforts*, Newbury Park, CA.

Nias, J., Southworth, G. and Yeomans, R. (1989) *Staff Relationships in the Primary School: A study of school cultures*, London: Cassell.

Nias, J., Southworth, G. and Campbell, P. (1992) *Whole School Curriculum Development in Primary Schools*, London: Falmer.

Smith, W.F. and Andrews, R. L. (1989) *Instructional Leadership: How principals make a difference*, Alexandria, VA: Association for Supervision & Curriculum Development.

Southworth, G. (1987) Primary school headteachers and collegiality, in Southworth, G. (ed.), *Readings in Primary School Management*, London: Falmer.

Southworth, G. (1990) Leadership, headship and effective primary schools, *School Organisation*, 10(1), 3–16.

Southworth, G. (1994) Trading places: job rotation in a primary school, in G. Southworth, (ed.), *Readings in Primary School Development*, London: Falmer Press, 48–66.

Southworth, G. (1995) *Talking Heads: Voices of experience; an investigation into primary headship in the 1990s*, Cambridge: University of Cambridge Institute of Education.

Southworth, G. (1995a) *Looking into Primary Headship: A research based interpretation*, London:, Falmer Press.

Southworth, G. (1997) Primary headship and leadership, in M. Crawford, L. Kydd and C. Riches (eds.), *Leadership and Teams in Educational Management*, Buckingham: Open University Press, 40–61.

Southworth, G. (1997a) Sweeping decentralisation of educational decision-making authority: lessons from England and New Zealand, *Phi Delta Kappan* 78(8), 626–632, with R. Williams, B. Harold and J. Robertson.

Southworth, G. (1998) *Leading Improving Primary Schools: The work of headteachers and deputy heads*, London: Falmer Press.

Webb, R. (1994) *After the Deluge: Changing roles and responsibilities in the primary school*, York: Association of Teachers & Lecturers.

# 5

## Primary Schools and the Nature of the Education Market Place

### LES BELL

### INTRODUCTION

This chapter considers the ways in which headteachers in primary schools in England have responded to an educational policy based on the establishment of an educational market place. It will look briefly at the nature of that policy and identify the main characteristics of the educational market. It will consider the reported activities of primary school heads in relation to the competitive nature of the educational market place and the strategic marketing of their schools within that environment. It will conclude by offering some observations on the interpretation of those activities in the light of what heads say about their own professional values and the educational market place, a critique of the concept of the market as a means of allocating resources and the extent to which heads of primary schools operate from a position of organisational ambiguity in respect of the educational market and the ways in which they manage within that context.

Management and the market were closely interrelated in Conservative Government policy on the reform and restructuring of state schooling. Both the local management of schools (LMS) and grant maintained (GM) schools policies occasioned not only new conceptions of what it meant to manage a school, but also altered relations between schools and local communities. As Ball (1993) observed, the market and management reforms replaced collective, bureaucratic controls, structures and relationships with individualistic and competitive ones. The model for this fundamental change in perspective and practice is derived from the private sector within which fee-charging schools, managed like small businesses, market and sell their services to parents whose educational requirements they must anticipate and whose confidence they must retain in order to survive. Studies of the impact of particular markets on the management practices of schools, and theorising about the relationship between local market conditions and the education identities promoted by individual schools, have chiefly been directed at the secondary sector. These studies highlight the extent to which, in secondary schools, management styles are being adopted that stress stricter and more bureaucratic divisions of labour between senior managers and teacher subordinates and involve more explicit ways of managing and marketing the reputation of those schools (see Ball, 1992 and 1993). The little research currently available on the impact of recent educational reform on the work of primary school heads and primary school management points up similar developments. For example, findings from the PACE project (Pollard *et al.*, 1994), in which 48 primary heads were interviewed, suggest that the local management of primary schools is giving rise to a gradual shift away from collective decision-making towards a more 'top-down' directive approach entailing a form of contrived collegiality or 'managed participation'. Similar conclusions are reached by Menter (1997) in a study of the effects of education marketisation on a group of primary schools in one city. The research reported in this chapter challenges such earlier work by concluding that individualism and competitiveness, while latent in the work of some heads, is not sufficiently pronounced as to lead to the establishment of an education market place and thus preclude genuine forms of inter school collaboration.

The data on which this chapter is based is derived from a recently completed Economic and Social Science Research Council funded project (R000221271). The main aim of this project was to examine the extent to which management practices, defined as the formulation of policy and day-to-day decision-making, varied between primary schools that had different degrees of managerial responsibility devolved to them. Schools (200) from the LEA maintained and grant maintained (GM) sectors were included in the sample. This provided a comparison between two parts of the maintained sector that had been granted different degrees of institutional autonomy by government legislation. Fieldwork was conducted in two phases. In the first phase a lengthy questionnaire was sent to the heads of 289 primary schools. This sample included every all-through primary school which, at the time of starting the research, had been operating as a GM establishment for a minimum of one year (49 in total), and a randomly selected group of all-through self-governing local authority maintained primary schools located in five LEAs in central England (208 in total). The questionnaire elicited data on 137 primary schools, including 29 from the GM sector. These data comprised basic information on the schools, the perceptions of their heads concerning a range of management roles, practices and functions and details of the characteristics of the education market within which each one operated. The questionnaire data were analysed using the social science statistical package SPSS. These tests enabled us to identify features for each group of respondents which were typical of that group. The principle of typicality, tempered by considerations of geographical proximity, determined the choice of heads for the interview phase of the research. 'Typicality' refers to heads whose responses to the questionnaire in terms of how they described their style of management matched other respondents working in the *same* school sector. This produced a sample of heads whose responses approximated to those that were typical of their sector and a smaller group whose responses were atypical.

The second phase of the research followed the analysis of the question-naire data. Detailed semi-structured (audio-recorded) interviews were conducted with 12 LEA and six GM school heads who had returned a completed questionnaire. These interviews explored further the nature and extent of respondents' sense of professional empowerment and efficacy including management style and level of job satisfaction. The interviews were also used to obtain additional background information about individual schools and, in particular, the character of the education market environment in which they were set.

## CHARACTERISTICS OF THE EDUCATIONAL MARKET PLACE

A plethora of policy documents bombarded schools, colleges and local education authorities in Britain during the 1980s. These culminated in the Education Reform Act (Department for Education and Science[DES], 1988a) and the series of circulars and education acts (e.g. DES, 1988b, 1991) which followed it. This legislation was largely derived from a socio-political philosophy based on the work of right wing political economists such as Friedman (1980) and Hayek (1973) who believed that market forces were the most appropriate way of allocating resources and structuring choices in all aspects of human endeavour, including social and educational policy. This belief was translated into a set of organisational principles for public sector institutions by, among others, Harris (1980), Joseph (1974) and Scruton (1984), the main tenets of which were:

- the absolute liberty of individuals to make choices based on their own self interest
- the freedom of individuals to exercise such choices without being subject to coercion from others
- the freedom to choose being exercised daily through spending choices rather than every five years through the ballot box.

Competition becomes the motive force for policy implementation and through it improvement in the nature and quality of service will be brought about as the family becomes a unit of economic consumption, its members make choices about products and public sector institutions behave as firms seeking to maximise both profits and market share.

Since 1988 legislation has been introduced to implement an educational policy based on creating and sustaining an educational market place. Much of this legislation focused on making schools accountable, providing parents with information on which to make judgements about the relative performance of schools and ensuring that funding followed pupils so that schools gained financially if they recruited pupils and suffered financial penalties if they lost pupils. Most of the elements of accountability that provided the impetus for the education market remain under New Labour. Results will still be published; league tables will still be produced but will provide more detail and will have a value added element; increasingly rigorous inspections by OFSTED continue, still surprisingly under the leadership of Her Majesty's Chief Inspector of Schools, Chris Woodhead. Its judgements are now even more telling since the Secretary of State's 'Fresh Start' idea has been incorporated into OFSTED strategy. As a result, where a school is significantly underachieving it will immediately be closed, perhaps over an extended summer break, and a new school opened with a new staff and a new governing body. Thus, some of the key legislative features designed to foster the education market place remain intact or have been strengthened. But how far has an educational market been created? What effect has the attempt to create such a market place had on the small and medium sized enterprises of the educational world, the primary schools?

If schools are to operate in the education market place, this presupposes that heads and governors accept the philosophical justifications for the creation of that market which emanate from the wider socio-political environment. If they are to embrace the education market philosophy and operate in accord with its basic tenets, heads will recognise the need for competition as a motive force and accept it as a mechanism for resource allocation and structuring parental choice. This recognition will then be translated into action in several ways. Heads will seek to recruit the maximum possible number of pupils and, by so doing, maximising the income of the school. In order to achieve this heads and their governing bodies will develop a coherent marketing plan based on an assessment of parental expectations and the need to communicate the benefits to be accrued from sending children to a particular school. In so doing, heads will understand that:

> Marketing . . . can just mean selling, promotion and aggressive competition, or it can mean making the market's requirements central to decision making.
>
> (Pardey, 1994, 203–4)

Most heads in our sample denied the importance of the educational market place to decision-making in their schools. They did not acknowledge the centrality of competition to their thinking about the relationship between their school and others in the neighbourhood. Heads of LEA schools, in particular, were more likely to espouse values of collaboration and co-operation with local schools than to recognise that they were in direct competition. A few heads, mainly in GM schools, did see themselves as directly in competition with both LEA and independent schools. One head of a Catholic GM school stated:

> Yes I am in competition. My competitors are the local junior schools and then the private schools. There is a big independent Catholic school which is my main competitor.

Other GM heads recognised the reality of competition but in a less overt way and sought to minimise its extent and importance as a contributing factor to pupil recruitment:

> Yes I think we are in competition but hopefully competition with a small 'c'. We try to help parents make the right choices for their children and for some it might be this school.

This head reported that his school was not quite full but he was not prepared to encourage parents to send their children to the school if its pedagogy and ethos did not appear to suit the child. Fully fledged competition was not part of his overall strategy for the school. At most it was an operational exigency. The head sought to deny the centrality of competition and acted to optimise rather than maximise the school's income through the pupil recruitment process.

Heads of LEA maintained primary schools were even less likely to acknowledge the competitive nature of the market place. A typical comment when asked if they were in direct competition with other schools was the following from the head of an inner city primary school:

> I don't see us in competition. Although we take children from outside our area we are not aggressively competing.

To the same question, a head of a primary school in North Oxfordshire responded:

> Not really, it's sort of swings and roundabouts. There are a number of children in this catchment area that I know go to other schools and I have a number from other areas. We are not competing in that way. There is one school that has very low pupil numbers in our partnership. We support that school as much as possible.

When asked if she would act differently if her school was not full, the same head replied:

> I would like to think not but when it comes to the implications of losing staff I think you would be fighting to keep your numbers up.

The heads of primary schools in this area tended to co-operate over organising events and to collaborate over pupil numbers. Another head whose school was under-subscribed and which has a GM primary school in its catchment area claimed that:

> We work very closely. We have a close cluster around our secondary school and we are not in competition.

Schools with declining numbers might compete more aggressively although there appears to be a degree of tolerance about numbers of pupils on roll. Heads appear to be unwilling to use competition as the main mechanism through which to manage their external environment.

Surprisingly, however, the provision of nursery places was one area in which there was competition amongst LEA schools. Heads with nursery schools were perceived by their peers to have a significant advantage over schools which could not recruit children at such an early age. One head noted that:

> The competition in all honesty has been made by the nursery classes. For a long time we had no problem in filling our numbers but a nearby school has now got newer accommodation and a nursery and so has our next nearest.

The concern here is that once parents place their children in a school they are unlikely to exercise choice and move them. Another head highlighted the importance of a nursery when he remarked that:

> Every other school in this area has got a nursery school. What does that mean? It means that over a period of six years £180,000 is being poured into those schools which is not being poured into mine.

This head perhaps identified the main reasons for such concern. The allocation of nursery provision appears to give some schools a competitive advantage over others on the basis of an allocation process from which some heads felt excluded. Such a process, for those excluded from it, reflected the individualistic, even atomistic nature of the market place rather than an approach to socially just decision-making based on equality of access and opportunity. Understandably, therefore, heads reacted to what they regarded as an unfair allocation of resources.

In general, however, primary school heads tended not to see themselves as being in competition. They were more concerned about falling below a threshold above which they could staff their schools and sustain an internal structure that was compatible with what they wanted to achieve, than they were about maximising pupil numbers and thus maximising their income. Although the overall tenor of responses from heads in GM schools did recognise the need to compete for the attention of parents and to attract the optimum number of children, heads in both LEA and GM schools sought to minimise the importance of competition as a strategy. They tended to deny that it formed a significant part of school management at an organisational level, while recognising, in some instances, that it might become an operational necessity.

## STRATEGIC MARKETING OF PRIMARY SCHOOLS

If heads reject competition as a motive force within the market place, to what extent do they manage their schools in accordance with a market ideology? Do they take a strategic view of what it means to exist in a market environment, scan their market for information about consumer preferences and translate these into organisational principles which can then be operationalised through marketing processes? How far are marketing and promotion clearly distinguished at both the organisational and operational levels? Sullivan notes that effective marketing of schools must be based on meeting customer needs by offering a high quality product using market research and analysis (Sullivan, 1991). For heads to market their schools, therefore, they need to have a strategy which, it is argued, should include a concern for the 'Seven Ps of Marketing', namely price, product, people, promotion, place, processes and proof (James and Phillips, 1995). Our research, like that of James and Phillips (1995) indicates that such an approach to marketing is not evident. None of the heads in our survey had a clearly formulated and written marketing policy or a marketing plan.

Many heads were fairly explicit about the nature of schools nearby and about the main selling points of their own schools. Our findings support the view that heads were clear about the distinctive features of their schools and :

> had a good understanding of what it was they offered ... Although they did not refer to this explicitly as their product ... they described it confidently and unambiguously.
>
> (James and Phillips, 1995, 276)

In the light of this it was interesting to note that these strengths were based far more on what the heads had decided that the school could and should offer than on any analysis of parental choice and preference.

The heads differed in the degree to which they said they employed marketing strategies. At least one appeared not to have a strategy at all. The head of this school, in response to a question about how he marketed the school, replied that he did not advertise. He attracted pupils:

> By standing for principles and standards. By satisfied customers and by talking to parents.

A similar reluctance to become involved in marketing was identified among other heads, one of whom was firm in the view that he did not market his school and he did not often seek coverage in the local press. Nevertheless, the school paid considerable attention to the appearance of the building, which had a revamped entrance, a new technology area and a strictly enforced dress code for the children. The school also ensured that the school logo was on every advertisement for staff in the local press. At the very least, this school was implicitly promoting itself through emphasising the visible or symbolic aspects of the school as a distinctive place. The head believed that word of mouth and family tradition were far more powerful networks for pupil recruitment than the overt use of advertisements and press coverage. If first impressions count for anything then any head wishing to benefit from a good local reputation must pay attention to the symbolic aspects of the school, the nature of the place. This emphasis on the visible aspects of the school does not only include the appearance of the building. Clubs, societies and extra curricular activities are a significant part of schools' self presentation:

> This school is popular for its extra curricular clubs and its emphasis on music and performing arts. We employ peripatetic music teachers. We achieve good standards, certainly in the standardised test results.

Another GM school head identified other aspects of the school that played a major part in marketing:

> What we do is work very hard at the external face that we present so we put an incredible amount of money into the arts. We put, for example, £1,500 into peripatetic musicians to come in and teach in the school. We have two very good choirs and we sing in the community. We enter national chess competitions and we put a lot of energy into PE. We organise local sports which would not operate unless the school ran them, and then we win them.

This head acknowledged that this was his approach to promoting his school. It is an obvious attempt to benefit from a particular reputation within the local community. His counterparts in LEA schools were far less forthright and were less inclined to believe that it was necessary to have any formal strategy for directly publicising their schools. Many of these heads claimed not to market their schools at all. They did, however, recognise the importance of the local information network:

> I do give a lot of time to parents that are interested in looking round the school. We set out to be attractive to parents. You can't disregard parents any more.

Some heads noted the importance of the school brochure:

> Our school prospectus I know needs to be good. It needs to fulfil the many regulations that the government has imposed on it but it needs to be good in the sense that it provides good information and promotes the school in a positive way. But I don't want to go down the road of being competitive.

Others argued that they make use of the press to celebrate the work of their schools, to give children a sense of pride in their achievements and to locate the school within its local community, rather than to advertise or promote the school. For example, one head commented that he did ensure that his school appeared in the local press but that this was not marketing, it was:

> The celebration of good education and a shared pride in what we are doing. Yes and it's about the self-esteem of the children. Their efforts can be brought to the attention of a wider audience.

An LEA primary school head denied marketing the school but recognised the importance of some aspects of place such as the importance of easy access:

> We try to be genuinely open door. We use the grapevine rather than the *Birmingham Evening Mail*.

Another head said of his school:

> I know it has a good reputation. It takes a long time to build a good reputation and it could be lost overnight. By far the most important marketing force I have got is word of mouth ... But the old fashioned thing that people judge a school's performance by, it's the ... grades. So we have a ... tangible record of academic success. One of the other very attractive features to parents is extra curricular activities. We have an inordinate number. This has led to a significant amount of success

in all sorts of fields of endeavour. If we feel that any group or individual in the school has done something worthy of public recognition, we will let the local press know.

In spite of this extremely perceptive analysis of a well developed set of promotional and public relations activities based mainly upon the visible, the symbolic and upon the extremely effective use of the information network within the local community, this head stated quite categorically:

I have never advertised the school in any way, shape or form.

Almost all of the primary school heads in our sample confused the term marketing with promotional activities, much of which took the form of public relations exercises. They tended to use local press and television rather than either formal advertising or outreach material, except for prospectuses. Several heads indicated that they had recently increased expenditure on school brochures, although an analysis of the brochures from each school in our sample revealed that these are not of a consistently high standard. Heads obviously treat much of what they termed marketing as an add-on activity and not part of the main stream of their work. They certainly did not take a rigorous look at:

what the school most wishes to achieve as a result of a public relations programme ... pinpointing the most relevant target audiences ... decide on the best strategy to reach them ... and ... the most important priorities

(Devlin, 1989, 94–5)

Even though promotional activities and public relations tended to be the main, if not the only, element of marketing these were, to a large extent, a marginal exercise. They were not based on a strategic view either of the school or the market place and were not underpinned by clear organisational principles. The heads in our sample, therefore, did not act in an informed and rational manner in respect of the educational market place.


COMPETITIVENESS AND THE EDUCATIONAL MARKET PLACE

How, then, can such behaviour be explained? At least part of the answer to this question can be found in the way in which the educational market is conceptualised. The free market is a hypothetical construct within the discipline of Economics. As a construct it exists within the Newtonian paradigm (Zohar, 1997), which presents the world generally, and the market place in particular, as an ordered, simple entity that conforms to specific rules. This, in turn, means that its activities should be rational, predictable and controllable. In essence, the rules of the market place can be summed up in the statement that firms will seek to maximise profits through competition and consumers make choices based on price and quality.

The perfect market, however, does not exist. It does not obey simple rules, cannot easily be controlled or its outcomes predicted. Those operating in the market place do not necessarily follow its tenets. Many firms do not seek to maximise their profits. They continue to trade even when it is unprofitable to do so and when liquidising assets and reinvesting them would be the most effective way of maximising profit. Many firms strive for profit optimisation rather than maximisation, survival being a more attractive option than profit maximisation. In every market firms set out to control and influence market operations through such tactics as fixing prices, selling below cost, limiting the supply of products or creating monopolies. Even where firms may choose to behave in accordance with the rules of the market, it cannot be assumed that either they or their customers always have the necessary knowledge to make informed decisions.

Similarly consumers may not necessarily act as the market place dictates that they should. Many consumers may make choices for a wide variety of reasons of which price and the nature of the product are but two. Harmony, equity, geographical proximity, personal convictions and even prejudice may also shape consumer decisions. Furthermore, the concept of the free market presents choice only in the context of competition, ignoring the possibility of other decision-making frameworks within which choice might be made, such as co-operation and collaboration. The possibility of co-operative smart partnerships based on trust, reciprocity of interest and mutual support for the benefit of all is discounted (Hampden-Turner, 1997). The market characterises and explains the totality of human behaviour in terms of self-interest expressed through buying, selling, consuming and producing. This denies the possibility of altruism, selflessness and concern for others outside the immediate family unit. It also fails to acknowledge that individual self-interest in the market place does not operate in isolation. Individual decisions may be, and indeed are, isolated but they impact on the decisions of others and may restrict the choices that others are able to make. This is to deny the existence of community or group interest. The poverty of the market ideology stems from its inability to recognise the existence of community in either an organic or personal sense. Clearly, here is an atomistic view of society within which the public institutions which serve its members are fragmented and placed in opposition to each other. The market, even as a hypothetical construct, therefore, is imperfect. It is not surprising, therefore, that many heads in primary schools do not act as they might were a true educational market to exist.

It is clear, for example, that competitiveness and individualism, while latent in the work of some heads, is not pronounced in the work of most of them. On the contrary, the extent to which most heads have resisted the temptation to enter in direct competition is surprising. They still, in many instances, prefer to co-operate and collaborate in a number of ways. Husband (1996), for example, draws attention to the existence of patterns of collaboration that include purchasing consortia, professional interchange and partnership development, all of which are inimical to the basic operating tenets of an educational market. Thus, there is, as James and Phillips (1995) note, a special quality about educational relationships. Education is about much more than responding to customer needs in a commercial way. In so doing, they are rejecting the market ideology.

## THE REJECTION OF THE EDUCATION MARKET

Heads have not marketed their schools intensively nor have they adopted an explicit recruitment strategy for their school. Although they claim to base much of what they do in their schools on parental expectations, scanning the education market place in relation to parents and identifying their preferences as consumers of education is not a high priority for many heads (Glatter and Woods, 1995). They have preferred instead to rely on word-of-mouth, presentational, symbolic and opportunist means of commending their institution to parent consumers. Heads have demonstrated a reluctance to become active participants in the educational market place. They have not been driven by market forces to maximise income by increasing pupil numbers to excessive levels. Instead, heads in this study have tended to optimise rather than maximise pupil numbers in their schools. They may vary in the extent to which they are willing to adopt accommodatory positions in respect of the education market place but, on the whole, they appear to show no enthusiasm for it. It can be seen, therefore, that most heads have not subscribed to the market ideology.

The extent to which heads reject the concept of the market place can be seen in their behaviour. Heads appear to be supported by a strong set of educational values based on mutual trust, the provision of professional support, the welfare of their pupils and shared views of primary education that transcend their immediate concerns and exist beyond the confines of their schools. It is possible that, for many heads, their socialisation into the professional culture of teaching and the extension of this into the realms of primary headship is so strong that it remains uppermost as a predeterminant of their world view. The existence of this professional culture, in itself, provides a foundation upon which supportive networks of like-minded colleagues can be established and sustained. This culture focuses on the educational needs of children and on collegial rather than hierarchical styles of management. As Grace reports of the heads in his sample, their professional caution about the philosophy of the market place:

> arose in most cases because they believed that market forces and market values in education would be inimical to educational and professional values.
>
> (Grace, 1995, 208)

This value position in respect of the educational market place adopted by many heads in our sample finds support among both parents and governors, whose participation is essential if market forces are to operate within an educational environment.

In the theoretical construct of the market parents are required to act as consumers. It is unclear, however, exactly how far parents are prepared to act in this way. They do not appear to be willing or able to treat the education of their children as a commodity. Parents tend to make educational choices on their perceptions of the best interests of their children. These interests are often couched in terms of sustaining existing friendship groups and proximity of school to home rather than on market considerations such as schools' performance in the standard attainment test league tables. Often children themselves play a central role in this process.

> It is commonplace to assume that parents make choices and yet . . . children's own choice of school is a major factor in parental considerations.
>
> (Smedley, 1995, 99)

Nor is it certain just how many parents do exercise the right to move their children during a specific stage of education. There is some evidence to suggest that parents do not have and, in many cases do not seek, full access either to information or processes that might enable them to make these choices (Martin, 1995). Furthermore, as Bridges has noted, parents may play many roles in relation to the education of their children of which that of consumer is but one. These might include supporter, partner, co-educator or even puzzled bystander (Bridges, 1994).

At the same time, many governing bodies are equally reticent about managing primary schools as they would in a free market, not least because in many cases they have only partly shouldered the burden of the detailed management of schools. In so doing they also appear to be reluctant to accept the ideology of the market. The range of values espoused by school governors frequently does not include an endorsement of the educational market place (Deem *et al.*, 1995). There is little evidence that governors are anxious to encourage those activities that might be appropriate if a fully fledged educational market were to exist. Thus, there are reservations about this ideology in each of the three key groups whose support is necessary if the educational market place is to become a reality.

## CONCLUSION: AMBIGUITY AND THE EDUCATION MARKET PLACE

There is no doubt, however, that the attempt to introduce market forces to the education sector has had a significant effect (Bottery, 1992). Taken as part of a package of measures to re-shape the education system, it has been instrumental in creating an extremely turbulent environment. The mechanisms for allocating pupils to schools, the levels of resourcing and processes of accountability and quality assurance are now far more problematic than was the case prior to 1988. As a result, the educational world in England (for Scotland, Northern Ireland and, to a lesser extent, Wales, have been spared some of the more excessive turbulence) can be seen for what it has truly become, a complex set of ambiguous relationships which do not conform readily to any set of rules, the outcomes of which appear to be both uncertain and uncontrollable to those in schools.

In spite of the extremely turbulent nature of their educational environment, many of the primary school heads in this sample did report an increased empowerment and ability to control aspects of work in their schools (Bell, Halpin and Neill, 1996a). Nevertheless, they recognised the new realities of this environment. Their sense of empowerment related largely to matters internal to their schools. They felt far less confident about managing their external environment. This is evident both in their relatively unconsidered approach to marketing their schools and in their general unwillingness to become involved in strategic approaches to marketing. This position is based on far more than a lack of knowledge or expertise. It is rooted in value systems which reject, or at least fail to legitimate, marketing as an appropriate activity for this group. Once this is recognised, it is possible to understand how heads can repeatedly deny any involvement in activities which might be termed marketing. There is a clear value conflict here, the result of which is that many heads display those characteristics in relation to the educational market place which lead to what Cohen and March (1974) have termed organisational ambiguity.

Organisational ambiguity is characterised by unclear goals, a poorly understood technology and fluid membership. In this context, heads in our sample were, in many cases, extremely equivocal about their position in respect of the education market place. Some sought to ignore its operation by seeking to collaborate with colleagues in other schools. Others denied that they were influenced by market forces at all, even where their actions might lead observers to conclude otherwise. Still others believed that they had been unfairly treated in some aspects of resource allocation, notably the establishment of nursery schools, and felt compelled to respond to this. When asked what their goals were, each group of heads would reply unambiguously, to do the best for their school. The ambiguity lies in the definition of what is best for primary schools.

Considerable ambiguity also surrounds the technology to be deployed. As James and Philips (1995) have shown, heads have not developed or even set out to develop coherent marketing strategies. At the same time, most heads do not believe that becoming a market leader is necessarily a good thing or something that can be sustained to advantage over time. Even if heads understood the relevant technology, therefore, they are doubtful about its effectiveness and its long term outcomes, believing that too high a price would have to be paid for becoming an accomplished exponent of the technology derived from the educational market place.

The price to be paid might be in terms of a loss of support and professional acceptance by head teacher colleagues. This community of heads, like that in North Oxfordshire, is valued beyond the exigencies of the market place and the value of any benefits that participating in the market place might bestow. Nevertheless, for some heads, the membership of such professional groupings is fluid to the extent that those heads who felt challenged by the nurseries established in nearby schools were prepared to forego the support of colleagues and seek to maximise pupil recruitment. This fluidity of membership is also found, but in a different way, in the schools. The amount of time and effort which heads and their staff are prepared to devote to activities relating to the educational market is very limited. For the staff of most schools operating within the market place is not accorded a high priority. Much of what is done in this regard is a by-product of and incidental to the core business of the school and is seen as such by most heads, teachers and governors (Bell, Halpin and Neill, 1996b). Marketing the school and competing aggressively within a market environment is not part of the ethos of heads in primary schools.

## REFERENCES

Ball, S. J. (1992) Changing management and the management of change. Paper presented at the Annual Meeting of the American Educational Research Association, San Francisco, April.

Ball, S. J. (1993) Education policy, power relations and teachers' work, *British Journal of Educational Studies*, Vol. 41, No. 2, 106–121.

Bell, L., Halpin, D and Neill, S. (1996a) Managing self governing primary schools in the local authority, grant maintained and private sectors, in *Educational Management and Administration*, Vol. 24, No. 2.

Bell, L., Halpin., D. and Neill, S. (1996b) Management and the market place: perspectives from primary head teachers. Paper presented to the British Educational Management and Administration Society Research Conference, Cambridge.

Bolman, L. G. and Deal, T. E. (1991) *Reforming Organisations: Artistry, choice and leadership*, San Francisco: Jossey-Bass.

Bottery, M. (1992) *The Ethics of Educational Management: Personal, social and political perspectives on school organisation*, London: Cassell.

Bridges, D. (1994) Parents: customers or partners? in D. Bridges and T. H. McLaughlin (eds.) (1994), *Education and the Market Place*, London: The Falmer Press, 65–79.

Cohen, M. D. and March, J. D. (1974) *Leadership and Ambiguity: The American college president*, New York: McGraw-Hill.

Deem, R., Brehony, K. and Heath, S. (1995) *Active Citizenship and the Governing of Schools*, Buckingham: Open University Press.

Department of Education and Science (1988a) *The Education Reform Act*, London: HMSO.

Department of Education and Science (1988b) *Circular 7/88. The Education Reform Act: Local management of schools*, London: HMSO.

Department of Education and Science (1991) *The Education [School Teacher*

*Appraisal] Regulations*, London: HMSO.

Devlin, T. (1989) Planning an effective public relations programme, in J. Sayer and V. Williams (eds.) (1989), *School External Relations*, London: Cassell, 85–92.

Friedman, M and Friedman, R. (1980) *Free to Choose*, New York: Harcourt, Brace and Jovanovich.

Glatter, R. and Woods, P.A. (1995) Parental choice and school decision-making: operating in a market-like environment, in A. K. C. Wong and K. M. Cheng (eds.) (1995), *Educational Leaders and Change*, Hong Kong: Hong Kong University Press.

Grace, G. (1995) *School Leadership: Beyond Educational Management: An essay in policy scholarship*, London: The Falmer Press.

Hampden-Turner, C. (1997) Globalisation/global values: Two concepts of globalising value. Paper presented at the 26th International Federation of Training and Development Organisations. New Paradigms in Human Resource Development, Kuala Lumpur, 28–30 October.

Harris, R. (1980) *The End of Government . . .?* London: Institute of Economic Affairs Occasional Paper 58.

Hayek, F. (1973) *Law, Legislation and Liberty*, Vol. 1. London: Routledge and Keagan Paul.

Husband, C. (1996) Schools, markets and collaboration: New models for educational policy, in D. Bridges and C. Husband (1996) (eds.), *Consorting and Collaborating in the Educational Market Place*, London: The Falmer Press, 9–20.

James, C. and Phillips, P. (1995) The practice of educational marketing in schools, in M. Preedy *et al.* (eds.) (1997), *Educational Management: Strategy, quality and resources*, Buckingham: Open University Press, 271–289.

Joseph, Sir K. (1974) *Stranded on the Middle Ground*, London: Centre for Policy Studies.

Martin, S. (1995) *Choices of Secondary School: The experiences of eight urban families*, unpublished Ed.D. thesis: University of Bristol.

Menter, I., Muschamp, Y., Nicholls, P., Ozga, J. with Pollard, A. (1997) *Work and Identity in the Primary School: a post-Fordiat analysis*, Buckingham: Open University Press.

Pardey, D. (1994) Marketing for schools, in H. Green (ed.), *The School Management Handbook*, London: Kogan Page, 203–208.

Pollard, A., Croll, P., Broadfoot, P., Osbourne, M. and Abbott, D. (1994) *Changing English Primary Schools*, London: Cassell.

Preedy, M., Glatter, R., and Levačić R. (eds.) (1997) *Educational Management: Strategy, quality and resources*, Buckingham: Open University Press.

Smedley, D. (1995) Marketing secondary schools to parents – some lessons from the research on parental choice, in *Educational Management and Administration*, Vol. 22, No. 2, 96–103.

Sullivan, M. (1991) *Marketing Your School: A handbook*, London: Longmans.

Scruton, R. (1984) *The Meaning of Conservatism*, London: Macmillan.

Zohar, D. (1997) Rewiring the corporate brain: Re-discovering human potential. Paper presented at the 26th International Federation of Training and Development Organisations. New Paradigms in Human Resource Development, Kuala Lumpur, 28–30 October.

# SECTION 2

# PROFESSIONAL DEVELOPMENT

## Edited by Ray Bolam

# 6

## Understanding Leadership: Developing Headteachers

### PETER RIBBINS

### 1. THREE QUESTIONS: THREE THEMES

For 25 years I have been an avid headteacher watcher. In this chapter I will consider what we know of the production and development of educational leaders, especially headteachers. In tackling this task, my thinking has been influenced greatly by three key sets of questions. Although I have substantially modified them, in their original form they were first voiced by the Canadian scholar Benjamin Levin. He put them to the Chief Executive of the Teacher Training Agency at the end of a lecture on the TTA's proposals for headteacher training she had just given to the National Conference of the British Educational Management and Administration Society held in 1997. Anthea Millett seemed to accept their legitimacy, but it would not, perhaps, be unfair to suggest that she struggled to meet their challenge. If so, then she, and I, and many others, are in good company; I doubt, for example, if the authors of the latest Green Paper on education have been any more successful. Even so, I believe that all who seek to be involved in the development of schools leaders should attempt to think through how they might respond to Levin's agenda:

1. What is good leadership? What is a good leader? How can those with good potential be identified and encouraged to prepare for leadership? How can those with significant leadership responsibilities be encouraged to improve? How good is the evidence?
2. What should a curriculum for developing and sustaining good leaders and leadership look like? How should it be taught? What standards should it entail? How should it be assessed? How good is the evidence?
3. What is the evidence that if such a curriculum were to be developed and taught, it would have a significant beneficial effect on how those graduating actually lead, on the quality of schools and, ultimately, on pupil achievement?

A comprehensive discussion of issues of such magnitude is beyond the scope of a single short chapter. Instead, I will keep them in mind in tackling three more modest themes: headteachers in England and Wales and their development; headteachers elsewhere and the relevance of the experience of England and Wales: and, researching headteachers and headship. In doing so, I should stress that since my initial attempt to write this chapter for the ESRC Seminar in July 1998, much has changed: the third and fourth of my on-the-record studies of 34 heads working in secondary, primary and special education in England and Wales have been published (Ribbins and Marland, 1994; Ribbins, 1997; Pascal and Ribbins, 1998; Rayner and Ribbins, 1998); I have made presentations on much the same as this paper in response to invitations from groups in Canada, Cyprus, Hong Kong and Singapore, all of whom have challenged me to think carefully about what they could hope to make of and take from the British experience; I have read the papers and heard the debates at the ESRC seminars; and, the Green Paper *Teachers: Meeting the Challenge of Change* and its attendant *Technical Consultation Document on Pay and Performance Management* (DfEE, 1998, 1999) have been published.

## 2. HEADTEACHERS AND THEIR DEVELOPMENT: TOWARDS A CAREER-BASED UNDERSTANDING

The development of a strategic approach for the continuing professional development of teachers and leaders of teachers in England and Wales has not been straightforward. The James Committee of 1972 was the first public body to suggest that an effective teaching profession required appropriate initial *and* substantial subsequent in-service training: its ideas were largely ignored at the time, but exercised a major influence on later thinking. Thus in 1974, the Advisory Committee on the Supply and Training of Teachers proposed a five-phase, career long approach to meet the in-service needs of teachers (induction, consolidation, reorientation, advanced training and refreshment). In the late 1980s a Task Force was set up to improve school management. Like the James Report it advocated a career-long approach from initial training to retirement, with all staff entitled to be treated as managers. This entailed a commitment to preparation and induction for all who were to assume new managerial responsibilities and not just to those already appointed to headship (Styan, 1991).

Since 1995, under the leadership of the Teacher Training Agency, a number of important developments have taken place. In an initial letter to the Minister, the TTA proposed the identification of agreed national standards to help set targets for teachers' development and career progression designed to establish clear and explicit expectations of teachers in different key roles. In commenting on its achievements Glatter (1997) claims that 'the TTA, with their new headship qualifications and their initiatives in middle management, have set out a hugely ambitious programme – nothing of its scale or complexity has been attempted elsewhere' (190).

The 'new headship qualification' described above is the National Professional Qualification for Headteachers (NPQH). To be awarded the NPQH candidates must have:

- undertaken an initial needs assessment designed to help them identify their training needs against the national standards for headteachers, which results in an action plan for training and development
- completed successfully the compulsory strategic leadership and accountability module and any further training and development that is necessary
- be successfully assessed against all designated national standards during training and in a final assessment designed to guarantee that the candidate has demonstrated overall fitness for headship.

In December 1997 an evaluation report on trials for the NPQH was published (TTA, 1997). Its findings are largely positive. Reflecting on the limitations of functional competencies methods of training for management development, Glatter (1997) warns that the TTA must avoid implementing an approach which is too narrow, atomistic and bureaucratic (190). He believes that in its emphasis on school improvement there is reason to hope these evils are being avoided. This may be so but it is too early to be sure. Much turns on how good school leadership and leaders are to be described. Even those who support the TTA's competency approach tend also to stress the need to emphasise what Cave and Wilkinson (1992) 'have called the "higher order capacities" to do with judgement, intuition, political acumen and the like. Personal qualities like integrity, stamina and commitment as well as value systems were seen as fundamental' (in Glatter, 1997, 190). In my view, it is not obvious in what respect and how the package which the TTA is developing and implementing is designed, or intended, to enable NPQH candidates to develop, let alone to demonstrate, such higher order capacities.

To date, such unsystematic feedback as I have been able to obtain from a small number of trainers and 'candidates' on the 'needs assessment' and 'training' which they have experienced has been more negative than the views expressed in the evaluation report. I await with interest the findings of the substantial evaluation currently being undertaken by the National Foundation for Educational Research.

On **needs assessment** the 1997 report concludes 'The great majority of candidates expressed strong appreciation for this stage of the qualification. Indeed, many reported that they had never before received such concentrated attention to help them define their needs and plan a way forward' (TTA, 1997, 4). In contrast, some of my informants suggested that candidates were not clear about what the needs assessment exercise was intended to achieve and voiced the suspicion that a key purpose was to encourage candidates to register for as many of the training modules as possible, whether or not they felt they really needed all of these, on the grounds that if they did not then they might struggle when faced with their final assessment.

On **training** the report found

> Candidates overwhelmingly approved . . . where it was practical and professional. The great majority reported that the training they received was clearly matched to their needs, was rooted in the practice of school improvement and addressed effectively those aspects arising from different phases and types of schools. However, in some regions the training was reported to be too theoretical . . . (Conversely) the vast majority of trainers, particularly those who were experienced headteachers, were seen to be effective in using candidates' knowledge, understanding, skills and attributes

(4).

This may be so, but I have heard the training described as highly prescriptive and focused narrowly on the delivery of a package of material developed centrally and, initially at least, produced in haste. It is hard to see how this could hope to meet the individual needs and local circumstances of particular candidates drawn from a wide variety of contexts. Furthermore, it was suggested that in practice opportunities for trainer feedback have been very limited and that little attempt was made to enable candidates to reflect critically and analytically. Finally, the idea that the training exercises could be regarded by some as 'too theoretical', was regarded with incredulity. As one put it 'the course tries very hard to be as untheoretical as possible and largely succeeds. If I were not also attending a masters degree course I would have no frameworks in which to locate what we are doing. Most feel the same.' Another described her experience as 'death by a thousand case studies.' Should we worry about this? I am, like Glatter, not biased against 'practically focused education'. But, as Kay (1993) has observed: 'Practical knowledge which is not based on some more fundamental analysis is usually knowledge of the most superficial kind' (quoted in Glatter, 1997, 190).

So much for the past, what of the future envisaged in the Green Paper? I find myself sharing the views of SHA that there is much to appreciate, subject only to 14 major reservations about what is proposed. Duffy (1999) commends it for its clarity and consistence, but concludes 'the Devil . . . is in the detail'. He demonstrates this by raising a series of 'nit-picking' questions and reservations. I must restrict myself to two observations.

First, I find aspects of the language of the Green Paper hard to square with its acknowledgement that teachers matter and that they should be regarded as 'higher professionals' and treated and paid accordingly. In contrast, its defining concepts seem to be 'standards' and 'skills' (yesterday's word, competency, is almost wholly absent). Both terms are repeated frequently. This, and the prescriptive nature of much of what is proposed, could indicate a government seeking to make teaching as teacher-proof and school leadership as headteacher-proof as possible. If so, then whilst many teachers and heads can anticipate being better paid, supported and resourced they may also face a future in which their professional status is progressively diminished.

Second, for a government which puts such stress on 'evidence based' approaches, the Green Paper contains many unsubstantiated ideas and claims. Thus, for example, in discussing the role of the head it is asserted that 'all the evidence shows that heads are the key to a school's success'. My own view, supported by much of my research, is highly sympathetic to the proposition that headteachers, in the United Kingdom anyway, have a key role to play in determining the quality of a school and the achievements of its pupils. But to suggest that 'all the evidence' demonstrates this to be the case is simply not true. On the contrary, much research takes a very different view. Ouston, a member of the Rutter team, claims that 'the [school effectiveness/school improvement] movement has over-emphasised the role of the head . . . and top-down management' (page 175 in this volume) (see also Slee and Weiner, 1998). She quotes Torrington's and Weightman's (1989) view that 'the empha- sis on the headteacher-as-leader . . . was far in excess of that found in orga- nizations outside education'. They question 'this dangerous dependence on one person'. This last idea has been developed by many others. Gronn (1999), for example, rejects traditional notions of the dominance of the solo or stand- alone leader and advocates instead an alternative conception of leadership as a distributed function. Finally, in the fullest survey currently available, Hallinger and Heck (1999) report on a review of some 50 major research studies published between 1980 and 1998 in 11 countries. Summarising what scholars have learned about the substance of claims that principal leadership makes a difference in school effectiveness, they conclude that

1. Leadership, as measured in the behaviour of school principals, does *not* exert a measurable *direct effect* on school effectiveness and student achievement.
2. Leadership, as measured in the behaviours of school principals, *does* exert a measurable *indirect effect* on school effectiveness and student achieve- ment.
3. Leadership, as measured in the behaviours of schools principals, is itself influenced by the context of the school and its environment.

If this last study is an example of what we can learn from other countries, what can they can learn from us?

## 3.   HEADTEACHERS ELSEWHERE: WHAT CAN OTHERS HOPE TO LEARN FROM ENGLAND AND WALES?

With the globilisation of key features of education, the issue of what differ- ent countries can, and cannot, hope to learn from each other has attracted growing attention. As such, England and Wales are widely regarded as having taken an important lead in the evolution of a distinct, and possible transfer- able, strategic approach to the initial preparation and continuing development of headteachers. I can illustrate what I mean by drawing on the experience of recent visits to Hong Kong and Cyprus to fulfil invitations to report on developments in school leader preparation in England and Wales and, if possible, to identify their relevance to the countries of my hosts.

In Hong Kong the idea of a standards based competency approach has attracted a great deal of attention and much heated debate. That this should be so, is not surprising given that amongst the ideas being aired is the proposal that continuing leadership training should be compulsory for all principals and that those who fail to achieve the required standards should have their contracts terminated.

That Hong Kong, given the historical influence of British ideas, should wish to hear of developments in England and Wales is not remarkable. That the same should be true of Cyprus, given its very different Greek legacy, is much more so. Even so, I was asked to contribute to a symposium on *Current School Leader Preparation Practices: The Way to the Future* (Ribbins, 1998). In important respects, things are very different in Cyprus. First, principals when initially appointed are normally much older than their British counterparts. Second, the typical career of a principal is much shorter than is usual in Britain. Third, principals currently exercise a much more restricted, and, a much less demanding role than is the norm in Britain (18).

A recent UNESCO report reveals that

> appointment to Deputy Principal posts occurs at about 45 years of age for teachers in Primary schools and between 50 and 55 for teachers in Secondary schools, appointments to Principals occurring not long before retirement age . . . the principal criterion [for promotion] is age and seniority . . . competence in performing the work is scarcely taken into account. . . On the long climb up the promotion ladder . . . the system establishes what can only be described as a 'gerontology in education'.
>
> (Drake *et al.*, 1997, 56,58)

The report warns that, 'when the education service focuses so clearly upon the career structure of the teachers there is a danger that this is achieved at the expense of the education of the children' (26).

To correct this imbalance, the consultants advocate a decision-making approach emphasising competency in the appointment and promotion of teachers. They propose, in a section which could have been written by the TTA or the drafters of the Green Paper, that

> each stage in promotion . . . should be preceded by training appropriate to the new duties with evaluation at the end of the training used to decide on the appointment.
>
> (59)

However, the report also stresses that if the benefits of such an approach are to be realised, this would require principals in Cyprus to be accorded the kind of independence normally to be found in educational systems characterised by devolved school management.

The experience of working in many countries has led me to conclude that any attempt to achieve a worthwhile understanding of leaders, leading or leadership, and therefore of leadership preparation and development, must be alert to the significance of variations due to specific contextual and cultural factors (Ribbins, 1996). As I have argued elsewhere, I believe that whilst it is possible to employ similar methodological instruments, procedures and approaches, and even explanatory theoretical frameworks, with profit in a wide variety of cultural contexts, what they find may vary a great deal (Ribbins, 1999). As such, the importation of substantive ideas from one cultural setting to another can be beneficial but is fraught with risk and should be undertaken with care. As Hofstede (1991) points to the need for some 'suspension of judgement when dealing with groups of societies different from one's own' and therefore 'information about the nature of the cultural differences between societies, their roots, and their consequences should precede judgement and action' (7).

What might an approach to the study of school leaders and their development over time which is sensitive to the considerations discussed above look like? I have spent many years devising and testing a framework relevant to a wide variety of historical, social and cultural contexts. Applied to the study of headship within, for example, a period of radical reform, such an approach would require the collection of data on:

1. The reforms in their specific historical, social, cultural and values framework.
2. The contemporary scope, dimension and character of the reforms.
3. The interpretation of, and responses to, the reforms of key national/local stakeholders.
4. The interpretation of, and responses to, the reforms by key institutional stakeholders as seen from the perspective of particular schools.
5. And the interpretations of, and responses to, the reforms by individual headteachers within the schools identified in 4 above.

Propositions 1 and 2 constitute macro-level, longitudinal and comparative elements of relational context. Three, 4 and 5 cover actors and agencies operating in a variety of interpretive contexts and at a variety of levels. At the ESRC seminars, Glatter (1999) and Fitz (1999) argued against misguided attempts to separate the study of educational management from that of educational policy. My framework assumes an integrative approach. Even so, much of my field work has focused on propositions 4 and 5 and reflects my belief in the need for meso and micro level ethnographies of educational leaders and leadership. In this, three elements of interpretive contexts are implicit, building collectively to a cumulative approach at three levels. I have termed these **situated, individual portrayals** [Level 1]; **multi-actor perspectives** [Level 2]; and, **multi-actor perspectives in action** [Level 3] (see Ribbins, 1996, 1999). In what follows, I will say something of what is involved in such an approach.

## 4.   REGARDING THE LIVES AND CAREERS OF HEADTEACHERS

I believe that the generation of a worthwhile strategic approach to meeting the developmental needs of teachers and headteachers requires an understanding of characteristic patterns of careers within the profession. I propose a 'natural history' approach to achieve this (see Pascal and Ribbins, 1998; Rayner and Ribbins, 1998) based on two models. The first, developed by Gronn (1993) from a study of headship, detects four phases in the **lives of school leaders**. The second, from Day and Backioglu (1996) identifies four stages in the **career of headteachers**. The models can be combined to identify two ideal typical pathways as follows:

Formation, Accession, Incumbency [initiation, development, autonomy, disenchantment], Moving On [divestiture].

Formation, Accession, Incumbency [initiation, development, autonomy, enchantment], Moving On [reinvention].

### 4.1   Formation: Making Headteachers

The process of formation is made up of all the influences which shape the kinds of people prospective heads become. In this process future headteachers are socialised into deep rooted norms and values by the action and interaction of key agencies including the family, school and other reference groups. These agencies, particularly those exerting their influence during the early years, shape personality by generating a conception of self, along with the rudiments of a work style, attitude and outlook.

### 4.2   Accession: Achieving Headship

Following formation candidates for headship must enter their chosen career. They then seek advancement and in due course prepare for promotion to headship. This means developing their capacity and testing their readiness in comparison with existing heads and likely rivals. They develop networks of peers and patrons and learn to present themselves and jockey for position in the competition for preferment. I am particularly interested in how heads regard their earlier career as teachers as a preparation, planned or not, for achieving headship.

### 4.3   Incumbency: Enacting Headship

Incumbency marks the period of headship and runs from the time a head is first appointed to headship to when he/she finally leaves headship. Over the course of such a career, incumbency may take two possible routes, each with four successive sub-phases. The first three sub-phases are common to both routes and are entitled *initiation, development* and *autonomy*. The fourth sub-phase can take one or other of two different directions, one negative *(disenchantment)* and the other positive *(enchantment)*.

## Initiation

Following appointment there is an immediate period of initiation. During this time new heads become familiar with the workplace norms of their new school and its community and of the roles they will be expected to fulfil. This first phase normally takes at least three years before a head feels fully initiated. During this phase most heads experience a broadly similar range of emotions – beginning with feelings of initial elation and enthusiasm quickly followed by a growing sense of realism and adjustment to what the real parameters of the job will be. New heads tend to feel ill prepared and uncertain about what was expected of them. They view these first years as exhausting and demanding. A few claim to have enjoyed a smooth transition; some faced great difficulties. The nature of this experience is shaped by factors such as: self-confidence and belief; scope and relevance of previous experience; the ability to transfer previous experience; the scope and relevance of prior preparation and training; the ability to transfer prior preparation and training; the ability to learn from working with appropriate and inappropriate role models; ability to learn on the job; and, the quality of the institutional and local support structures in place.

## Development

This phase is characterised by enthusiasm and growth and normally takes four to eight years. By then the head feels in control, and has made good progress in developing the enormously wide range of competencies it requires. Such heads have developed confidence in their ability to manage the school. This allows them to maintain self-belief in the face of the pressure which is a head's lot today. Such growing confidence can be expressed in a new vision for the school or in the development of new ways of working. Heads tend to recall this as the period of their careers in which they were most effective and made the most progress.

## Autonomy

This phase usually comes into play after eight years or more in the job. By then the head is generally very confident and competent. Experience and survival give them a sense of control and the knowledge that they have largely mastered the demands of headship. They have learnt a variety of strategies to cope with the strains of the job and can take a more open and longer term perspective. Some believe this makes them even more effective as leaders. Their day-to-day professional life is usually easier than it used to be. Having put in place management posts and teams and delegated responsibilities to them, the school may appear to be running smoothly without much apparent hands-on management from the head. Such heads tend to advocate a collegial or team work approach to managing the school as both right and good. Of course not all who have been in post for eight years and more achieve all of this. And even those who have may yet take very different routes in the next and final phase of headship.

## Disenchantment

The final period of incumbency is a transitional time for the long-serving heads in this category. For some there is the prospect of disenchantment; the seeds of disillusion and loss of commitment may stem from the previous phase. They may have seemed at the height of their power and authority, but it is at just such a time that feelings of stagnation and loss of enthusiasm can set in. If they have not achieved much of what they wished they may begin to feel trapped in post with nowhere to go. There were hints of this amongst a few of the longest serving of the heads I have interviewed. Day and Bakioglu (1996) go further and depict a downwardly spiralling process leading towards disillusion and divestiture. They describe such heads as increasingly autocratic in style and reluctant to respond to any demand for change.

## Enchantment

Some long-serving heads do seem discouraged and disenchanted, but others do not. We spoke to several who despite their long years in post remain enchanted with headship. If anything they appear more confident and optimistic about what is possible than some in the previous phase. They express feelings of much left to do, of new challenges to face, of looking forward to this. They still see their work as focusing on children and their achievements and speak with passionate commitment on teaching and of the life of the headteacher. Huberman (1993) identifies four conditions for sustaining high levels of professional satisfaction: enduring commitment; manageable job expectations; good relations with colleagues; and, a balanced home and school life. I would add two more: a balance between leisure and work; and, good opportunities for continuing professional development.

## 4.4  Moving On: Leaving Headship

This final phase focuses on leaving headship. It deals with how heads anticipate and divest themselves of office, whether to a new occupation or to retire. The manner of this transition can depend on the way in which they experienced the final phase of incumbency. The *disenchanted* face the prospect of **divestiture** whilst the *enchanted* can look forward to **reinvention**.

## 4.5   Future Prospects

In terms of the model described earlier, much of this account of the lives and careers of selected headteachers has been at Level 1. It has also focused on heads in England and Wales. There is a need for more Level 2 and 3 studies and for the model to be tested in a variety of international contexts. To date I have used a similar approach with colleagues from the Institut Ammudin Baki in Malaysia to undertake a Level 1 on-the-record study of 24 primary and secondary principals. I am also involved, albeit at an early stage, in similar exercises with staff from the Universities of Hong Kong and Cyprus. To date, the approach seems promising within each of these three very different contexts. What, then, are the lessons for the professional development of headteachers which we might learn from all this?

## 5.   Lessons for Continuing Professional Development

The heads I have studied prepared for headship in many different ways. Many sought to learn from experience, their own or others. Most engaged in further studies. As somebody who spends much of his professional life involved in the provision of award bearing in-service courses, I have been encouraged to hear, again and again, from heads how important they feel such courses have been in enabling their professional development – one even suggested 'This has kept me sane'. In conclusion I would argue for an approach which:

- is centrally concerned with improving the quality of schooling and the achievements of pupils
- is systematic and comprehensive and of high quality
- makes available continuing professional development opportunities at every career phase
- has a concern for practical skills but also for a more philosophical approach
- involves a range of providers, with the universities engaged fully and at a variety of levels
- provides core training, but supports developmental opportunities that mean more than this
- is based on the best available evidence and fosters the research which generates this.

## REFERENCES

ASCTT (1974) *The In-Service Education and Training of School Teachers*, London: HMSO.

Cave, E. and Wilkinson, E. (1992) Developing managerial capabilities in education, in

Bennett, N., Crawford, M. and Riches, C. (eds.) *Managing Change in Education: Individual and Organisational Perspectives*, London: Paul Chapman.

Day, C. and Backioglu, A. (1996) Development and disenchantment in the professional lives of headteachers, in I. Goodson and A. Hargreaves (eds.) *Teachers' Professional Lives*, London: Falmer.

DfEE (1998) *Teachers: meeting the challenge of change*, London: DfEE.

DfEE (1999) *Technical consultation document on pay and performance management*, London: DfEE.

Drake, P. *et al.* (1997) *Appraisal Study on the Cyprus Educational System*, Paris: International Institute for Educational Planning [for UNESCO].

Duffy, M. (1999) Future perfect, in *Headlines*, February.

Fitz, J. (1999) Reflections on the field of educational management studies, *Educational Management and Administration*, 27, 3.

Glatter, R. (1997) Context and capability in educational management, in *Educational Management and Administration*, 25, 2.

Glatter, R. (1999) From struggling to juggling: towards a redefinition of the field of educational leadership and management, in *Educational Management and Administration*, 27, 3.

Gronn, P. (1993) Psychobiography on the couch: character, biography and the comparative study of leaders, in *Journal of Applied Behavioural Science*, 29(3).

Gronn, P. (1999) Systems of distributed leadership in organizations, paper given at the Annual Meeting of the American Educational Research Association, Montreal, April 1999.

Hallinger, P. and Heck, R. (1999) Can leadership enhance school effectiveness? in Bush *et al.* (1999) *Redefining Educational Leadership and Management*, London: Sage.

Hofstede, G. (1991) *Cultures and Organizations: International cooperation and its importance for survival*, Harper: Collins.

Huberman, M. (1993) *The Lives of Teachers*, London: Cassell.

James Report (1972) *Teacher Education and Training*, London: HMSO.

Kay, J. (1993) *Foundations of Corporate Success: How business strategies add value*, Oxford: Oxford University Press.

Pascal, C. and Ribbins, P. (1998) *Understanding Heads and Headship in Primary Education*, London: Cassell.

Rayner, S. and Ribbins, P. (1998) *Headteachers and Leadership in Special Education*, London: Cassell.

Ribbins, P. (1996) Producing portraits of educational leaders in context: cultural relativism and methodological absolutism?, keynote paper given at the Eighth International Conference of the CCEA on Indigenous Perspectives of Educational Management, Malaysia, August 1996.

Ribbins, P. (1997) (ed.), *Leaders and Leadership in the School, College and University*, London: Cassell.

Ribbins, P. (1999) Context and praxis in the study of school leadership: a case of three?, in P. Begley and P. Leonard (eds.) *The Values of Educational Administration*, London: Falmer.

Ribbins, P. and Marland, M. (1994) *Headship Matters: Conversations with seven secondary headteachers*, London: Longman.

School Management Task Force (1990) *Developing School Management: The way forward*, London: HMSO.

Slee, R. and Weiner, G. (1998) (eds.) *School Effectiveness for Whom?*, London: Falmer.

Styan, D. (1991) Developing educational managers, in P. Ribbins (ed.) *Developing Educational Leaders*, London: Longman.

Torrington, D. and Weightman, J. (1989) *The Reality of School Management*, London: Blackwell.

TTA (1995) *Initial Advice to the Secretary of State on the Continuing Professional Development of Teachers*, London: TTA.

TTA (1997) *National Professional Qualification for Headship: Report of evaluation of trials*, London: TTA.

# 7

# Stages of Headship

## DICK WEINDLING

### 1. INTRODUCTION

This chapter uses socialisation theory to re-examine the NFER longitudinal study of headteachers (Weindling and Earley, 1987; Earley *et al.*, 1990 and 1994/5) in order to study the stages of headship transition. Previous models of leadership transition and succession in both business and schools are outlined. Finally, the NFER findings are integrated with the earlier work to produce a stage theory of headship which can be used as a research tool and to assist the development of heads and prospective heads.

### 2. STAGE THEORIES OF SOCIALISATION

A useful approach to understanding leadership and headship development derives from Merton's (1963) socialisation theory. The stress here is on the two-way interaction between the new leader and the school situation (with each trying to change and influence the other). In this view of socialisation, which is prevalent in the North American research, there are two main overlapping phases:

- professional socialisation which involves learning what it is to be a headteacher, prior to taking up the role, from personal experience of schooling and teaching and from formal courses;
- organisational socialisation which involves learning the knowledge, values, and behaviours required to perform a specific role within a particular organisation (Schein, 1968), after appointment.

A large body of work exists, drawn largely from the non-educational field, where previous writers have suggested stage theories to explain the transition phases experienced by leaders. Although various labels are used by different authors, they commonly identify three periods of organisational socialisation. Hart (1993) provides the most detailed synthesis and critical analysis of the field and the following is adapted from her book.

### Stage 1. Encounter, anticipation, or confrontation

The initial arrival stage requires considerable learning on the part of new heads as they encounter the people and the organisation. Cognitive approaches focus on rational interpretations and the understandings that new heads construct, what Louis (1980) called the *sense making* process in an unfamiliar situation.

### Stage 2. Adjustment, accommodation, clarity

This involves the task of attempting to fit in. New leaders must reach accommodation with the work role, the people with whom they interact and the school culture. They look for role clarity in this new setting and may face resistance from established group members.

### Stage 3. Stabilisation

In this stage, stable patterns emerge but this is only visible in data from longitudinal studies. Nicholson and West (1988), using a cyclic model, treat the stages of stabilisation and preparation (for the next change) together, because they found that stabilisation did not occur for some managers who had moved on to their next post.

## 3. PREVIOUS RESEARCH

A few studies have looked at the period as a deputy as preparation for headship. Ribbins (1997), for example, interviewed 34 heads and found that, while some enjoyed the experience as an appropriate preparation for headship, relatively few remembered it with enthusiasm or their former heads with unqualified warmth. Although most felt that their heads had not positively prepared them for headship, they believed that they had learned from the negative experiences, often vowing never to act like that themselves.

Gender issues and headship were explored in two important, life history studies by Evetts (1994) and Hall (1996) who found that women heads' career paths, and the way they approached management, differed from that of men, but these authors did not use stage theory.

Parkay and Hall (1992) conducted a US project modelled on the NFER research. They surveyed 113 new high school principals and carried out case studies of 12 throughout their first year in post. A return visit was made after three years. The authors derived a five-stage developmental model to describe the career patterns of new principals:

1. Survival
2. Control

3. Stability
4. Educational leadership
5. Professional actualisation.

Four basic assumptions underlie the model:

- principals begin at different stages and not all start at Stage 1;
- principals develop through the stages at different rates;
- no single factor determines a principal's stage of development. Personal characteristics, the school context and the previous principal all play a part;
- principals may operate at more than one stage simultaneously, *ie* the stage is their predominant orientation.

In this country, Day and Bakioglu (1996) questionnaired 196 headteachers and interviewed a sample of 34, and derived a four-phase, developmental model:

1. Initiation: idealism, uncertainty and adjustment.
   This lasted about three years and involved two key processes: learning on the job and accommodating to the existing framework and structure of the school.
2. Development: consolidation and extension.
   Heads with four to eight years' experience were still enthusiastic, saw this as more satisfactory and rewarding with fewer difficulties than the other phases, built new management teams as inherited senior staff left, and delegated more.
3. Autonomy.
   Here heads continued to be self-confident, felt they had management expertise but had less energy, a nostalgia for the past, and saw externally imposed national initiatives as causing lack of enthusiasm. 'Autonomy' was positive in that they felt in control of the school, but negative because this was threatened by external change and pressure to work with governors.
4. Disenchantment.
   A decline in confidence, enthusiasm and fatigue were the characteristics here. Heads started to ease off and their health (physical and mental) deteriorated as they approached retirement. The Education Reform Act had a major impact on many of them.

Ribbins (1998) adapted Day and Bakioglu's phases and a stage model developed by Gronn (1993, 1999) to produce a model of typical pathways for school leaders:

- Formation – the early socialisation influences from agencies such as the family, school and other reference groups which shape the personality of a future head.
- Accession – career advancement and preparation for headship.

- Incumbency – the total period of headship, from appointment to leaving, sub-divided into Day and Bakioglu's four phases, to which Ribbins adds enchantment as an alternative to disenchantment for some long-serving heads.
- Moving on – leaving headship which may involve divestiture for the disenchanted or reinvention for the enchanted.

Gabarro (1987) conducted research on 17 senior management successions in business and industry in the US and Europe (including three case studies in the UK), pointing out that while there has been research on management succession, very little work has examined the activities and problems facing a new manager after they take up their post. He calls this process 'taking charge':

> ... I do not mean just orienting oneself to a new assignment. Taking charge, as I use the term, refers to the process by which a manager establishes mastery and influence in a new assignment. By mastery, I mean acquiring a grounded understanding of the organisation, its tasks, people, environment, and problems. By influence, I mean having an impact on the organisation, its structure, practices, and performance. The process begins when a manager starts a new assignment and ends when he or she has mastered it in sufficient depth to be managing the organisation as efficiently as the resources, constraints, and the manager's own ability allow.
> (Gabarro, 1987)

He characterised the process as a series of five predictable, chronological stages of learning and action. The timings are approximate:

- Taking hold (the first six months).
  This period involves intense learning as the manager develops a cognitive map of the organisation using processes of orientation, evaluation (an assessment of staff, understanding where the problems lie) and establishing priorities. 'Corrective' actions are taken to address emerging problems and 'turnaround' actions to deal with urgent problems.

- Immersion (six to 12 months).
  This very important period of deeper learning and diagnosis involves relatively little organisational change activity. Managers develop a much better understanding of the basic issues and underlying problems. They often question more sharply if they have the right people in place as they understand their strengths and weaknesses.

- Reshaping (12 to 21 months).
  This is a time of major change, organisational reconfiguration and implementation. The transition to reshaping often involves the use of task groups and external consultants.

- Consolidation (21 to 27 months).
  Earlier changes are consolidated. Learning and diagnosis tend to be evaluative. The manager and key colleagues assess the consequences and the unanticipated problems of earlier changes and take corrective actions.

- Refinement (27 to 36 months).
  A period of fine-tuning with relatively little major additional learning. The managers had 'taken charge', were no longer 'new' and had either established their credibility and power base, or not. This relative calm could be disturbed by changes in the external world.

Gabarro found that the organisational changes managers made as they worked through these stages characteristically occurred in three waves: the first wave occurs during the Taking-Hold stage, the second, and typically largest, during the Reshaping stage, and the last and smallest during the Consolidation stage. These stage and wave patterns are found in successful transitions regardless of the kind of succession (insider versus outsider; turn-around versus non-turnaround cases), the industry of the organisation involved, or the manager's prior functional background.

## 4.   THE NFER SECONDARY HEADS PROJECT

This unique project, which followed a cohort of headteachers for over ten years, falls into three stages:

1. Stage 1 began in 1982 with everybody who took up their first post as a head of a secondary school in England and Wales. Questionnaire data were obtained from 188 heads. Forty-seven new heads were interviewed towards the end of their first term in post and 16 of them were then chosen for detailed case studies covering the first two years of headship. A total of three visits were made to each of the schools in this part of the project and individual interviews conducted with the heads, each of the senior management team, a cross-section of teachers, the chair of governors and a senior LEA adviser. A total of over 300 interviews was conducted.
2. In 1988, the cohort of 188 heads was surveyed after they had been in post for five to six years and the 16 heads were re-interviewed.
3. In 1993, survey data were collected from 100 heads who were still in post some ten–11 years after they began their headships.

This chapter concentrates on the problems the heads experienced and the changes they made in this ten year period.

### a.   The First Years

The key point to make is that new heads do not start with a clean slate (as some seem to think). The shadow of 'headteachers past' hangs over them for longer than they expect. The previous head had often retired, having been in post for 15 to 20 years. They had 'shaped the school in their image' and while this might be apparent in the form of structure, it was harder to see the school culture. New heads were often surprised, when they confronted existing routines, to be told, 'That's the way we have always done it'. They soon found that their approach differed from that of their predecessor and this affected the period of settling in and the kind of changes they made. Many teachers said the new heads and their predecessor differed considerably – they were like 'chalk and cheese'.

The main problems reported by new heads were: difficulties caused by the style and practice of the previous head, the school buildings, communication and consultation with staff, creating a better public image of the school, coping with a weak member of the SMT, dealing with incompetent staff, and low staff morale.

The heads differed in their approaches to change. Some deliberately chose to make early changes, others to move cautiously, while some were delayed and hindered by a poor SMT.

Almost all the changes made in the first year were organisational. Curricular changes began in the second year and continued into the third year and beyond. A few of the changes to the pastoral system occurred in the first year, but these were mainly introduced in years two and three.

The organisational changes made soon after the new head's arrival were frequently concerned with communication and consultation. Another group of early changes was concerned with promoting a positive image for the school, something of particular concern to the new heads especially where the community held it in low esteem or student numbers were falling.

Today it is hard to remember the pre-National Curriculum and OFSTED inspection period when these heads first took up their posts. They had to initiate curricular changes. Timetable changes could not be implemented until the beginning of their second year, but much preparatory work was undertaken in the first year. This usually took the form of a curriculum review, where each department was required to set out its aims, objectives, schemes of work and, in some cases, methods of assessment.

Of the 200-plus changes introduced in the first three years in the 16 case study schools, it was noticeable that only a handful did not originate with the new heads themselves. Once the decision to adopt a change had been made, day-to-day responsibility was usually delegated either to a deputy head or a head of department.

### b. Ten years on

The external changes produced by the Educational Reform Act and other legislation had only just begun when we conducted the second phase of the research in 1988. The following five years saw the heads attempting to cope with substantial changes imposed from outside.

One hundred of the original cohort 1982/83 returned a completed questionnaire in 1993. Seventy-seven were still in their first school, while 23 had moved to a second headship. We were not able to track down the fate of those

(104) who did not return a questionnaire, but we believe that most had retired.

To gauge their feelings after ten years the heads were asked a set of questions about their current level of enthusiasm. Two-thirds said they had the same enthusiasm as when they started as heads but there were noticeable differences between those who were still at their first school compared with those who had moved to second headships. For example, 40 per cent of those still in their original school said they did not have the same enthusiasm as when they started, compared with only 14 per cent of those in second headships. This may not be an unexpected result, but it is difficult to tell whether those who moved to a second school were more highly motivated people, or whether the challenge of a new school boosted their enthusiasm. It is most likely to be an interaction of the two.

In order to explore how the problems changed over time a set of core questions was used in the first and last surveys. Table 7.1 shows heads' perceptions in 1984 and 1993 on the core questions where a direct comparison is possible.

**Table 7.1** *Comparison of problems perceived by secondary heads in 1984 and 1993*

| Percentages | V. serious or serious | | Moderate or minor | | Not a problem | |
|---|---|---|---|---|---|---|
| | 1984 | 1993 | 1984 | 1993 | 1984 | 1993 |
| Getting staff to accept new ideas | 47 | 20 | 47 | 68 | 6 | 12 |
| Creating a good public image | 42 | 21 | 43 | 60 | 15 | 19 |
| Dealing with a weak member of SMT | 38 | 27 | 36 | 39 | 26 | 34 |
| Dealing with incompetent staff | 37 | 31 | 32 | 63 | 31 | 6 |
| Dealing with poor staff morale | 36 | 16 | 51 | 58 | 13 | 26 |
| Improving consultation/communication | 35 | 18 | 46 | 66 | 9 | 16 |
| Managing staff dev. and INSET | 30 | 5 | 60 | 60 | 10 | 35 |
| Establishing good standards of discipline | 27 | 6 | 51 | 65 | 22 | 29 |
| Managing time and priorities | 21 | 40 | 54 | 50 | 25 | 10 |
| Dealing with LMS and finance | 19 | 10 | 58 | 57 | 23 | 33 |
| Issues concerning non-teaching staff | 19 | 11 | 57 | 52 | 24 | 35 |
| Working with LEA officers | 7 | 7 | 42 | 27 | 51 | 66 |
| Working with the governors | 6 | 11 | 42 | 50 | 52 | 39 |
| Working with LEA inspectors | 5 | 3 | 32 | 28 | 61 | 69 |

Most problems were perceived to lessen over time, e.g. getting staff to accept new ideas; creating a good public image of the school; dealing with poor staff morale; improving communication and consultation; managing staff development and INSET; establishing discipline; dealing with finance; and issues concerning non-teaching staff. However, a few problems seemed to have increased, e.g. managing time and priorities; working with the governors. Dealing with incompetent staff appeared to have continued over time. Working with LEA officers and advisers remained a very minor problem for most heads.

These findings are likely to be due to the interaction of several complex factors. With time, heads and staff get to know each others' strengths and weaknesses; the heads have made some key staff appointments; they have gained a deeper understanding of the school and have introduced most of their intended changes. But the world outside has also changed. During the ten-year period a large number of external changes occurred, such as: the role of governors, LMS, GM, NC, league tables, and OFSTED inspection.

The 100 heads were also asked to outline how they thought the school had improved in the five years since the previous survey. It is interesting to compare these results with the heads' replies to the same question in 1988 when they had been in post about five years.

Half the heads reported improved exam results in their first five years, while 29 per cent said the results had improved in the last five years. It seems possible that some sort of 'levelling off' may have occurred. However, without more detailed information it is not possible to say exactly what has happened over the total ten-year period.

Similarly, in the 1988 study, half the heads mentioned improvements in the curriculum. Not surprisingly, this again emerged as a focal area. In fact, the comments were very similar, usually describing a more relevant curriculum, but after ten years just over a quarter of the heads mentioned the curriculum.

Approximately the same number – about a quarter – talked about physical improvements in the buildings and facilities in 1988 and 1993. At each point in the study very similar comments were also made about improvements in the main areas of staff, students, parents and the community.

School improvement, in all its forms, is obviously the major quest for all heads. From our longitudinal research it seems that most of the groundwork is put in place during the first five years or so, and then further refinements are made. This involves setting up a number of working parties, curriculum and organisational restructuring, modelling appropriate behaviour, and most crucially, appointing key staff (particularly at senior and middle management).

## 5.   TRANSITION TO HEADSHIP: STAGES OF SOCIALISATION

A problem with much of the previous research in schools or businesses is the lack of a sufficiently long time-frame to see all the phases of development. Hence the value of the NFER ten-year study.

Gabarro's work shows interesting parallels with the NFER study where the new heads attempt to 'take charge'. But heads are more constrained than business managers in their ability to hire and fire, and the school year and timetable delay major curricular changes. Nevertheless, the waves of changes described by Gabarro have great similarity to the way that the heads introduced change. Another common finding was that internally appointed heads/managers appear to make fewer changes and to move more slowly than external appointees.

Day and Bakioglu's final phase of disenchantment produces a new perspective, while Ribbins offers the alternative of enchantment for some long-serving heads. The NFER data shows that, as Ribbins believes, some heads are enchanted and others disenchanted by their experience of headship.

The NFER results and the work of Hart, Gabarro, Day and Bakioglu, and Ribbins and Gronn, have been used to produce the following model which maps out the stages of transition through headship. The timings are approximate.

### Stage 0 – Preparation prior to headship

Throughout their career people develop a conception of headship during their professional socialisation which is learned through both formal and informal processes. As the NFER and other studies (e.g. Ribbins, 1997) show, they learn from both good and bad headteacher role models.

The NFER heads said they learned about headship throughout their career but they particularly stressed the value of the following experiences prior to appointment: the need for a wide variety of experience, especially as a deputy head; the value of a period as acting head; the importance of delegation by the head; the rotation of deputies' responsibilities; and the need to work with heads who saw deputy headship as a preparation for headship. Some heads spoke highly of management courses that they had attended as deputies, but most agreed that off-the-job training and development complemented experiences gained as a deputy working with 'a good practitioner'. The gulf from deputy to head was, nevertheless, seen as enormous: 'no course or reading matter can really prepare you for the job'. It will be interesting to see to what extent the National Professional Qualification for Headship (NPQH) improves the preparation for headship.

### Stage 1 – Entry and encounter (first months)

The first few days and weeks are a critical period when the new head's notions of headship meet the reality of a particular school. It is a time of 'surprise' and the importance of sense-making is highlighted as organisational socialisation begins and the new head attempts to develop a cognitive map of the complexities of the situation, the people, the problems and the school culture.

### Stage 2 – Taking hold (three to 12 months)

The newcomer strives to 'take hold' in Gabarro's terms, and the new heads begin to challenge the 'taken for granted' nature of the school. The NFER heads introduced a number of organisational changes. They develop a deeper understanding and their diagnosis of key issues during this stage was used to decide priorities.

This is also part of the 'honeymoon period', when staff are more lenient and open to change. In the NFER study we found that all new heads had such a period, though some did not realise it! The length of time varied, from about a term to possibly a year. It was often ended suddenly by negative staff reaction to an action of the new head e.g. an internal appointment whom the majority of the staff considered the wrong person for the job.

### Stage 3 – Reshaping (second year)

After a year in post most heads felt more confident and were beginning to feel that they could take off their 'L' plates! They had experienced a complete annual cycle of school events and learned about the strengths and weaknesses of the staff. Conversely, the staff had also learned about their strengths and weakness, and their mutual expectations had become more realistic. The seeds planted in the previous stage now produced the implementation of major changes to reshape the school. This was the period of major change.

### Stage 4 – Refinement (years three to four)

After two years many of the structural changes were in place. But during this stage further curriculum changes were introduced and a number of refinements made. Previous innovations were fine-tuned and heads felt they were 'hitting their stride'.

### Stage 5 – Consolidation (years five to seven)

After about five years a period of consolidation seems to occur after the heads have introduced most of their planned changes. However, in the NFER study this was affected by the introduction of legislative and external changes. These, as Gabarro found, required attention as their impact may hit the school during any of the stages.

### Stage 6 – Plateau (years eight and onwards)

The NFER heads suggested that about seven years in one school was sufficient to see through a cohort of pupils and to have initiated most of the changes they wanted. This period corresponds with Day and Bakioglu's phase of disenchantment or Ribbins' enchantment. The NFER data showed that about a third of the cohort felt they had reached a plateau after ten years but that this was far less likely if they had moved to a second headship. Motivating heads who stay in one school until the end of their career can be a problem. However, many of the NFER heads said they still enjoyed their work and, despite the changes to the role, considered it to be the 'best job in education'.

The model is in the form of an ideal type and some caveats are necessary. Clearly the time periods attached to each stage must be treated as approximations. It is also likely that different heads may move at different speeds, as Parkay and Hall suggest. Also, the situation in the UK has changed considerably due to ERA and other legislation. Whereas the NFER heads were able to introduce almost all the changes internally, today's headteacher has to manage major multiple initiatives which originate externally, and attempt to integrate themselves and shape the culture of the school. Unfortunately, the NFER study of secondary heads had too few women heads to make a comparison. This means that it is not possible to say how gender differences might affect the stages of headship.

The model is offered as a means of helping headteachers and prospective heads to understand the likely phases they will experience during headship. Although the particular circumstances in each school make it unique there are common patterns, knowledge of which can be used to improve the preparation and support for heads.

## REFERENCES

Day, C. and Bakioglu, A. (1996) Development and disenchantment in the professional lives of headteachers, in I. Goodison and A. Hargreaves (eds.) *Teachers' Professional Lives*, London: Falmer Press.

Earley, P., Baker, L. and Weindling, D. (1990) *Keeping the Raft Afloat: Secondary headship five years on*, Slough: NFER.

Earley, P., Weindling, D. and Baker, L. (1994/95) Secondary headship ten years on. A series of ten articles in *Managing Schools Today*, Vol. 4 (1) onwards.

Evetts, J. (1994) *Becoming a Secondary Headteacher*, London: Cassell.

Gabarro, J. (1987) *The Dynamics of Taking Charge*, Boston: Harvard Business School Press.

Gronn, P. (1993) Psychobiography on the couch: character, biography and the comparative study of leaders, *Journal of Applied Behavioural Science*, 29 (3).

Gronn, P. (1999) *The Making of Educational Leaders*, London: Cassell.

Hall, V. (1996) *Dancing on the Ceiling*, London: Paul Chapman.

Hart, A. W. (1993) *Principal Succession: Establishing leadership in schools*, New York: State University of New York Press.

Louis, M. R. (1980) Surprise and sense making: what newcomers experience in entering unfamiliar organisational settings, *Administrative Science Quarterly*, 25 (2) 226–251.

Merton, R. K. (1963) *Social Theory and Social Structure*, NY: Free Press.

Nicholson, N. and West, M. (1988) *Managerial Job Change: Men and women in transition*, Cambridge: Cambridge University Press.

Parkay, F. and Hall, G. (eds.) (1992) *Becoming a Principal*, Boston: Allyn and Bacon.

Ribbins, P. (1997) Heads on deputy headship, *Educational Management and Administration*, 25 (3) 295–308.

Ribbins, P. (1998) On ladders and greasy poles; developing school leaders careers. Paper presented at the Third ESRC Seminar, Milton Keynes, June 1998.

Schein, E.H. (1968) Organisational socialisation and the profession of management, *Industrial Management Review*, 9 (1) 1–15.

Weindling, D. and Earley, P. (1987) *Secondary Headship: The first years*, Windsor: NFER-Nelson.

# 8

# Promoting Continuing Professional Development for Teachers: An Achievable Target for School Leaders?

AGNES McMAHON

## 1. INTRODUCTION

Promoting the continuing professional development (CPD) of teachers must be a priority for any government which aims to raise educational standards. The challenge is to decide how best to do this within the context of recent reforms. The scope of the reforms and the speed of implementation have been well documented but the impact on CPD is less well known. They demonstrate a mix of tight central regulation (e.g. over teachers' conditions of service) and local autonomy (e.g. decisions about the selection and appointment of teachers). The consequences for CPD have been profound, for two main reasons:

- teachers have had to acquire new knowledge and skills to implement the reforms;
- there have been radical changes in provision (e.g. five professional development days; successive training grant schemes; delegated school budgets; the Teacher Training Agency).

In addition, the teacher force is ageing, two-thirds are 40 or older (House of Commons, 1997); work long hours, on average 50.3 per week for secondary classroom teachers and 53 for middle managers (School Teachers' Review Body, 1997); and is experiencing intensification of work and high stress levels (Gewirtz, 1997; Crawford, 1997).

Accordingly, the questions discussed here are: how has CPD been influenced by the post-1998 reform agenda and are current strategies likely to promote teacher growth? To answer them this chapter draws upon selected findings from a Leverhulme-funded study of teachers' perceptions of CPD, conducted in four contrasting English local education authorities. Data were collected in 1995-1997 through interviews with LEA personnel, a headteacher and provider in each authority; a survey of CPD provision in 66 secondary schools; and case studies in three schools.

## 2. THE PURPOSES OF CPD

A broad statement that the purpose of teacher professional development is to improve the teaching and learning process seems unexceptionable. However, questions about what forms of CPD are likely to lead to this improvement and who should take decisions about the most appropriate type of provision and the priority areas to focus upon are highly debatable. The tension between two views of what ought to be the overall purposes of CPD: to promote system (or institutional) improvement or individual teacher development, a tension which was predicted in an international context several years ago (Bolam, 1982) has not yet been resolved. Is there a difference between the needs of the individual teacher and of the school? Answers to this question will be shaped by the context in which it is asked and by varying perceptions of the role of the teacher and of school management.

The government has recognised that school improvement cannot be achieved without a high quality teacher force:

> Teachers and headteachers need to have opportunities to update their subject knowledge and teaching skills, and to gain new skills throughout their careers. They need to have opportunities to exchange ideas and best practice with others in the profession and to have access to the highest quality research and teaching materials.

> (DfEE, 1997, 5.2)

Hence, it sees the main purpose of CPD as being to improve teaching and learning, arguing that teachers:

> must be held accountable for their success in sustaining and raising the achievements of their pupils.

> (DfEE, 1997, 5.3)

The survey respondents' understanding of professional development was similarly instrumental, focusing on the training and experiences needed to enable them to do their job. Few of those interviewed spoke of engaging in professional development activities for their intrinsic value; the activities were assessed in terms of their potential to influence the work that the particular teacher was responsible for in school. A number of respondents distinguished between professional development to help them with their teaching tasks and other forms of training (e.g. management courses) geared to career development and promotion.

The younger and newly qualified teachers were concerned to gain practical training which would help them become more effective classroom teachers:

> I regard the training as providing me with strategies for coping, helping me to cope with the load effectively and helping me ensure that the children get the best out of their time.

> (Man, newly qualified languages teacher, 30s)

More experienced teachers also believed that the purpose of professional development was to help them in the classroom:

> I have to enjoy my teaching and my students have to enjoy it too. . . I've got to be changing, always making it more interesting and finding new ways to make it more interesting.
>
> (Woman, art teacher, 40s)

> I tend to think of my professional development as two strands, what I do in the classroom and what I need if I am to move into more senior positions as I move up the managerial side . . . at the moment I am more interested in and feel I need to know more about how to improve the classroom side of things.
>
> (Woman, recently qualified history teacher, 20s)

The evidence from this research is that teachers are keen to improve their knowledge and skills, although at any one time their learning priorities might differ from those of the school or government. Further, the interview data highlighted the difficulty of separating professional and career development. One man in his 30s made this point quite starkly. He drew a distinction between professional competence and professional development and said that development implied that you were going forward, but going forwards to where? He felt he was getting better but staying still. He saw no opportunities to further his career in the school or the local area.

## 3.  CPD PROVISION FOR SECONDARY TEACHERS

The introduction of site-based management was expected to improve CPD provision for individual teachers. Schools had time, five days per year, to use for education and training purposes; they had systems for identifying individual and organisational needs through teacher appraisal and the school development planning process and they had a delegated CPD budget. Moreover, they had been freed from the 'bureaucratic' control of the local education authorities and could decide what forms of professional development were required to improve the quality of teaching and learning in the school. In practice, this model has proved difficult to implement for four main, inter-related sets of reasons.

### (i)   Resources for CPD

First, schools did not have equal access to human and financial resources to support teacher professional development. It was clear that the school's geographical location influenced the opportunities available to its teachers. In the late 1980s and early 1990s all schools were able to call upon the free advice and support of LEA advisers, many of whom had expertise in particular aspects of the curriculum. However, the introduction of a regulated market for in-service training in which funds are allocated to schools to enable them to buy support had a great impact on LEA provision. In all four LEAs, the traditional pattern of local advisers routinely providing advice and running a range of in-service activities had ended; some LEAs, particularly those in urban areas, were more successful at fund-raising than others and continued to employ a team with curriculum-wide expertise. Schools in the large, rural authority were disadvantaged not only because they did not have easy access to any higher education institutions but also because there was comparatively little in-service support available from their LEA. If schools had sufficient funding and if there was someone with the appropriate expertise in post, they could buy adviser time (e.g. for half a day) but activities like the facilitation of local teacher networks which can be very valuable (Firestone and Pennell, 1997), which had been provided earlier, had largely ceased:

> . . . there used to be a local network, but we are all drifting apart; we don't have a home economics adviser as we used to. . .
>
> (Secondary school teacher)

There was considerable variation between schools in the financial resources available for CPD, most obviously between the maintained and Grant Maintained schools, with mean grants of £12,000 and £32,000 respectively. Schools also differed in the extent to which they were able to provide additional funding from the school budget (amounts varied from £400 to £30,000) or gain additional funding to support specific initiatives (e.g. training for the introduction of NVQs) or projects (amounts varied from £200 to £41,868). The range of opportunities available to teachers was largely determined by the availability of funding:

> Everything revolves around finances to support whatever it is you want to do and all the time it's restraints.
>
> (Secondary school teacher)

### (ii)    Supporting CPD Within Schools

Site-based management requires schools to take greater responsibility for the management of their teaching and non-teaching staff. At minimum, systems for identifying individual development needs, for planning appropriate development opportunities and providing support are necessary. However, a mixed picture was evident. Though the majority reported having someone with specific responsibility for CPD, in two-thirds of the schools this person was not allocated any specific time to do the job and less than one-third used appraisal reports when planning their CPD programme. It also became evident that appraisal was no longer operating in the case study schools. CPD priorities were largely determined by school needs, over two-thirds (71 per cent) of the schools reported that they mainly used the school development plan to identify CPD needs. A number of the teachers interviewed reported that they identified their training needs either through necessity:

> By what they ask me to teach next year.
>
> (Woman, business studies teacher)

or by focusing upon a career goal:

> I would like to go into school management . . . that's what prompted me to take
> the Open University course.
>
> (Woman, history teacher)

In the absence of any formal procedures for talking to teachers about their individual development needs the attitude of the head of department could be very significant. Variations in practice were apparent even in the same school: one would actively seek out opportunities to promote the development of colleagues, encouraging them to take up particular initiatives, others would not.

Schools had few mechanisms to support teacher development: only a minority reported arrangements for job rotation, work shadowing, classroom observation, teacher portfolios etc. The bulk of the school budget for CPD was normally devolved to heads of subject areas and was intended to be used to support their teaching plans. While few teachers would disagree with the spirit of this, in practice it meant that individual development needs were neglected unless they were in an area that was designated a school priority. Training opportunities might be available to staff in one subject area but not in others. Teachers interviewed in one of the case study schools believed that they would only receive support to attend an external course when it addressed an identified school need; even then resources would probably only permit one person to attend.

> I would love to have a placement in industry . . . I did have one week in a factory,
> that was nine years ago.
>
> (Science teacher)

A number of teachers had experienced training to implement innovations that were subsequently dropped and found this frustrating:

> This can happen once or twice but if it keeps on happening, people become very
> cynical. When people become cynical they become resistant to training.
>
> (English teacher)

These wide differences in organisational approaches to CPD and in the extent to which the school was promoting learning for the teachers were not all due to the availability of resources. They also represented the level of commitment to CPD by the headteacher and senior staff.

### (iii)   Use of the Five Non-Contact/Professional Development Days

The main resource that a school receives to support CPD is the five days each year when the teachers work but the pupils stay at home. Yet there is evidence from a number of sources that this time is not always well used. Sixty per cent of the schools responding to the survey reported that they used all five days for CPD; of the remainder, 18 per cent and 15 per cent used three and four days respectively. Only 40 per cent used all the time in whole days; the remainder used it in a combination of whole days and 'twilight' sessions (4.30–6.00pm). In most schools the time was used to investigate departmental and whole school issues (e.g. departmental planning); only 28 per cent said that they allocated one day for individual teacher professional development.

When asked what opportunities for professional development they had received in the previous year several teachers interviewed in the case study schools did not mention the five days until prompted. No one suggested that they had all been valuable though they often had very different responses to the same training event. Two broad concerns were expressed by those who were dissatisfied: first, that the content was inappropriate for them, either because it was delivered at too low a level or was not relevant to their particular work and responsibilities; second, that the quality of training was poor.

> Occasionally you get something interesting. . . I always think we've got to do something – how shall we fill the day.
>
> (Head of department)

> Unless you accept that on those days you need to have a variety of activities and allow staff to opt for what they wanted to do it is very difficult to meet people's needs – from my point of view they have been very variable.
>
> (Head of sixth form)

> Often they were just telling you (what special needs were) and you knew a lot of that anyway and rather than just having time in the department to plan it or do something about it you were just talked at and given a couple of worksheets and you went away with something which you felt wasn't going to help you.
>
> (Science teacher)

> The adviser was appalling . . . I used to feel I knew more than he did.
>
> (Geography teacher)

In-service training activities organised on these days were usually presented to the whole group of staff, often 50 people or more depending upon the size of the school. Little or no attempt was made in any of the case study schools to identify and take account of teachers' preferred learning styles. Yet interview data revealed that these were very different and what suited one individual would irritate another.

> I like lots of visuals, . . . I also learn a lot from participation.
>
> (Head of department)

> I like to be lectured at, told what the right answers are . . . I like to be sure where I am before I start on anything.
>
> (Newly qualified teacher)

## (iv)   Impact of In-Service Training Courses

The aims and content of external and school-based in-service activities focused primarily on the national reform agenda. External in-service courses were mainly short training events rather than longer, award-bearing, professional education programmes. Ninety-four per cent of survey schools reported that teachers commonly attended courses lasting one day only. Analysis of the programmes of CPD activities provided by LEAs confirmed this finding. A great deal of the provision was in the form of short (e.g. half-day or one-day) sessions. Given the time constraint trainers were able to do little more than raise teachers' awareness of innovations. In interview, the providers indicated that, although they were aware that this was not the most effective way of providing CPD, this was all that the market would bear.

The teachers had clear views about whether or not CPD activities had promoted their professional learning. First, if the training was to be useful it had to be relevant, they needed to see how they could use it to improve their teaching. Given the pressure under which the majority of teachers were working, relevance was usually defined quite narrowly:

> ... relevance to the job that I'm doing at the moment, for example, I'm teaching Key Stage 4 (age 16) but not Key Stage 3 (age 14) so if we had a whole day that was related to Key Stage 3 I'd feel that wasn't relevant.
>
> (Man, 30s, School A)

Teachers also judged the quality of INSET activities in terms of appropriateness for their needs and level of knowledge and skill, the provision of practical advice and suggestions and the quality of trainers.

> It was good because it gave me very practical ideas on how to set out the gym and the tutor also asked what ideas the participants wanted help with.
>
> (Woman, School C)

Most comments referred to short training courses which was all that the majority had experienced. However, a minority of older teachers in their 40s had experienced a period of secondment and this had undoubtedly been their best professional development experience. Memories remained vivid even after several years.

> [Studying for the degree was] Brilliant ... it's a completely different experience from doing an MA part-time. A lot of colleagues that I know have done a part-time MA which is obviously weekends and after work, the've got work to do before that and they can't immerse themselves in the culture of learning ... it was good for me personally and I think it was good for the school.
>
> (Man, 40s, about an experience some 12 years earlier)

> It made me realise what it was like out there, you quite forget because you become quite isolated. It was nice to be with a different group of adults ... they don't have the tension of having children there as well. It was invaluable [for the job] because I've written case studies about what I saw and the information I gathered.
>
> (Woman business studies teacher about an earlier secondment to industry)

## 4.  DISCUSSION

The findings reported here do not lead one to be optimistic about the quality of CPD that secondary teachers currently receive. But do we know what forms of professional development would be likely to enhance teacher learning and help them to become more effective practitioners? How might head-teachers promote the development of their staff and is it realistic to set this target for them? I suggest that there are a number of issues that we have to consider.

### (i)   CPD for Teacher Learning and Growth

What models of CPD do we want to use? A model which focuses tightly on training for specific tasks and purposes or something which is broader and more open ended? How seriously does the profession take the frequently stated belief that all teachers should be reflective practitioners? Little (1993) argued that, although training models intended to develop particular skills may work well for technical innovations or particular classroom practices, if used alone they will not help teachers to develop the range of intellectual skills need for handling the reform agenda. Hargreaves (1995:126) was similarly critical of narrow training models of professional development, suggesting that, as well as addressing technical competence, professional development should include '. . . the place of moral purpose in teaching, political awareness, acuity, and adeptness among teachers, and teachers' emotional attachment to and engagement with their work.' Fullan (1993) argued that '. . . teacher education must drive and be driven by new conceptions of teaching as a skilled, morally committed learning profession' and that in order to achieve growth they should: 'practice reflection in, on and about action; seek variety; redefine their role to extend beyond the classroom, balance work and life (Fullan and Hargreaves, 1991). Huberman (1995) reported findings which showed that teachers who were more likely to be 'satisfied' later in their careers had steered clear of reforms and multiple classroom innovations but invested in classroom experiments with their teaching; had sought a change in role when they began to feel stale; and had experienced success by achieving significant results in the classroom.

In sharp contrast the research in four LEAS shows that for the majority of teachers CPD provision consists of short training courses which can do little more than raise awareness of innovations; follow up activities or in-school coaching is very rare. Professional education, in the form of longer award bearing programmes, is being neglected by schools. Site-based management of CPD assumes that schools have the capacity to manage and deliver a comprehensive programme, but whether they all have this capacity is questionable. The survey data reported here indicated that management of CPD was frequently not given high priority, and the infrastructure to support teacher development was rarely in place. Teacher appraisal schemes had ceased to function. Planning for school professional development days was often poor. In consequence, opportunities for growth-enhancing CPD were very limited. Ideally, CPD should include all three components, training, education and in-school support. Eraut (1994) has argued that professional knowledge '... cannot be characterised in a manner that is independent of how it is learned and how it is used ... professional knowledge is constructed through experience.' If teachers are exposed to only a limited range of experiences will their development be constrained?

### (ii)   Saved by the National Standards?

Millet has suggested (1997:5) that one reason potential teachers do not join the profession is the perceived lack of development opportunities and career structure. She argued that the national standards for teachers set out the knowledge, understanding, skills and attributes required for the job(s) as well as the key tasks and the expected outcomes and so can be used to assess the professional development needs of teachers and to help teachers draw up their individual development plans. But, while the concept of a framework for professional development is likely to be welcomed by many teachers as a means of helping them to think more clearly about their involvement in CPD at different stages in their career, there is no indication as yet that the existence of national standards will substantially alter the pattern of CPD provision for the majority of teachers.

In recent years the CPD agenda has been skewed by the need to implement centrally imposed innovations. The topic areas for funding have been determined by government (e.g. special education needs) and schools have felt compelled to give priority to training teachers to implement centrally imposed innovations (e.g. national assessment). In practice schools have little scope to choose the content of their CPD programme given the degree of central control of priorities. This situation seems set to continue with the Labour Government's determination to improve pupil skills in literacy and numeracy and train teachers for this initiative. The Standards Fund for in-service expenditure for 1998-99 (DfEE, 1997a) suggests that training for school-based teachers should '... where possible, be explicitly linked to the national framework for professional development and take account of the priorities for continuing professional development identified by the TTA.' The TTA has also introduced a bidding process for funds for in-service teacher training which have been used to support award-bearing HE programmes; bids were requested against a short list of designated priority areas. Glatter (1999) has suggested that this is producing a pressure towards convergence which makes it less likely that the profession will be able to respond to new challenges. As a result, several well-established higher education providers have had their funding removed and teachers in those areas will have reduced access to award-bearing CPD programmes. It does not appear that the notion of individual teacher entitlement to training and development is being given serious consideration at national level (with the exception of the five 'professional development' days) so most decisions about who gets access to training will continue to be made at school level and this will disadvantage a number of teachers.

### (iii)    Can Headteachers Promote Growth-Orientated CPD for their Staff?

While there is much that headteachers can do to promote and encourage the professional development of their staff, their efforts will be limited not just by the extent of their personal commitment to CPD but also by the resources that they have available and the need to take account of the national regulations and framework of designated priority areas. For as Eraut (1995) has noted, schools can provide a challenging range of professional development opportunities but, if activities are to be properly developmental, teachers will also need time and stimulus for reflection, something that many schools find it hard to provide.

Hall (1997) has suggested that the purpose of human resource management (HRM) in autonomous schools is '. . . to get the best from staff in order to achieve the school's strategic goals, represented in improved opportunities for learning.' She argues that autonomy gives schools the freedom to choose the philosopy and value system that will underpin their HRM strategy, by implication this philosophy could be more or less supportive of individuals. Riches (1997) argued that 'People need to be managed to optimise their own and institutional performance and value being managed.' But do we know exactly what forms of development will maximise an individual teacher's performance? Texts about the management of professional development often seem to focus on structures (e.g. induction and appraisal programmes, coordination) rather than content but as Claxton (1996) reminds us, 'We are not yet at the point where the intricate interweaving of professional competence and personality is fully understood or fully respected . . .'

The intensification of the teacher's workload, the quantity and pace of change that they are having to cope with has led many to want to leave the profession. Poor working conditions are likely to have an adverse effect on teachers' commitment and sense of efficacy (Seashore Louis, 1998). If individuals are to grow and develop as teachers and enjoy and take pride in their work, more flexible and diverse approaches to CPD than those currently used will be required. For example, it might be the case that giving teachers a regular entitlement to periods of study leave (suggested in the James Report, 1972, but never implemented) would do more to raise the quality of teaching and learning than further investment in short skill training programmes. Certainly the majority of the teachers interviewed in my research did not feel that the INSET that they experienced was contributing to their professional development, many felt that their CPD needs were being neglected. Their schools differed in their commitment to CPD and in the number of opportunities that they made available to staff but the conclusion must be that even the most supportive headteachers were constrained in what they could make available to staff. Since so many key decisions about CPD are taken at national level (e.g. funding, priority areas and standards) significant changes will have to be made in the policy framework if all teachers are to have access to high quality CPD experiences.

## REFERENCES

Barber, M. (1996) *The Learning Game*, London : Victor Gollancz.

Bolam, R. (1982) *In-Service Education and Training for Teachers: A condition for educational change*, Paris: OECD.

Claxton, G. (1996) Put it all together and what have you got? in G. Claxton, T. Atkinson, M. Osborn and M. Wallace (eds) *Liberating the Learner*, London: Routledge.

Crawford, M. (1997) Managing stress in education, in T. Bush and D. Middlewood (eds) *Managing People in Education*, London: Paul Chapman.

Department for Education (1972) *Teacher Education and Training – The James Report*, London: HMSO.

Department of Education and Employment (DfEE) (1997) *Excellence in Schools*, London: HMSO.

Department of Education and Employment (DfEE) *The Standards Fund 1998–99 Circular number 13/97*, London: DfEE.

Eraut, M. (1994) *Developing Professional Knowledge and Competence*, London: Falmer.

Eraut, M. (1995) Developing professional knowledge within a client-centred orientation, in T. R. Guskey and M. Huberman (eds) *Professional Development in Action*, New York: Teachers' College Press.

Firestone, W. A. and Pennell, J. R. (1997) Designing state-sponsored teacher networks: a comparison of two cases, *American Educational Research Journal* 34, 2: 237–266.

Fullan, M. (1993) *Change Forces*, London: Falmer.

Fullan, M. and Hargreaves, A (1991) *What's Worth Fighting for in Your School?* Buckingham: Open University Press.

Gewirtz, S. (1997) Post-welfarism and the reconstruction of teachers' work in the UK, *Journal of Education Policy* 12, 4: 217–231.

Glatter, R. (1999) Reconceptualising educational management, *Educational Management and Administration,* forthcoming.

Hall, V. (1997) Managing staff, in B. Fidler, S. Russell and T. Simkins (eds) *Choices for Self Managing Schools*, London: Paul Chapman.

Hargreaves, A. (1995) Development and desire : A postmodern perspective, in T. R. Guskey and M. Huberman (eds) *Professional Development in Action*, New York: Teachers' College Press.

Huberman, M. (1995) Professional careers and professional development, in T. R. Guskey and M. Huberman (eds) *Professional Development in Education,* New York: Teachers' College Press.

House of Commons (1997) *The Professional Status, Recruitment and Training of Teachers: education and employment committee Sixth Report*, London: HMSO.

Little, Judith Warren (1993) Teachers' professional development in a climate of educational reform, *Educational Evaluation and Policy Analysis* 15, 2: 129–151.

McMahon, A. and Bolam, R. (1990) *Management Development and Educational Reform: A handbook for LEAs*, London: Paul Chapman.

Millet, A. (1997) Tackling a long standing malaise, *Professional Development Today* 1, 1: 5–8.

Office for Standards in Education (OFSTED) (1996) *The Appraisal of Teachers 1991–96*, London: OFSTED.

Riches, C. (1997) Managing for people and performance, in T. Bush and D. Middlewood *(op. cit.)*.

School Teachers' Review Body (1997) *Sixth Report 1997*, London: HMSO.

Seashore Louis, K. (1998) Effects of teacher quality of work life in secondary schools on commitment and sense of efficacy, *School Effectiveness and School Improvement* 9, 1: 1–27.

Teacher Training Agency (1995) *Advice to the Secretary of State on the Continuing Professional Development of Teachers*, London: Teacher Training Agency.

UCET (1993) *A National Framework for the Professional Development of Teachers: A case for the 1990s*, submission to the National Commission on Education (mimeo), London: UCET.

# 9

# Headteachers' Knowledge, Practice and Mode of Cognition

## MICHAEL ERAUT

## INTRODUCTION

The term 'knowledge' carries several meanings in professional discourse, but for our purposes these can be reduced to two. Type A, which I shall call public knowledge,

> is defined in terms of propositional knowledge, codified and stored in publications, libraries, databases and so on, subject to quality control by editors and peer review, and given foundational status by incorporation into examinations and qualifications. Under this definition, skills are regarded as separate from knowledge (although some of them, such as reading and reporting, are essential for acquiring knowledge and passing it on to others). Hence there is a potential problem when an educational system, which has evolved with propositional knowledge as its main focus, is also expected to deliver certain skills and competences.
>
> (Eraut, 1997b)

Type B knowledge, which I call personal knowledge is defined as

> what people bring to practical situations that enables them to think and perform. Such personal knowledge is not only acquired through the use of public knowledge but also constructed from personal experience and reflection. It includes propositional knowledge along with procedural and process knowledge, tacit knowledge, and memories of images, episodes, incidents and events. Under this definition, skills are treated as part of knowledge rather than as separate from it. This allows for representations of competence, capability or expertise in which the use of skills and propositional knowledge are closely integrated.
>
> (Eraut, 1997b)

I define the terms 'professional knowledge' and 'management knowledge' as forms of Type B knowledge. Thus, the personal knowledge of a headteacher includes both professional knowledge developed as a teacher and management knowledge, as well as knowledge acquired outside school contexts but still relevant to them, e.g. from living in the local community or through experience of being a parent, not to mention several years of experience as a pupil. To explore the nature of headteachers' knowledge more deeply, let us consider three diverse examples.

## 1.  The Relationship with Governors

Every headteacher and governing body have to develop or negotiate their own interpretation of their respective roles. This will be influenced by some members' prior experience of governing bodies or similar kinds of group and by other members' lack of such experience. Governors' prior expectations may not match those of the headteacher; and the development of the group will also depend on the interests and personalities of its members. What knowledge, then, do headteachers bring to this situation? Their public knowledge will come from statutes, inspectors' reports, books and articles. More private knowledge may be gained from their own experience and from hearing about other headteachers' experiences. In addition they bring with them a range of relevant skills in listening, presenting oral and written reports and getting to know people and understand their viewpoints both as individuals and group members. Most of the skills of communication and acquiring situational understanding will have been acquired in a wide range of contexts, many of them unconnected with schools; but some newly appointed heads may not be well prepared in all these areas. This whole gamut of knowledge, personal experience and skills for communication and developing understanding is likely to be used by experienced headteachers in some integrated form, both reflectively in preparation and intuitively in response to unexpected events.

## 2.  Relationships with Individual Teachers

In order to manage teachers appropriately, heads need to make judgements about their individual performance and potential, to understand their social and political situation in school, to have some understanding of relevant aspects of their life outside school and to relate to each teacher in a way that suits them both. How do heads acquire sufficient valid knowledge of individual teachers to do this? Their files will include job applications, appraisal reports and correspondence – all compiled for specific purposes. Any evidence of their students' performance will rarely be of a value-added kind. Heads receive oral comments about a teacher from a range of sources, but usually as incidental comments rather than considered reports. Otherwise the information comes from a series of incidents: one-to-one conversations; group meetings; observations of the teacher interacting with pupils and colleagues in various settings. Apart from formal interviews for appraisal or appointment, few of these incidents will have had the intention to learn about the teacher concerned. Even incidental knowledge from direct contact tends to be regarded as more authentic. What is remembered will be determined by what was perceived at the time and stored in episodic memory as a series of impressions. Though not sufficiently processed by reflection to yield propositions, these observations and encounters will nevertheless contribute to heads' knowledge of the teacher but without them being aware of how the selection, integration and reorganisation of knowledge in episodic memory had occurred.

These remembered episodes are likely to be a highly atypical sample of a teacher's behaviour, partly because the head was present and partly because the most typical incidents are often the least memorable. Salient and recent incidents are the most likely to be remembered, and there will also be other sources of bias (Nisbett and Ross, 1980). For example:

a) In order to sustain human interaction, rapid interpretations of the other person have to be made early in order to make a response: but this response itself affects the ongoing interaction and affects later interpretations, often in ways which tend to confirm the original and possibly inaccurate interpretation.

b) Headteachers' personal constructs, developed by experiences before they even met the teacher, will affect how that teacher is perceived.

c) Preconceptions, gathered from earlier incidents, affect the interpretation of later incidents, so that the sample is not constructed from genuinely independent events.

In general, we may conclude that headteachers' construction of their knowledge of individual teachers is often a mainly intuitive process, which is significantly affected by potentially biasing factors of which they are unlikely to be aware. Both a head's current communication with each teacher and those past interactions which have constructed their relationship (including occasions when the teacher has not been a specific recipient but one of a larger group of staff) will depend on interpersonal skills developed over a lifetime as well as their ability to make appropriate use of their knowledge and prior experience of that teacher. Thus informally acquired skills are integrated in performance with knowledge of people which has been mainly acquired by informal and implicit learning. Without such knowledge, the skill dimension of a headteacher's performance is likely to be of only limited effectiveness.

### 3.  Understanding Schools as Organisations

This example has been chosen as an area of personal knowledge where theory makes a particularly significant contribution. The experience of myself and my colleagues in teaching masters level courses to mid-career teachers and public service managers has been that many theoretical concepts link easily with people's experiences of working in organisations and provide frameworks which enable them to make sense of that experience and transform it into useful knowledge for decision-making. When combined with training in qualitative research, they acquire a capability to investigate the nature of organisations more quickly and at greater depth, using other people's experiences as evidence as well as their own. Their own experience is likely to have been acquired informally and incidentally as in the previous example; but becomes far more useful when set alongside that of other people and when theoretical frameworks are available to help develop more considered and generally recognised analyses. Given the complexity of organisations, different theoretical perspectives are needed as well as multiple sources of evidence. My research on learning at work found strong support for mid-career management qualifications in the finance, engineering and healthcare sectors (Eraut *et al.*, 1998) and several respondents noted without prompting that modules on organisational behaviour had been particularly useful.

We need to recognise, however, that acquiring this useful knowledge is not a simple process. Having relevant prior experience enables managers to quickly appreciate that theories of this kind may help them in their current work and future careers. They then need the time and opportunity to think and talk about it, and gradually expand their personal cognitive framework to accommodate it. They may note that others have interpreted the same theories in different ways and argued about their relative significance. After a while, those theories they find particularly convincing become part of their normal way of looking at organisations, a platform for their future learning. The total learning time involved will ultimately be much greater than that allocated to that particular course module.

## TRANSFER, CHANGE AND LEARNING

This last example involved the transfer and personalisation of public knowledge about organisational behaviour from an academic to a school context. This was not an event in which managers applied (or failed to apply) a piece of recently learned public knowledge, but a lengthy learning process during which that knowledge was transformed through use. Transfer might also occur when a head of department becomes a deputy headteacher in another secondary school in a different part of the country. Given the change of role, school and location, how much knowledge of schools as organisations would be relevant to the new context and what would be involved in learning to use it? Research indicates that a theoretical framework would help by suggesting ways of sorting out the similarities and differences between the two schools and reducing the risk of imprudent transfer (i.e. overgeneralisation). The new deputy will need to be aware of the challenge and prepared to learn a lot about the new school before making strategic decisions, then to reinterpret their prior knowledge – both theoretical and practical – in ways that suit the new organisational context. Similar considerations will apply to changes in the community context, pupil culture, individual colleagues and so on. When the contexts are very similar, for example from one governors' or staff meeting to the next, little further learning may be necessary; but even then circumstances may have been changed by external events. Interpersonal skills, in particular, have to be resituated for every new encounter in the light of one's best knowledge of the people and circumstances involved. Any performance or management process involves the integration of skill with knowledge of people and situations and often with conceptual knowledge. This knowledge has to be constantly updated, the skills retuned and the action sensitively monitored in case a change of direction is needed. Such integration is rarely recognised in the literature about headteachers' knowledge, competence and expertise.

Another neglected aspect of change is the amount of unlearning which has to occur. We have already mentioned the inevitable acquisition of unbalanced perspectives of people and situations, as a result of the uncritical way in which informal information is collected, selected and aggregated. Unless this is periodically checked against more carefully collected evidence, inappropriate decisions and behaviour will result; and relationships and understandings will gradually become more difficult to adjust or modify. Routines and habits are even more difficult to change. They are needed to avoid information overload and to cope with busy contexts, so one comes to depend on them. As circumstances change, routines become dysfunctional; and people take shortcuts which save effort but reduce effectiveness, often without being aware of it. Yet abandoning them leads to disorientation and an inability to cope until new routines have been developed to replace them. The problem for headteachers is not only to evaluate and, where necessary, change their own practice but also to facilitate this learning process for all their staff.

The recently introduced National Standards for Headteachers uses the word 'effective' nearly 40 times in order to emphasise a commitment to improving pupils' achievement. But having the will, contrary to popular belief, does not ensure finding the way. What expertise do headteachers need in order to be able to improve their schools? Evidence suggests that there is both a sociopsychological dimension, generic to all organisations, and a technical dimension specific to schools. The implication of my earlier discussion is that expertise is a dynamic capability which constantly changes and develops. Hence school improvement depends on all staff being committed to continuing learning focused on this purpose. My own research (Eraut *et al.*, 1998) suggests that workplace learning arises mainly from the challenge of the work itself and through interacting with other people (colleagues, customers and clients). Such learning depends on confidence, motivation and capability (knowledge and skills previously acquired), which in turn depend on how they are managed and on the microculture of their immediate work environment.

> The key person is the local manager whose management of people and role in establishing a climate favourable to learning, in which people seek advice and help each other to learn quite naturally, is critical for those who are managed.
>
> (Eraut, 1998a)

Few schools are organised to support and facilitate this kind of teachers' learning.

The technical dimension is highly dependent on theories of what constitutes effective teaching, an area where the Standards are not entirely consistent. Sometimes effectiveness appears to be treated as an absolute unproblematic judgement, as when heads are expected to have knowledge and understanding of 'effective teaching and assessment methods' (Section 3d) and to 'secure and sustain effective teaching and learning throughout a school' (Section 5b). Sometimes effective teaching is more contextualised as, for example, when teachers are expected 'to employ the most effective approach(es) for any given context and group of pupils' (Section 2b). In this latter case, the head could not reasonably be expected to know the group of pupils that well nor even the context of the lesson; and would not therefore be in a position to judge the most effective approach, although bad teaching might be more obvious. This distinction is important because the first interpretation implies that knowledge of effective teaching is public propositional knowledge, while the second suggests that it is mainly personal process knowledge. Significantly the contextual interpretation is accompanied by process criteria which could be applied to almost any teaching method: pacing lessons appropriately, using time and resources effectively, extending pupils' learning and achievement through setting consistent and challenging homework.

The notion of 'effective methods' has great political appeal, especially when linked to ideas of evidence-based practice imported from the field of medicine. But not more than 20 per cent of medical decisions and virtually no teaching decisions can be made on the basis of 'gold standard' evidence from meta-analyses and randomised control trials. Educational 'diagnoses' and 'treatments' show so much natural variation that the construct of an 'effective method' is highly questionable. Elsewhere the Standards accompany statements about effective practice by discussion of standards of achievement, the use of benchmarks and setting targets; which suggests that effectiveness is to be judged only by the outcomes and not by the method employed. But it is difficult to tell whether it is the method or its application that is effective, which brings us back to a contextual interpretation of effectiveness. This depends more on teacher expertise than prescribed methods, so heads have to work with teachers to continually develop that expertise. Agreed targets between headteacher and teacher or teacher and pupil may signify rising expectations and confidence in their ability; imposed targets may be perceived as threats and lower their sense of self-efficacy.

## HEADTEACHERS' PRACTICE AND MODE OF COGNITION

During the last decade the nature of professional expertise has become increasingly an issue for debate. The traditional academic stance, by no means as dominant as often presented, defines the professional knowledge base in terms of Type A knowledge – public, propositional and grounded in established research traditions. In so far as it is theoretical, the relevant expertise lies with the academicians; in so far as it is empirical, the relevant expertise lies with researchers. The modernist stance, often described as hyper-rational, focuses on competences and achievements. Expertise is attributed to those who achieve good results even though the attribution of such success to individual merit may be highly questionable. Neither approach tells us much about how experts actually do their job. To do that we have to identify and deconstruct the various processes which constitute their practice, then find out what enables them to conduct these processes with (or without) quality and expertise.

Those processes which constitute a manager's or a professional's practice can be usefully analysed in terms of four types of sub-process, linked in a variety of sequences and combinations:

i   Acquiring situational understanding through collecting and interpreting information about people and situations.
ii  Deciding how to respond to this current representation of the situation, both immediately and over a longer period.
iii Activities required for implementing one's own or other people's decisions: routine actions, special techniques, giving advice, referral, delegation, further inquiry etc.
iv  Meta-processes concerned with directing and controlling one's own behaviour in accordance with one's main purpose, whilst also monitoring one's clients and their environment (*vide* Eraut, 1999).

These sub-processes are most often described in the context of a deliberative process in which professionals assess a situation, think of alternative options and their implications, plan an appropriate course of action then modify it in the light of information from ongoing monitoring. This model of practice gives prominence to analytic reasoning; and is favoured both by academics, who see it as an essential framework for research-based practice, and by government who recognise that public defence of policy requires a reasoned approach which is difficult to criticise. However, this approach is limited by the amount and quality of evidence available.

In a seminal paper, the McMaster University Working Group (1992) on evidence-based medicine argued that: evidence of all kinds should be gathered more systematically and interpreted more critically; the balance between patient evidence, personal experience, theoretical reasoning, research evidence and advice from local experts should be altered to give more weight to systematically gathered patient evidence and research evidence. More systematic observation and recording of patients is needed to construct a valid personal knowledge-base, alongside regular consultation and critical appraisal of the literature. Advice from local experts should be sought (rather than rejected) but used more critically. They also argue that

> clinicians must be ready to accept and live with uncertainty and to acknowledge that management decisions are often made in the face of relative ignorance of their true impact.

The Government and TTA now advocate this approach for teaching. However, as noted above, the research evidence on the respective merits of different classroom 'treatments' is neither available nor likely to become available in the future. While it is clearly desirable to attend to as much class-room-generated evidence as possible, the absence of valid and relevant research imperatives significantly changes the decision-making context from that found in medicine. There are also practical difficulties. Hospital doctors can concentrate on diagnosis and decision-making while relying on healthcare teams to look after their patients and imaging and pathology departments to provide scientific evidence. General Practitioners can refer more complex, urgent or critical cases to hospitals. Teachers are the equivalent of the whole healthcare team (doctors, nurses, scientist, therapists, porters); and there is nobody to mind their classes while they make individual diagnoses of pupils' learning. Even at school level, where there are strong arguments for collecting evidence about critical issues before making decisions, the allocation of staff time has to be carefully considered when making pre-decisions about the scope and scale of such inquiries.

The alternative for professionals, but not necessarily for managers, is to locate prime authority with acknowledged expert practitioners. Such people become experts as a result of years of experience in a particular domain of professional practice, usually quite specialised. In some professions such experts may need to be very familiar with research, but it is their use of research knowledge rather than their creation of it, that characterises the expert practitioner. It would be wrong to suggest that experts do not use analytic reasoning; but their superior performance will have been primarily constructed through learning from experience and being able to call upon that experience quickly and appropriately. This perspective receives considerable backing from psychological research contrasting novices with experts. A particularly attractive model for many professional practitioners is that of Dreyfus and Dreyfus (1986). They define skill as an integrative overarching approach to professional action and identify five stages of skill acquisition: novice, advanced beginner, competent, proficient and expert.

Their model's early and middle stages involve:

- the development of situational recognition and understanding;
- the development of standard routines which enable one to cope with crowded busy contexts;
- the later abandonment of explicit rules and guidelines as behaviour becomes more automatic; and
- a peaking of the deliberative mode of cognition (not usually very analytic) at the competence stage.

Progression beyond competence is then associated with the gradual replacement of analysis by more intuitive forms of cognition. Their claim that experts make considerable use of rapid decision-making is well substantiated by research (Eraut, 1999); but they do not establish their claim that deliberation has become virtually redundant. Benner (1984) recognises two situations where analytic approaches by experts might be required: when confronted with a situation of which they have no previous experience or when they mis-diagnose a situation and then find that events and behaviours are not occur-ring as expected. Thus it can be argued that the Dreyfus model neglects the self-evaluative dimension of professional work. The gradual development of experience-based intuition may enable a person to become an expert, but without a more explicit evaluative dimension it can become so self-confirm-ing that it slips into decline. Is there not a danger that an almost wholly intu-itive model of professional expertise will perpetuate the myth of an almost infallible expert? The problems of sharing intuitive expertise with colleagues or explaining the basis for their 'expert opinions' will severely constrain par-ticipation in collaborative endeavours, thus minimising their exposure to dif-ferent, possibly critical, perspectives.

The term deliberation has been used hitherto in the sense of taking time to think about a situation, decision or problem. As Aristotle observed over 2,000 year ago, many practical problems in society require thought but cannot be resolved by logical argument and evidence alone. The 'real world' is too complex. Managers need to mull over problems, consult and discuss, then judge the probable best course of action; more likely, they settle for an option good enough for the purpose, even if it might not turn out to have been the best. According to the context, deliberative decision-making may vary from 'just sorting something out' to making 'high stakes' decisions after a period of careful consideration, consultation, predicting consequences then finally deciding. In this latter context headteachers would normally aspire to that maturity of judge-ment we sometimes call wisdom. Wisdom implies experience in making diffi-cult decisions, access to multiple perspectives, a balanced viewpoint and an ability to situate the expertise of others in a broader social context. It conveys neither the analytic reasoning of the researcher, nor the confident, intuitive grasp of the expert practitioner, but an ability to deliberate about issues and problems, to see how different people might be affected and to put them into longer term perspective. Part of the skill of a manager is to recognise which problems can be dealt with fairly quickly by satisficing strategies and which require prolonged attention and more evidence.

The most important variables affecting the time devoted to decision-making are likely to be the significance and complexity of the decision, the timespan during which it has to be made and other demands on the decision-maker's time. The less the time available, the more headteachers will have to rely on more rapid, intuitive approaches. Figure 9.1 depicts the effect of time (and indirectly also complexity and busyness) on three of the four types of sub-process identified earlier (Eraut, 1995). Since thinking time is the focus, action itself has been omitted and the thought accompanying action treated as interpretation, decision-making or reflection.

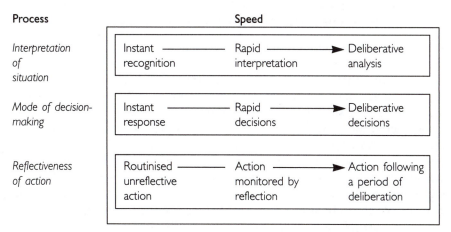

**Figure 9.1**  The effect of speed on the nature of professional work

The relationship between time and mode of cognition is probably interactive: shortage of time forces people to adopt a more intuitive approach, while the intuitive routines developed by experience enable people to do things more quickly. Crowded contexts also force people to be more selective with their attention and to process their incoming information more rapidly. Under conditions of rapid interpretation and decision-making, reflectiveness is necessarily intuitive, in accordance with Schon's (1983) concept of reflection-in-action. But as the time scale expands, the role of meta-processes becomes more complex, expanding beyond self-awareness and monitoring to include the framing of problems, thinking about the deliberative process itself and how it is being handled, searching for relevant knowledge, introducing value considerations, etc.

Headteachers do not start as novices in quite the same way as beginning teachers; but neither, especially at primary level, do they have experience of the headteacher role before their first headship. Many important relationships will have been constructed and major decisions made before significant expertise has been developed. By then, patterns of work will have been formed which may be considerably less effective than they might have wished, and changing them will require a significant amount of determination and effort. For headteachers to maintain critical control over their own practice they will need to be aware of their habits and routines and their ways of thinking about people and situations, even if they cannot easily explain them (Eraut, 1994). Otherwise they are, in effect, abdicating their responsibility for the outcomes that follow. This is why the self-evaluation dimension of headship is extremely important, as well as being a strong argument for facilitating constructive criticism within the senior management team and governors rather than seeking to avoid uncomfortable or time-consuming debate.

## THE RELATIONSHIP BETWEEN CAPABILITY AND PERFORMANCE IN A CHANGING CONTEXT

Another important consideration is the problem for new headteachers in both converting their current capability into competence in a new role and context and converting that competence into performance. When the expected level of performance does not result, there is a natural tendency to look for dispositional factors, such as drive and motivation. But often closer inspection reveals significant factors in the work context which constrain performance. Capacity to perform is affected by the total demands of the job, emotional as well as physical. Headteachers' performance will depend not only on their expertise but also on their overall workload and the expectations of governors, senior managers, teachers and parents about access to them and about what they ought to be doing. It is easy to forget when formulating standards that the 'whole job' role is the most important of all.

This 'whole job' role, however, still needs to be seen in the context of the whole management function of the school. Ultimately it is the performance of the school's management which counts. Some headteachers are much better supported by governors and their management team than others. This is partly their own responsibility but they normally inherit both groups and working conventions, and have little control over the loss of valued people through illness or promotion. Developing the capability of the management team as a whole has to be a major priority, even though it may be periodically upset by changes. Thus, depending on the senior management team's expertise, the head's personal role in many of the activities listed in the Standards may vary from 'do it yourself' to monitoring and occasionally advising capable colleagues, thus affecting their priorities for time management and professional development.

This emphasis on the 'whole job' role of the headteacher and the 'whole team' approach to the management function emphasises the over-riding importance of prioritisation and the deployment and development of management expertise. Thus the key requirements for a headteacher are to:

- make an accurate and balanced assessment of the school's current state and of trends, risks and opportunities;
- formulate, through consultation, short- and long-term priorities for action;
- ascertain how staff can best attend to the priorities without causing negative side-effects.

This may entail some staff, including the headteacher, developing new capabilities; and this overall management development plan should determine the head's own professional development priorities.

Finally, it should be recognised that government and school policy and practice change. Views about the relative merits of different types of learning outcomes will change. So also will views about the teacher's role and how schools should be managed. Staff will also have to change their roles or practices because of internal reorganisation, promotion or new external mandates. What constitutes competence or expertise today will not be the same tomorrow. Hence it is important for people to have capabilities which extend beyond the confines of their current job but may be valuable in future.

Conceptually it is important to distinguish between a head's capability, which is individually defined in terms of what that particular person can think and do, given the appropriate context and opportunity, and the competence required to be the headteacher of a particular school, which is socially defined in terms of the performance expected from the holder of that post (Eraut, 1998b). That definition of competence will also change; and in responding to that change the headteacher will need to call upon or develop additional capability. Equally important for headteachers in the modern world will be their ability to redesign their own job in accordance with the changing needs of their school; and this of course will change what counts as being competent in that job. Should they not also expect such proactive innovation from others? Rapidly changing organisations are not only dependent on the current competence of their staff but also on their additional capabilities and understandings. These need to be continually developed in the interests of the school's mission; but they also need to be properly appreciated and used. Individual capabilities and understandings relevant to group or whole school issues have to be incorporated into the capabilities and understandings of the school as a whole and its constituent sub-groups (Eraut, 1997b). Where there is synergy, the potential of groups will be greater than that of their members; where there is division, stratification or mutual isolation, the group potential will be less. That is what transforms learning professionals into learning groups and learning organisations; and what headteachers in rapidly changing contexts need to develop in their schools.

## CONCLUSION

My conclusions from the above analysis of headteachers' knowledge, practice, mode of cognition, job priorities and leadership role are that training for new headteachers should concentrate on:

1. Aspects of the management role which can be undertaken only by the headteacher.
2. Assessing the school's current state and determining priorities for action, by enabling rather than prescribing.
3. Collecting evidence to complement informal learning.
4. Understanding the school's culture and sub-cultures and the symbolic impact of their behaviour and thinking about the promotion (if desired) of cultural change over a period of time.
5. Leadership of the senior management team and sharing duties among them.

6. Their own self-evaluation and continuing professional learning.
7. Supporting and developing managers, groups of staff and learning throughout the school.
8. Organising the administration of the school to give its professional staff thinking time.
9. Strategies for school improvement which take the above into account, and avoiding pressures from documents like the Standards to try to do too much.


## REFERENCES

Benner, P. (1984) *From Novice to Expert: Excellence and power in clinical nursing practice*, Menlo Park, Calif: Addison-Wesley.

Dreyfus, H.L. and Dreyfus, S.E. (1986) *Mind over Machine: The power of human intuition and expertise in the era of the computer*, Oxford: Basil Blackwell.

Eraut, M.R. (1994) *Developing Knowledge and Competence*, London: Falmer.

Eraut, M.R. (1995) Schön Shock: A case for reframing reflection-in-action?, *Teachers and Teaching*, 1 (1). 9–22.

Eraut, M.R. (1997a) Professional knowledge in teacher education, in P. Nuutinen (ed.) *Inquiring Teacher – from Experience to Pedagogy, Bulletins of the Faculty of Education No. 64*, University of Joensuu: Finland.

Eraut, M.R. (1997b) Perspectives on defining 'the learning society', *Journal of Educational Policy*, 12 (6), 531–538.

Eraut, M.R. (1998a) Managers hold key to developing knowledge and skills, *Professional Manager*, 7 (2), 41.

Eraut, M.R. (1998b) Concepts of competence, *Journal of Interprofessional Care*, 12 (2), 127–139.

Eraut, M.R. (1999) Professional knowledge, practice and mode of cognition, in R. Foucher (ed.) *Proceedings of International Conference on Self-Directed Learning*, Montreal.

Eraut, M.R. *et al.* (1998) Developing knowledge and skills in employment, *Research Report 5*, University of Sussex Institute of Education.

McMaster University Evidence-Based Medicine Working Group (1992) Evidence-based medicine: a new approach to teaching the practice of medicine, *J. American Medical Association*, 268 (17), 2420–2425.

Nisbett, R.E. and Ross, L. (1980) *Human Inference: Strategies and Shortcomings of Social Judgement*, Englewood Cliffs, N.J.: Prentice Hall.

Schön, D. (1983) *Educating the Reflective Practitioner: Towards a new design for teaching and learning in the professions*, San Francisco: Jossey-Bass.

# SECTION 3

# THEORY DEVELOPMENT

### Edited by Peter Ribbins

# 10

# Combining Cultural and Political Perspectives: The Best of Both Conceptual Worlds?

## MIKE WALLACE

This chapter advocates combining two commonly employed perspectives – the cultural and the political – to overcome limitations of using either alone to explain and evaluate interaction in organisations. The mix of concepts adopted within either perspective varies, leading researchers to look for different things and give a different conceptual spin to what they find. A way forward is to combine the two to reap the analytical benefit of insights that each perspective can bring while avoiding tunnel vision following from adherence to one or other.

Combining perspectives is, however, easier said than done. If each offers a lens for viewing the social world, will the combination of lenses produce enhanced stereoscopic vision or merely a blur? The remainder of the chapter explores, first, the nature of perspectives as metaphors and alternative strategies for combining them. Second, examples are critically reviewed of research on school management from either the cultural or the political perspective. Third, key concepts incorporated in the proposed dual perspective are stipulatively defined. Fourth, application of this dual perspective is illustrated through interpretation of findings from an investigation of school reorganisation. Finally, advantages and drawbacks of the strategy for combining perspectives are reviewed and the wider applicability of the dual perspective is considered.

## MIXED VERSUS MULTIPLE METAPHOR

Any quest for one best theory to explain the social world is probably futile. Social phenomena are too complex for such reductionist explanation, and theories in the social sciences are both normative and culturally relative, reflecting beliefs and values of their creators who cannot escape their location within the social climate of their time. Theories orientate us towards phenomena in particular ways; it therefore seems more realistic to adopt the metatheoretical position that they constitute metaphors (Morgan, 1986) highlighting some features of social phenomena while ignoring aspects that other metaphors would address. If no metaphor can be taken as gospel, it follows that we may deepen analysis by using more than one metaphor to examine the same phenomenon. Mixing metaphors from different traditions is increasingly advocated to transcend the limited insight a single metaphor can give: Cuthbert (1984) identifies five; Bolman and Deal (1991) four; and Bush (1995), drawing on Cuthbert's work, six.

These metaphors, according to Bush (146–148):

> represent conceptually distinct approaches to the management of educational institutions. However, it is rare for a single theory to capture the reality of management in any particular school or college. Rather, aspects of several perspectives are present in different proportions within each institution. The applicability of each approach may vary with the event, the situation and the participants.

He argues that the validity of applying any metaphor depends on organisational characteristics like size. The political perspective is deemed less relevant to decision-making in small primary schools than in large secondary schools and colleges where staff compete for resources. Bush apparently assumes, first, that each perspective addresses an exclusive proportion of the 'reality' of particular organisational phenomena; and second, that certain phenomena may be present or absent in different situations. This view of metaphors seems overly restrictive. Surely it is more valid to assume that any perspective may bear on any situation in the social world. One limitation of much research from a single perspective into primary and secondary schools stems from the possibility of interpreting the same phenomenon (like decision-making) in both kinds of institution from alternative perspectives. Secondary schools no more have a monopoly on political conflict over decisions about scarce resources than primary schools have on cultural cohesion leading to consensual decisions.

The approach of Bolman and Deal (1991) rests on the assumption that organisational phenomena may be interpreted from more than one perspective or 'frame'. They argue that most managers become stuck with their pet frame, whereas:

> The ability to reframe experience enriches and broadens a leader's repertoire and serves as a powerful antidote to self-entrapment. Expanded choice enables managers to generate creative responses to the broad range of problems that they encounter . . . it can be enormously liberating for managers to realise that there is *always* more than one way to respond to any organisational problem or dilemma. Managers are imprisoned only to the degree that their palette of ideas is impoverished.

> (4, original emphasis)

Each frame contains a set of concepts enabling managers to develop their interpretation and normative image of how organisations should be managed, giving them something to emulate or reject according to their values. By switching between frames, managers enlarge the basis of understanding which informs their practice. However, concepts within different frames are not compatible: the cultural frame leads to interpretation of what holds people in organisations together, the political frame to what pulls them apart. As a consequence of adopting incompatible assumptions underpinning each frame, Bolman and Deal are forced to employ them sequentially in what may be termed a 'mixed metaphor' approach. In parallel with the managers they seek to help, they appear to be stuck with their pet 'metaframe'.

We can go further with integrating perspectives through a 'multiple metaphor' approach. Cultural and political perspectives may be merged into a dual metaphor by adopting mutually compatible definitions of concepts drawn from each constituent perspective. Table 10.1 compares approaches of several researchers using these perspectives to examine school management. It is intended, heuristically, to indicate how the approach towards perspectives moulds interpretation of findings, and how concepts must be rendered compatible for integration in a multiple metaphor.

These writers have different purposes for theory development affecting their use of perspectives. Hoyle (1986) distinguishes between 'theory for understanding', whose purpose is to provide explanation (which may be antithetical to action) and 'theory for action', whose purpose is to guide practice. The 'theory for understanding' category may be subdivided according to the place of writers' value orientation. Some investigators have adopted an explicit critical stance either from the outset, framing their theory building and empirical efforts, or in the light of their findings. Others have retained a more distanced orientation towards what they variably acknowledge as value laden fields of enquiry, seeking explanations as a platform for making judgements based on diverse value positions. 'Theory for understanding', where a distanced orientation is adopted, may usefully be distinguished from what I will call 'theory for critical evaluation' where commitment to an overtly critical stance is made.

Second, the different perspectives are associated with varying approaches towards metaphors – whether single, mixed or multiple. Third, assumptions differ about the compass of central concepts underlying each perspective, with consequences for interpretation. Fourth, for single or mixed metaphor approaches, concepts within the analysis are identified which may be construed as belonging to the alternative metaphor. The final two points of comparison address contrasting interpretations of interaction between headteachers and other staff which is either synergistic or conflictual.

## OVERCOMING CONCEPTUAL MYOPIA

Nias *et al.* (1989) employ a cultural perspective to explain interaction among primary school staff, portraying how they developed shared beliefs and values about the way colleagues related to each other. The analysis emphasises subtle ways in which staff contribute to developing and maintaining their shared culture. Arguably, this single perspective may have distracted the researchers'

**Table 10.1:** *Contrasting approaches to employment of cultural and political perspectives*

| Criterion | Nias et al., 1989 | Ball, 1987 | Southworth, 1995 | Blase and Anderson, 1995 | Bolman and Deal, 1991 | Wallace and Hall, 1994 |
|---|---|---|---|---|---|---|
| *Focus of study* | Research on staff relationships in UK primary schools | Research on secondary teachers' views of UK heads' behaviour | Research on a UK primary head's approach to management | US teachers' views of principals' behaviour, case studies of two principals | Management handbook based on US experience and research | Research on UK secondary school senior management teams |
| *Purpose of theorising* | Understanding leading to advice on action | Critical evaluation | Critical evaluation leading to conception of leadership and advice on action | Critical evaluation leading to leadership theory | Advice about action | Understanding leading to advice on action |
| *Type of metaphor* | Single | Single | Single | Single | Mixed, including separate cultural and political | Multiple, combined cultural and political |
| *Assumptions about key concept in main perspective* | Culture becomes widely shared among staff | Power is conflictual | Power is largely conflictual | Power may be conflictual or synergistic | Culture – leaders promote shared culture through vision, power conflictual | Culture – beliefs and values shared within subcultures, power may be conflictual or synergistic, beliefs and values reciprocally shape use of power |
| *Use of concepts from alternative perspective* | Use of power, especially by heads | Norms and rules govern routine interaction | Normative control by head and other staff | Principals attempt to manage staff culture through manipulation | Sequential use of different frames including cultural, political | Simultaneous use of concepts from cultural and political perspectives |
| *Interpretation of synergistic interaction between head and other staff* | Cohesion due to shared beliefs and values | Heads dominate other staff through controlling activity, so avoiding conflict | Head dominates other staff through controlling activity, so avoiding conflict | Most principals dominate, a few share power with other staff | Cohesion due to leaders' promotion of shared beliefs and values | Cohesion due to shared beliefs and values resulting from use of power by heads and other staff |
| *Interpretation of conflictual interaction between head and other staff* | Shared beliefs and values about compromise enable conflicts to be avoided or resolved | Each actor uses power in struggle to realise incompatible interests | Head resolves conflicts through normative control or personal interventions | Each actor uses power in struggle to realise incompatible interests | Each actor uses power in struggle to realise incompatible interests | Each actor uses power according to beliefs and values to realise incompatible interests |

attention from the possibility of differential use of power by heads and other staff in moulding the culture, of emergence of subcultures, or of conflict as the explanation for some interactions. Power may be underplayed but it does creep in, suggesting that the notion of organisational culture cannot grasp all that was significant. For example, they state:

> normative *control* was so pervasive that it is easy to lose sight of the fact that it too was the product of a *power differential*. Each school had a head with a strong 'mission' and well developed *political skills* who had been in post for at least ten years and to whom had accrued during that time a considerable amount of personal *authority*.
>
> (15)

The power related concepts I have italicised surface because they explain how headteachers were uniquely placed to persuade other staff to accept their managerial values, even in situations of cultural accord. Synergistic interaction is explained as expressing shared beliefs and values, whereas conflicts are interpreted as being confronted or avoided consistent with underlying shared values about working towards compromise solutions.

Ball (1987), in contrast, aims to inform educational improvement according to explicit values:

> An understanding of the way that schools change (or stay the same) and therefore of the practical limits and possibilities of educational development, must take account of intra-organisational processes. This is particularly crucial in examining developments which are related to the achievement of more equal, more just, as well as more effective education.
>
> (3)

His single metaphor approach is based on a political orientation he calls a 'conflict perspective':

> I take schools . . . to be *arenas of struggle*; to be riven with actual or potential conflict between members; to be poorly coordinated; to be ideologically diverse.
>
> (19, original emphasis)

Power is linked with struggle, whether overt or suppressed. Yet the narrowly conflictual view of power favours interpreting all interaction conflictually, a danger Ball acknowledges:

> having set an agenda for the study of micropolitics and institutional conflict in schools, I do not want to fall into the same trap as the social system theorists, of seeing conflict everywhere, where they saw consensus.
>
> (19)

Conflict, however, dominates the analysis. Apparently harmonious interaction is interpreted as masking covert conflict, and cultural concepts creep in:

> interaction is centred upon the *routine*, mundane and, for the most part, uncontroversial running of the institution . . . routine organisational life is set within the *'negotiated order'* . . . a patterned construct of contrasts, *understandings, agreements*

and *'rules'* which provides the basis of concerted action... In this way conflicts may
remain normally implicit and subterranean, only occasionally bursting into full
view.

(20, emphasis added)

The cultural concepts I have italicised play a subordinate role in Ball's
approach but are akin to those featuring centrally in the interpretation of
Nias and her colleagues. In both single metaphor analyses, concepts from the
perspective *not* employed are present. The 'norm' of cabinet responsibility
articulated by Ball is a cultural idea; the 'personal authority' of the head articulated by Nias and her co-workers is a political concept. Concepts associated
with the alternative perspective were required to grasp the range of phenomena found.

Southworth's (1995) single metaphor approach was developed to interpret
and evaluate findings from a case study. It draws on Ball's perspective and
appears similarly constrained, but his purposes reach further towards constructing an alternative normative theory. Ball (280) concludes with the statement: 'the alternative lies in the direction of *school democracy*. But that, as
they say, is another story' (original emphasis). Southworth begins to tell the
story by articulating a preferred critical approach to school leadership, offering advice on supporting heads with moving in this direction.

A conception of power as conflictual takes his analysis of a primary headteacher's management practice along parallel lines with Ball's, developing the
idea of 'normative control' to explain how the head used subtle means to get
his way, such as promoting teachers who shared his values to management
positions. The 'normative' element of the concept has cultural overtones,
linked with the political notion of control. Harmonious interaction is viewed
as resulting from the head's successful 'domination', acting to deflect or pre-
empt most potential conflict and, on rare occasions when staff disputes arose,
using normative control strategies such as deploying senior staff on his behalf.

The opposing interpretations following from these separate cultural and
political perspectives are symptomatic of their incompatibility. One
researcher's cultural cohesion is another's political domination. Concepts
from both perspectives cannot be integrated with a cultural perspective
restricted to cohesion and a political perspective restricted to conflict. How
is a marriage of (my) convenience between these perspectives to be achieved?

One response is to broaden the constituent perspectives: the cultural orientation may allow for conflict between subcultures, while the political orientation may allow for synergistic use of resources to achieve shared interests.
The political perspective adopted by Blase and Anderson (1995) goes part
way. Their purposes are aligned with Southworth's, and they construct a normative theory of 'democratic, empowering leadership' embracing a more comprehensive definition of power. It is conceived as expressed in all interaction
which may vary from conflictual ('power over'), through facilitative ('power
through') to synergistic, where individuals participate as equals ('power

with'). This conception circumvents limitations of the narrower conflict perspective where power disappears unless actors are interpreted as wielding power *over* others, whether through conflict or domination. The critically evaluative purpose of Blase and Anderson leads them to interpret much interaction in terms of domination by principals whether through overt, authoritarian means or the covert, manipulative means of more facilitative approaches where principals secure commitment of other staff to their agenda.

Their single metaphor approach also includes cultural concepts in the analysis. They argue that collaborative or 'diplomatic' interactions among teachers reflect a mutually supportive culture:

> the politics of diplomacy were consistent with the norms of equitable exchange and mutual benefit. Diplomatic actions, such as support among teachers, promoted networks of indebtedness and mutual assistance.

(69)

Principals' approach to power has a significant impact in 'setting the political "tone" of the school' (73), either promoting collaborative and reciprocal or conflictual and self-oriented interactions by other staff. Significantly for my analysis, they postulate that both forms of interaction may coexist – the bottom line interpretation here is not predetermined as necessarily either synergistic or conflictual.

This more comprehensive view of power avoids the problem conflict perspectives face over allowing for synergistic interaction. Yet even a single metaphor approach which allows for synergistic and conflictual interaction gives limited purchase on why people use power. Blase and Anderson appear to resort to cultural concepts because they help explain uses of power through inferences about beliefs and values guiding principals and other staff, how far these beliefs and values are shared, and how uses of power by different individuals and groups may contribute to changing or sustaining their own beliefs and values and those of other parties. Culture and power are intimately connected.

If the mixed metaphor approach of Bolman and Deal expands the number of concepts employed through sequential interpretation from each perspective, their definition nevertheless leads to alternate, incompatible explanations. The dual metaphor approach to integrating the cultural and political perspectives assumes that interaction may be synergistic and conflictual; relevant beliefs and values may or may not be shared; and concepts from each constituent perspective can be made compatible. In seeking to explain synergistic interaction inside senior management teams, the interpretation focused on how far team members shared beliefs and values about teamwork, how their past use of power engendered this shared culture and how the culture guided uses of power to achieve shared interests. Conflictual interaction was explained by examining the differing beliefs and values guiding use of power by team members in attempting to realise incompatible interests. The unique position of authority accorded to headteachers gave them greater power than their colleagues to shape the culture relating to teamwork, but the latter also had informal sources of power to support or reject the heads' model of teamwork and its cultural assumptions. Of these various approaches, only the dual metaphor explicitly links culture and power as equal components of the one analysis.

## THE DUAL CULTURAL AND POLITICAL PERSPECTIVE

Definitions of core concepts are as follows. A simple definition of organisational culture is 'the way we do things around here' (Bower, 1966), which implicitly encompasses rejecting ways we don't do things around here. Culture is largely internalised, and norms or rules of behaviour that guide interaction of those who subscribe to a culture rest on shared symbols, beliefs and values. Norms may be explicit, perhaps enshrined in a formal policy, or implicit, becoming noticeable only when transgressed. Symbolic elements of culture are those where actions represent a shared value, as where staff participate in a social event to mark the closing of a school. A school staff culture encompasses beliefs and values about education, management and relationships. Where groups share distinctive beliefs and values, they may form subcultures. In such 'differentiated cultures' (Meyerson and Martin, 1987), meanings are shared within subcultural boundaries, but there is disjunction between beliefs and values of different groups.

Following Giddens (1984), power is viewed as 'transformative capacity': the capability to intervene in events so as to alter their course. Expression of power need not imply conflict; parties to interaction who cooperate synergistically have ability to make things happen together. Equally, each protagonist in a conflict situation may employ transformative capacity to achieve opposing goals. It is useful to distinguish between two forms of power (Bacharach and Lawler, 1980): authority means use of resources legitimated by individuals' beliefs and values associated with status, including the right to apply sanctions. In contrast, influence refers to informal use of resources where there is no recourse to sanctions linked to authority, though others (such as withdrawal of support) may be available. While access to resources varies, any individual is likely to have recourse to some form of influence. Parties to interaction are implicated in what Giddens calls a 'dialectic of control', a flow of action and response where each actor acts to achieve her or his interest or goal and responds to others' attempt to achieve theirs, which may or may not coincide. Conversely, in everyday situations no individual has absolute power: it is (unequally) distributed within and between institutions and system levels. I will now illustrate the application of the dual metaphor (see Wallace and Pocklington, 1998).

## ORCHESTRATING REDEPLOYMENT: LEA RESPONSIBILITY WITHOUT POWER?

Implementation of LEA-wide reorganisation of schooling entails a network of interactions within and between schools, their communities, the diocesan authority for church schools, the LEA, the relevant central government department and inspectors. One question guiding the research into an LEA reorganisation initiative was:

- How were LEA staff able to broker redeployment of school staff whose jobs would be removed through reorganisation, so avoiding redundancies across the LEA, despite governors having exclusive authority over staff appointments in each school?

Reorganisation proposals approved by central government gave LEA staff authority to reduce overcapacity through closures, mergers and changing the age range for which schools catered. A substantial reduction was required, so many permanent staff faced possible redundancy. Under the local management of schools (LMS) initiative, authority to make staff appointments had passed from LEA to governors of 'self managing' institutions. LEA officers could only request governors to take staff threatened by redundancy. Governors' legitimate interest accompanying their new level of authority over appointments was to seek the best candidate for the job, rather than support the LEA by restricting the field to local candidates whom reorganisation had displaced. Within the dialectic of control between LEA officers, governors, school staff and their union representatives, what was the recipe for LEA staff success in placing all but three teachers by the time implementation was completed?

First, widespread belief in the authority of the LEA remained, a pre-LMS legacy, disposing school staff and governors favourably towards the LEA and so empowering its officers when negotiating appointments. One secondary head commented, 'the LEA is a good authority'. In handling reorganisation, he assumed '[the Chief Education Officer] is my boss'.

Second, LEA staff had credibility with most heads, governors, other staff and union representatives. Officers responsible for staffing were long-serving and highly respected. Their knowledge of local schools and their staff also helped empower them as they could usually offer acceptable staffing proposals, so sustaining their credibility. Other officers hinted at an LEA staff culture guiding such actions: one summed it up as the LEA's 'professional approach', another as the principle of ensuring consistent information was given to those affected by reorganisation.

Typical of this orientation was the effort one officer made to foster parity by persuading heads of expanding first schools to advertise their vacancies at the same time in the LEA staff bulletin issued to all schools: 'We would like to see them advertised as a bunch so that it doesn't appear that one [school] is trying to steal a march on the others.'

Third, a voluntary code of practice had been reached with all governing bodies, diocesan representatives and unions to support the LEA policy of avoiding redundancies wherever possible, stating that:

> The responsible body for the management of staff, the governing body or the Authority, will make every effort to avoid compulsory redundancy, and in avoiding compulsory redundancy will seek, in consultation with the Authority or the governing body respectively and staff representatives, to implement a policy of redeployment.

The code was solely a source of influence but it symbolised mutual commitment and shaped governors' use of their exclusive authority over appointments. They could be faced with tension between contradictory beliefs, either where officers proposed a displaced teacher with a reputation of marginal competence for redeployment, or where governors wished to seek candidates from outside the LEA. Belief in supporting LEA policy sat uneasily alongside belief in doing what was best for the school. Two years before a middle school was to close, the headteacher retired and governors insisted on promoting the deputy to a permanent headship in the face of LEA advice. This new head was thereby added to the list of staff whom LEA officers were committed to redeploying under the code of practice. Such instances were rare.

Fourth, LEA influence on governing bodies was strengthened through LEA governors. Although in a minority on any governing body, they had all been nominated by the ruling group of councillors and generally followed council policy. They had authority to contribute to appointment decisions, and supported LEA officers by acting on advice they had authority to offer, but governors had no obligation to heed. The strength of 'political will' to support redeployment was crucial to winning union support for reorganisation.

Fifth, the LEA had exclusive authority over decisions related to beneficiaries of a voluntary premature retirement (VPR) scheme introduced when reorganisation began. One officer dubbed it 'the oil in the gearbox' because VPR was an incentive, not only to eligible staff, but also to governors with an interest in the opportunity it created to appoint new staff, make savings by appointing a replacement on a lower salary, or shed a teacher whose competence they questioned. As another officer testified: 'VPR is one of the few sources of power left . . . without a scheme we could not under any circumstances have done this reorganisation.'

Norms framing LEA officers' actions rested on legal parameters for the scheme covering eligibility, salary enhancement and lump sum redundancy payments, and criteria that offers must be linked either to avoiding a compulsory redundancy or to improving the efficiency of the education service where a school's LMS budget was in deficit. Authority over VPR empowerd LEA officers to invite applications from anyone eligible in closing schools and so meet the LEA interest in reducing the number of staff to be redeployed.

LEA officers often suggested that a VPR in one school could be linked with avoiding redundancy in another. Where a deputy in an expanding first school applied for VPR, officers brokered an informal agreement with the head and governors that a teacher in the school would be promoted to the deputy headship. The vacancy created would be filled by appointing a teacher under threat of redundancy elsewhere. This agreement was not binding but, should governors opt to appoint a new deputy from outside the LEA and sever the link with avoiding a redundancy, the governing body would be liable for financing any enhancement of the pension through their LMS budget.

Union support had been won through LEA investment in the VPR package, suiting their members' interest in maximising compensation, coupled with the pressure that the present scheme was an unrepeatable offer with limited shelf life. An LEA administrator commented:

> We are a very generous employer and professional associations have been selling it to their members. The scheme may be revised following reorganisation; it will certainly be managed very differently and therefore it may be almost their [i.e. staff's] last opportunity to be released with very generous benefits and it's to their advantage to take it.

Sixth, LEA staff, heads and governors worked synergistically to maximise their influence over the appointment procedure. Headteacher and deputy posts must be advertised nationally, but legislation does not extend to wording of adverts or the selection process. Staff selection was guided by a belief that the letter of the law must be followed, but influence within the law was allowable to minimise the risk of the informal agreement being upset. The advertisement would be worded to discourage outsiders from applying. One advert for a deputy headship stated that 'a number of local schools will close. In this situation the Authority must look to protect the interests of all employees under threat of redundancy. The governors see the deputy head vacancy as an opportunity to assist the LEA in this task.'

Finally, the LEA had authority over other aspects of reorganisation which constituted a source of influence over staff appointments where they symbolised LEA support for school level interests. They included:

- investment in new building and refurbishment where reorganisation proposals required;
- 'transitional funding' – payments to schools to help staff prepare for changes;
- staff development support, including courses for staff redeployed to a different sector and servicing headteachers' meetings to air reorganisation issues;
- clerking for most governing bodies whereby officers could offer a direct line of communication between governors and LEA.

In sum, empowerment of LEA staff to reallocate staff among 'self managing' schools rested on nurturing a supportive culture through meeting interests of other groups where possible, coupled with appealing to their altruism.

## CONCLUSION

The cultural and political perspective helped show how, despite their loss of authority, LEA staff were not without power where they could foster acceptance of their influence as 'honest brokers' of staff appointment decisions. This application demonstrates the analytical purchase the combined perspective gives on the interrelationship between culture and power. Arguably, it offers the best of two conceptual worlds, enabling answers to be sought to questions linking culture with power, such as: who has power to shape the staff culture in educational organisations? How do cultural allegiances impact reciprocally on uses of power? How may actions according to contradictory cultural allegiances induce or avoid conflict?

The multiple metaphor approach also has disadvantages. First, the analysis is complex, with potentially double the concepts of either single perspective. Second, some fine-grained analysis possible within each single perspective is lost, since the totality of concepts they offer is not employed. Third, the necessity of adopting compatible versions of each constituent perspective rules out combining perspectives resting on incompatible assumptions. As Bolman and Deal recognised, a political perspective based on a conflictual view of interaction would not integrate with a cultural perspective based on a consensual view. Broadening conceptual horizons by combining perspectives may compromise the depth of analytical insight that incompatible versions of different perspectives provide. Those favouring a particular version of a single perspective would probably regard the multiple metaphor strategy as offering the worst of conceptual worlds because it weakens the analytical purchase of their pet perspective.

Nevertheless, such an approach has potential for wider application, as is happening elsewhere in the education sphere (e.g. Hall, 1996, incorporating gender in a triple metaphor). An agenda for further research and conceptual development could profitably include:

- empirical investigations using the cultural and political perspective, whether at the same or across different system levels, or amongst the diversity of institutional settings in different sectors of education;
- extension of the variety of concepts which might be incorporated in this dual metaphor;
- conceptual bridgework to create other multiple metaphors by seeking compatible areas of linkage and assessing their fitness for different analytical purposes.

## REFERENCES

Bacharach, S. and Lawler, E. (1980) *Power and Politics in Organisations*, San Francisco: Jossey-Bass.
Ball, S. (1987) *The Micropolitics of the School*, London: Methuen.

Blase, J. and Anderson, G. (1995) *The Micropolitics of Educational Leadership: From control to empowerment*, London: Cassell.

Bolman, L. and Deal, T. (1991) *Reframing Organisations: Artistry, choice and leadership*, San Francisco: Jossey-Bass.

Bower, M. (1966) *The Will to Manage: Corporate success through programmed management*, New York: McGraw-Hill.

Bush, T (1995) *Theories of Educational Management* (2nd edn), London: Paul Chapman.

Cuthbert, R. (1984) The Management Process, Block 3, Part 2, E324 *Management in Post-Compulsory Education*, Milton Keynes: Open University Press.

Giddens, A (1984) *The Constitution of Society*, Cambridge: Polity.

Hall, V. (1996) *Dancing on the Ceiling: A study of women managers in education*, London: Paul Chapman.

Hoyle, E. (1986) *The Politics of School Management*, London: Hodder and Stoughton.

Meyerson, D. and Martin, J. (1987) Cultural change: an integration of different views, *Journal of Management Studies* 24: 623–647.

Morgan, G. (1986) *Images of Organisation*, Newbury Park, CA: Sage.

Nias, J., Southworth, G. and Yeomans, R. (1989) *Staff Relationships in the Primary School*, London: Cassell.

Southworth, G. (1995) *Looking into Primary Headship: A research based interpretation*, London: Falmer Press.

Wallace, M. (1996) A crisis of identity: school merger and cultural transition, *British Educational Research Journal* 22, 4: 459–473.

Wallace, M. and Hall, V. (1994) *Inside the SMT: Team approaches to secondary school management*, London: Paul Chapman.

Wallace, M. and Pocklington, K. (1998) Realising the potential of large scale reorganisation for promoting school improvement, *Educational Management and Administration* 26, 3: 229–241.

# 11

## Institutional Transformation and Educational Management

### CHRIS JAMES

### INTRODUCTION

This chapter argues that institutional transformation theory, which integrates psychodynamic and social systems theory, is particularly relevant to the management of schools and can add an important dimension to educational management theory. The validity of the psychodynamic perspective on educational management is based on some simple propositions. First, educational institutions are locales for high levels of difficult emotions, especially anxiety. Secondly, educational institutions and the individuals within them will seek to defend themselves from these emotions and these defences will be reflected in their enculturation processes. Thirdly, the management of schools, particularly the management of their radical change, cannot be understood without a grasp of the underlying psychodynamic forces. While psychodynamic theory can give valuable insights and is highly appropriate to educational settings, used in isolation it does not provide answers to educational management problems nor enhance a school's capacity to move forward. Social systems theory links open systems theory, authority, leadership and power in organisations. It provides a heuristic framework for the diagnosis of organising processes and can provide answers to educational management questions. On its own, however, social systems theory does not address the underlying unconscious processes and is therefore likely to prove inadequate. The integration of the two themes, psychodynamics and the social systems theory, is therefore significant. Together they can be very powerful in helping to bring about radical change. Understandably, therefore, the term 'institutional transformation' is increasingly used to describe this approach (French and Vince, 1999).

The chapter begins with a summary of the central concepts that make up institutional transformation. It then explores from this perspective aspects of educational management that have emerged from a study of schools in South Wales which have implemented radical change in their practices in order to improve pupil achievement. The detailed findings of this study are not included in this chapter as they have been reported elsewhere (Connolly and James, 1998a and 1988b; Connolly, Connolly and James, 1998). The final section addresses the implications of the educational transformation perspective on educational management theory and outlines the conceptual analysis and empirical research needed to support the development of theory.

## THE THEMES IN INSTITUTIONAL TRANSFORMATION

### Psychodynamic Theory

The psychodynamic theme within educational transformation has a number of strands which have their origins in psychoanalysis, group dynamics and group relations. The different dimensions can be applied to individuals, groups within institutions and the institutions themselves and are as follows.

*The influence of the unconscious*
Thoughts and actions are influenced by unconscious processes which, while remaining covert, influence conscious behaviour. As a result of this influence, apparently rational acts by members of an institution and institutional rules, routines and rituals can have unconscious and non-rational origins (Obholzer and Zagier Roberts, 1994).

*Defence against emotional pain*
Institutions, just like individuals, seek to protect themselves against the pain associated with unpleasant emotions by protective patterns of behaviour. These social defences may have been learned over a long period and their origins perhaps date back to the earliest stages of an individual's or institution's life (Hirschhorn, 1990). It is likely that these social defences will be re-enacted in response to new anxieties. Because of the influence of previously learned behaviours, individual and institutional biographies can be important in understanding individual behaviours and institutional enculturation processes (Kets de Vries, 1991). Arguably, anxiety is the dominant emotion, in itself and because it is evoked at the prospect of experiencing other difficult feelings. Some defences against anxiety are useful but some obstruct change and impede contact with reality. Kets de Vries and Miller (1984) and Hirschhorn (1990) summarise these social defences as:

- repression which assigns anxiety-provoking recollections, urges and feelings to the unconscious;
- regression which is the process of resorting to behaviours that have been learned in earlier stages of development in order to limit anxiety;
- covert coalitions which represent a particular kind of regression where relationships are enacted in a way similar to significant relationships from the individuals' past;
- identification where individuals or institutions take on the behaviours of

those significant to them in order to limit the anxiety associated with enacting their own behaviours;

- reaction formation where the individual or institution becomes unaware of one of a pair of contradictory characteristics which is perhaps associated with anxiety by over-emphasising the opposite characteristic;
- denial which is an attempt to reject and deny the existence of an unacceptable and anxiety provoking aspect of the external reality;
- splitting and projection in which difficult feelings that give rise to internal conflicts are split off and located in others by a process of projection (Segal, 1974; Klein, 1975). In institutions, functional and structural divisions can exacerbate splitting and projection. Other consequences of splitting include **projective identification** and **counter-transference** (Krantz and Gilmour, 1991; Halton, 1994).

*Groups mentalities*
Wilfrid Bion (1961) identified two main tendencies in group life: the **work group mentality** where the tendency is to work on the primary task; and the **basic assumption mentality** which is the propensity to avoid work on the primary task thereby evading the anxiety inevitably associated with it.

## Social Systems Theory

The aspects of social systems theory which are particularly relevant here include open systems theory, leadership, authority and power. Systems theory, especially open systems theory, has considerable explanatory power and has made a significant contribution to understandings of institutional life. Arguably, it has been overtaken in the contemporary organisation literature by other images and metaphors (see, for example, Morgan, 1986), especially in explanations of organisational life in the post-modern epoch (Hatch, 1997). There has, however, been a recent resurgence of interest in systems theory in the context of organisational learning (Senge, 1990).

*Managing the system boundary*
From the institutional transformation perspective, managing the system boundary is crucial and is a key leadership role for individuals and institutions (Miller and Rice, 1967). For Zagier Roberts (1994), effective management of the system boundary involves:

- ascertaining and defining the primary task
- managing the information flux across the boundary
- ensuring that the system has the resources required to perform its primary task
- monitoring the primary task so that it relates to the wider system and to the environment.

The primary task of the system can be difficult to define and always carries anxiety (Bion, 1961). However, focusing on the primary task enables the development of on-task leadership, avoids the abuse of power and minimises basic assumption tendencies (Obholzer, 1994). Managers who relinquish their own boundary position cannot manage themselves. Managers who give up their position on the institution's boundary cannot adequately manage the institution.

*Authority and power*
Systems theory also helps in considering the flow of authority through the institution. Authority, as the right to make decisions which are binding on others, legitimises the exercise of power in an institution. It can arise from above through a system of delegation and from below sanctioned by the members who willingly join the organisation. Authority can also originate within the individual, under the influence of her/his relationship with figures in the individual's 'inner world' or past.

*Responsibility*
Responsibility means being answerable or accountable for outcomes either to a person in the institution or, importantly, in the individual's own mind (Obholzer, 1994). Having responsibility without the requisite authority to achieve outcomes relevant to the primary task can lead to high levels of anxiety. Improving the clarity of organisation structure through a systemic analysis helps to give explicitness of authorisation (Obholzer, 1994) and thereby reduces anxiety.

## SCHOOLS AS PARTICULAR LOCALES FOR ANXIETY

Emotion is one of the underlying links between the various themes in the institutional transformation perspective taken in this chapter. The most significant emotion is anxiety. It is linked with the initiation of primary tasks, it accompanies the doing of them and can prevent engagement with them. Social defences against anxiety will have played a part in an individual's and the institution's history. Further, management processes in the institution can both reduce and increase anxiety, and anxiety can be an imperative for change and also a barrier to it.

The link between anxiety and stress is significant. Stress in teaching is widely acknowledged and is referred to in both the professional and academic literature (see, for example, Travers and Cooper, 1996). The proposition here, however, is that stress in teaching has been treated uncritically and has remained at the level of discourse. As a result, the real reasons for it have been missed. From the institutional transformation perspective, stress is the mental, physical and emotional consequence of institutional/societal anxiety being projected onto individuals, in this case teachers, who are the ready and willing recipients of such projections. So, anxiety and the social defences against it are the issues, not stress.

Educational institutions have a number of features which particularly pre-dispose them to being locales for anxiety.

1. The special nature of the primary task of educational institutions. Teaching and learning are the primary tasks of educational institutions and will therefore carry anxiety (Bion, 1961). However, they are primary tasks cen-trally concerned with change, a process which is also almost always asso-ciated with anxiety either as an instigator of change or a consequence of it (Schein, 1992). So, the primary tasks of educational institutions carry additional anxiety.

2. Learning is associated with risk and uncertainty. The desire to learn, the learning process and the outcomes of learning are intimately associated with risk and uncertainty. Learners will be changed by their learning in a way they cannot predict. The results of learning are often judged, for example, in examinations. Learning may take place in a competitive envi-ronment where failure to learn may have unwanted consequences. Success or failure in learning might have an impact on the self-esteem of the learner and the teacher. A failure to learn may harm relationships with significant others.

3. The process of teaching. Teaching is likely to be associated with anxiety. The characteristics of teaching, its multidimensionality, simultaneity, imme-diacy, unpredictability, publicness and history (Doyle, 1986), are all poten-tial instigators of anxiety. In teaching, the teacher acts as a container of the anxiety associated with the learners' learning (French, 1997) which exacerbates the teacher's sense of anxiety. There is a good case for arguing that teachers are the repository of numerous substantial projections by the rest of society of the difficult feelings associated with any failure, defi-ciency or decline in any aspect of national life.

4. The nature of relationships in educational institutions. Relationships in schools can call up strong feelings and desires of a variety of kinds which can all potentially cause anxiety. There is a continual turnover of rela-tionships in schools. There is the sense of loss as older pupils in whom so much has been invested leave the institution perhaps never to be encoun-tered again. New relationships have to be forged as younger pupils join. The consequences of this turnover, which is not often acknowledged, can cause considerable emotional turbulence, and is a potential cause of anxiety.

5. New models of professional practice. New understandings of professional practice such as the 'reflective practitioner' model (Schon, 1983) place an onus on teachers to improve through reflection on action. Such models of teaching can easily be reconfigured into deficit models of continuous improvement which can provoke a fear in teachers that they will never be good enough.

6. Curriculum and management changes. In recent years, the level and extent of imposed change have increased levels of anxiety for teachers. Many of these changes have proscribed an extension of the teacher's responsibility into areas in which they may not have expertise. Changes in the management of schools, through for example the local management of schools, have increased institutional separation, responsibility and accountability which will have exacerbated anxiety.

7. Changes in the external environment. In recent times, technological and societal change, increased accountability, the eroding of the bases of professional authority, the undervaluing of the profession and the imposition of external 'snapshot' inspection will all have increased anxiety levels.

8. The centrality of education. Teaching and learning in educational institutions are about the management of central life processes. In schools, these include maturation to adulthood and the preparation for adult life in its widest sense and through the acquisition of qualifications which enable a pathway to life-time success and security. As such, teaching is associated with deep ambitions, motivations and desires. In this work, the teacher is not only accountable to the child but to her/his parents and to the rest of society.

The anxiety associated with teaching remains hidden and never explicitly asserted for a variety of reasons. Firstly, the task of containing emotion and anxiety in educational organisations is reified and thereby hidden or accepted in the taken-for-granted structures and processes of school life. Secondly, for teachers to affirm explicitly that they were anxious and that coping with that was a major determinant of their actions would undermine learners', colleagues' and society's confidence in their professional competence and authority.

## ASPECTS OF EDUCATIONAL MANAGEMENT FROM AN INSTITUTIONAL TRANSFORMATION PERSPECTIVE

This section explores aspects of educational management from an institutional transformation standpoint. The data for the examples used to illustrate the main aspects originated from research into the management of changes in schools which have been implemented to improve pupil achievement (Connolly and James, 1998a: and 1998b; Connolly, Connolly and James, 1998). In essence, the research has identified and documented the key themes in the school improvement 'journey' (Fullan, 1993; Hopkins, West & Ainscow, 1996).

## IMPROVING BOUNDARY MANAGEMENT

The changing nature of boundary management was a key feature of the school improvement journey. There are patterns in this improved boundary management.

Before the improvement journey began, the boundaries were not managed in any deliberate way. By default almost, the boundaries of many of the schools were practically impermeable to outside individuals and organisations. Typically, contacts with other organisations were rare. When they did occur, connections were unplanned, idiosyncratic and not purposeful. From a psychodynamic standpoint, this impermeability represents a social defence which reduces anxiety by creating separation. The impermeability of the boundary between the school and the environment was paralleled by similar impermeability within the institution. Communication between departments was poor and individual teachers' boundaries were relatively impenetrable. Collaborative activities such as joint working with other teachers were rare; the classroom door, with teacher and class inside, tended to remain shut.

Robust management of the boundaries was a feature of the very early stages of the improvement journey. In some instances, the boundary between the school and its environment was closed, a strategy which was combined with an increased focusing on the primary task of teaching and learning. In others, to accelerate the pace of change boundary permeability was increased significantly and links, connections and associations of all kinds were encouraged. Collaboration and co-working were stimulated often by the promotion of task-based, often practical, activities. Managing collaboration necessitated the breaking down of the teachers' boundaries, re-defining them and helping teachers to manage their own professional role boundaries more appropriately.

As the schools progressed further along the journey, the school boundary was managed with increasing sophistication, a process which allowed in appropriate resources for change and enabled beneficial contacts outwards with the environment. The strategic management of the school boundary was a characteristic of schools which were sustaining systematic improvement. Overall, during the improvement journey, individual teachers' boundaries moved from being impenetrable, to being open, to being managed.

Arguably, through the boundary management process, management defines the role of the whole institution and the constituent sub-systems. The process also defines the responsibilities of the system and sub-system and through a process of integration seeks to resolve the separations and splits and to move the institution into the integrated position (Klein, 1975). This reparation (Segal, 1974) in an institutional sense could be an important motivation for educational leaders in the challenging change management process. It has to be remembered that splitting and projection are defences against anxiety. The change management processes which tackle these and all social defences will therefore have additional anxiety associated with them.

## EDUCATIONAL ENCULTURATION

At the start of the school improvement journey, many of the schools, especially those that started from a low base, underwent some kind of 'fracturing of the culture' which initiated the process of change. This fracturing process was initiated by 'triggers' such as the appointment of a new headteacher and/or new staff, the merging of two schools, or an unfavourable inspection report. Momentarily, these events created a crisis that paradoxically may in turn have created anxiety which was a fundamental drive for change (Schein, 1992). What had to follow that moment of crisis was a process which overturned the existing social defences and prevented others from emerging. The process had to confront (or at least refuse to collude with) the illegimate power that had put extant defences in place and which may have built fresh ones.

Following the fracture, the creation of a climate of change and the engendering of a capacity to live with change was crucial but difficult to achieve. Simultaneously with a drive to become more effective, which is in itself heavily anxiety laden, the leaders of change were seeking to generate an ethos of continuous improvement through reflection on practice and adaptation which are also associated with anxiety. This interpretation may help to explain the particularly problematic nature of educational management. If teaching is centrally concerned with bringing about change, then educational management is concerned in a fundamental way with change management. If through educational management we then seek to adopt reflective practitioner models of teaching, then educational management is concerned with managing change in a change-making process and sustaining a process of continual change. Containing the anxieties associated with these changes is one of the tasks of the educational manager.

## LEADERSHIP IN RADICAL EDUCATIONAL CHANGE

From the perspective taken in this chapter, leadership in the improvement journey is worthy of especial consideration. Firstly, in radical educational change, a key leadership task is the dismantling of inappropriate social defences associated with the primary task of teaching and learning. These defences may be widely embedded with resistance to change coming from governors and parents as well as teachers and pupils. The leader has to contain the anxiety associated with the dismantling of the social defences anxiety, a process which adds additional challenge.

Secondly, the progressive transfer of leadership authority 'down' the organisation is a strong theme in the improvement journey. This transfer appears to be a way of establishing and clarifying roles and responsibilities and creating the systems. It also enables the leader to move to the boundary of the school system and to manage that boundary more effectively. The transfer of leadership authority is also a way of giving power to individuals so that they can enact their role assertively, with full authority and to the role boundary.

Thirdly, at any time, the educational institution will have basic assumption tendencies (Bion, 1961) which are influenced by anxiety. Appraising those tendencies is an important part of the vital initial diagnosis an incoming headteacher may have to make. These tendencies may vary in different parts of the school. Skilful and successful leaders are able to use the tendencies to their advantage and crucially without colluding with them in the long term (Stokes, 1994).

In the basic assumption dependency mentality, where the group has lost sight of the primary task and exists to satisfy the needs of its members, the leadership has to break down the social defences and encourage work on the primary task. In this work, the leader is likely to face inertia and a heaviness resulting from the projections of the group (Obholzer and Zagier Roberts, 1994).

In schools where the basic assumption fight and flight mentality is predominant, change may be brought about by using external 'enemies' such as 'league tables' of examination results, school inspection, or the Investors in People award. Some headteachers created very challenging high profile targets which the staff, because of their basic tendency, are willing and eager to attempt to achieve.

For schools with a basic assumption pairing tendency, the pairing is typically with a 'future' of some kind to take the group away from the anxiety of the present. It is perhaps understandable that articulating a 'vision' features strongly in the leadership literature (see Yukl, 1988 for a review).

Fourthly, leadership adaptability in the form of extreme contingency in leadership action is a significant feature of the improvement journey. Where there was willingness on the part of teachers and managers to change and engage in the primary tasks of teaching and managing, there was fulsome praise and support from the head; where there was opposition, it was resolutely confronted. Vince and Martin's (1993) model of the responses to anxiety associated with learning and change in groups gives some insights into this practice. The model has two alternative cycles. In the first, the amplifying loop, the group or individual lives with the uncertainty and risk and, through a process of struggle, gains insight and authority. In the balancing loop, the pathway is characterised by a fight or flight defence (classic biological responses to anxiety), which can encompasses denial, avoidance, defensiveness and resistance, and leads to a state of willing ignorance. Interestingly, both pathways lead back to anxiety but anxiety which has different bases and origins. The model is illustrated in Figure 11.1.

In terms of the leadership of educational change, the leader contains the anxiety of the other (a teacher or manager) in their work in the amplifying loop, and enables learning and development. In other contexts, the leader steadfastly refuses to give way or collude with those wishing to engage in the balancing loop process and as a consequence faces the accompanying individual and institutional projections, such as anger. In acting in this way, the leader manages change 'educationally'.

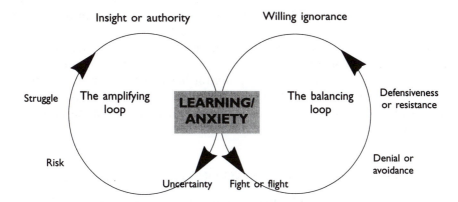

**Figure 11.1**    Responses to anxiety associated with learning and change (after Vince and Martin, 1993)

## MOVING TO A COLLABORATIVE CULTURE

Improved collaboration between individual teachers through the promotion of teamwork and collective school and department development planning was a key objective in the school improvement journey. This kind of collaboration, 'productive co-working', required a redefinition of professional boundaries and a refocusing on the improvement of teaching and learning. This view contrasts with collaboration in an anti-task sense (Obholzer and Zagier Roberts, 1994) as 'collusion in mediocrity'. Improving collaboration between the organisational sub-systems – sections, faculties or departments – was also a characteristic of the improvement journey as was collaboration with outside agencies. The development of productive collaborative linkages within and between the pupil and staff systems was also a feature. Collaboration as a process and an end-point of the journey could have a number of justifications:

* to facilitate the meaning-making process which is essential in professional work (Clarke, James and Kelly, 1996) and leadership in organisations (Oswick, Keenoy and Grant, 1997)
* to integrate the separated parts of the institution thus overcoming the organisational splitting and projection, thereby reducing the organisational difficulties which those behaviours can bring about
* as a way of exploiting the talent pool and maximising resources.

Collaboration, from a psychodynamic viewpoint, can also be a social defence. It can provide protection from the risk and uncertainty associated with learning and change. Put simply, facing 'the enemy' together is more comfortable than facing it alone. Collaboration can be a way of protecting individuals from competitive pressures (Lomax and Darley, 1995). It can provide a way of subverting leadership authority in the institution. For leaders who advocate collaboration, it is a way of reducing the anxiety associated with the deployment of their leadership authority. Simultaneously, collaboration can be a way of followers sanctioning leadership authority and projecting their anxieties onto the leader. For followers, it may be a way of limiting authority of the leaders and giving a subjective sensation of having control over the change forces. Collaboration's 'true beauty' though is that it can become the anti-task and can help to divert the individual and the institution from the normative primary task (Lawrence, 1977) as do many ideologies.

## PROGRESSIVE FOCUSING ON THE PRIMARY TASK

A key theme in the school improvement journey is the progressive focusing on the task of bringing about learning in the pupils and then seeking to improve that practice. As with any primary task, improving teaching and learning is associated with anxiety and is likely to have a number of social defences associated with it. In bringing about radical change for improvement, breaking down inappropriate defences against the anxiety is the key. Social defences include:

- self-induced teacher isolation
- teachers using the closed classroom door to hide their social defences from the outside world and to enable a retreat from the role boundary
- low aspirations which reduce the scale of the primary task and thereby the risk (and anxiety) associated with it
- low expectations, that is, effectively saying that the task of teaching and learning is doomed to failure, a strategy which discounts the anxiety before the task is begun.

## SOME IMPLICATIONS OF THE INSTITUTIONAL TRANSFORMATION PERSPECTIVE ON EDUCATIONAL MANAGEMENT

The issues raised in this chapter have implications for educational management and educational management theory and research. If educational management theory does not take account of the institutional transformation perspective, particularly the psychodynamic dimension, it is unlikely to be comprehensive. Those who look to educational management theories which do not encompass the non-rational and emotional dimensions may not find the answers they are seeking. Any guidance which may be gleaned from such theories will be inadequate.

There is a need for a conceptual analysis of the nature of anxiety in schools and colleges, the social defences against it and the impact those defences can have on teaching, learning and management. Anxiety in schools and in teachers needs to be problematised. What are the main sources? Are some institutions and individuals more susceptible and sensitive to it than others and why? What are the main defences and how are they characterised? What part do anxiety and defences against it play in apparently rational educational management actions? To support a conceptual analysis, there is a need for research which takes account of the emotional and non-rational aspects of education and educational management.

The author is grateful to Professor Russ Vince of the University of Glamorgan Business School for his helpful advice and insights in the preparation of this chapter.

## REFERENCES

Bion, W. (1961) *Experiences in Groups,* New York: Basic Books.

Clarke, B. A., James, C. R. and Kelly, J. (1996) Reflective practice: reviewing and refocusing the debate, *International Journal of Nursing Studies*, Vol. 33, No. 2, 171–180.

Connolly, U. and James, C. R. (1998a) The role of continuing professional development in managing the school improvement journey, *Journal of In-service Education* (in press).

Connolly, U. and James, C. R. (1998b) *Final Report of the Improving Schools Project,* Pontypridd: University of Glamorgan.

Connolly, M., Connolly, U. and James, C. R. (1998) Dimensions of leadership in the school improvement journey, paper presented at the British Educational Management and Administration Society Annual Conference, University of Warwick, England 18th–20th September, 1998.

Doyle, W. (1986) Classroom organisation and management, in M. C. Wittrock (ed.) *Handbook of Research on Teaching* (third edition), New York: Macmillan.

French, R. B. (1997) The teacher as container of anxiety. Psychoanalysis and the role of the teacher, *Journal of Management Education*, Vol. 21, No. 4, 483–495.

French, R. B. and Vince, R. (1999) *Group Relations, Management and Organisation*, Oxford: Oxford University Press.

Fullan, M. (1993) *Change Forces*, London: Falmer.

Halton, W. (1994) Some unconscious aspects of organisational life, in A. Obholzer and V. Vagier Roberts (eds.) *The Unconscious at Work*, London: Routledge.

Hatch, M. J. (1997) *Organization Theory*, Oxford: Oxford University Press.

Hopkins, D., West, M. and Ainscow, M. (1996) *Improving the Quality of Education for All*, London: David Fulton Publishers.

Hirschhorn, L. (1990) *The Workplace Within*, London: The MIT Press.

Kets de Vries, M. F. R. and Miller, D. (1984) *The Neurotic Organisation: Diagnosing and changing counter-productive styles of management*, San Francisco: Jossey Bass.

Kets de Vries, M. F. R. (ed.) (1991) *Organisations on the Couch*, San Francisco: Jossey Bass.

Klein, M. (1975) *Envy and Gratitude and Other Works*, New York: Dell.

Krantz, J. and Gilmour, T. N. (1991) Understanding the dynamics between consulting teams and client systems, in M. F. R. Kets de Vries (ed.) (1991) *op. cit.*

Lawrence, G. (1977) Management development . . . some ideals images and realities, in A. D. Coleman and M. H. Geller (eds.) *Group Relations Reader 2*, (1985)

Washington, DC: A. K. Rice Institute Series.

Lomax, P. and Darley, J. (1995) Inter-school links, liaison and networking: collaboration or competition?, *Education Management and Administration*, Vol. 23, No. 3, 148–161.

Miller, E. J. and Rice, A. K. (1967) *Systems of Organisation: The control of task and sentient boundaries*, London: Tavistock Publications.

Morgan, G. (1986) *Images of Organisation*, London: Sage.

Obholzer, A. and Zagier Roberts, V. (eds.) (1994) *The Unconscious at Work*, London: Routledge.

Oswick, C., Keenoy, T. and Grant, D. (1997) Managerial discourses: words speak louder than actions, *Journal Applied Management Studies*, Vol. 6, No. 1, 5–12.

Schein, E. H. (1992) *Organisational Culture and Leadership*, San Francisco: Jossey Bass.

Schon, D. A. (1983) *The Reflective Practitioner*, New York: Basic Books.

Segal, H. (1974) *Introduction to the Work of Melanie Klein*, New York: Basic Books.

Senge, P. (1990) *The Fifth Discipline*, London: Random House.

Travers, C. J. and Cooper, C. L. (1996) *Teachers Under Pressure*, London: Routledge.

Vince, R. and Martin, L. (1993) Inside action learning: The psychology and the politics of the action learning model, *Management Education and Development*, Vol. 24, No. 3, 205–215.

Yukl, G. (1988) *Leadership in Organisations*, London: Prentice Hall.

Zagier Roberts, V. (1994) The organisation of work: contributions from open systems theory, in A. Obholzer and V. Zagier Roberts (eds.) (1994) *The Unconscious at Work*, London: Routledge.

# 12

# Gender and Education Management: Duel or Dialogue?

VALERIE HALL

## PROLOGUE

In the space between delivering a paper and revising it for publication ideas and priorities change and the world moves on. This paper was a response to an invitation from the ESRC Seminar Series organisers to contribute a gender perspective to the debate about educational management. The paper attempts to do precisely that but, in so doing, I am heavily aware of the limitations of a brief which once more segregates gender as an issue both from the main discourse of education management and from the other equity issues, of which gender is only one. It is not difficult to look at the plight of what are increasingly described both officially and unofficially as failing schools and colleges and wonder whether gender is an irrelevance. Or, alternatively, to wonder whether gender is central in all its aspects but inextricably entwined with class and race and beliefs and values about equity and democracy. A macro view of what is happening in education might point the finger at management itself as the villain and the failure of individual managers, both men and women, to challenge the appropriateness and morality of what governments expect. In this case our concern should not be with gender exclusively but with the ethics of public service. A micro view might agree that gender is an important aspect of the complexity of daily interactions that make up the life of schools and colleges, but question its isolation as a single determining factor.

A cynic might ask why we need yet another paper on gender and educational management when the bookshelves are heavy with them. Yet a look at the bibliography of this chapter compared with the bibliographies of other chapters in the book will demonstrate precisely why yet another paper is necessary, though not whether it will achieve anything by being written. As I try to show, the debate about gender and educational management continues to be carried out mainly by women about women. The few men represented in the bibliography have entered it by talking about men and neither group of authors is likely to have made it into the other bibliographies contained in this volume. The question that this paper should have addressed, but does

not, is not whether gender, race and class are relevant to the process of redefinition with which this Seminar Series is concerned, but why the case for
their centrality to our understanding still has to be made. Only when volumes
like this do not have a separate chapter on gender or equality and the chapter
bibliographies are peppered with references relating to these issues will we
know some progress has been made.


## THROWING DOWN THE GAUNTLET

Occasionally over the past two decades those with a specific concern about
equity and educational management, particularly where it relates to gender,
have been knocking on educational management doors asking to be let in.
Generally the doors have been slow in opening and, even when gender does
gain entry, it may be allocated a separate table and remain largely ignored.
Usually personified in the lone figure of a woman researcher or academic or,
less frequently, a leader or manager, it continues to fight a hard battle to be
not only listened to but heard and digested in a way that ensures a seat next
time at the main table. Those attempting to redefine educational management
are engaged in a form of learning, as well as seeking ways to support the
learning of others whose primary role is to lead and manage learning in
myriad contexts. As Freire (1972) has demonstrated, true learning is emancipatory; a vehicle for making learners critically aware of their own false consciousness, for developing a clearer perception of themselves, society and their
place in it; and for feeling able to act upon the world in order to create a
better society. Any learning about educational management must include an
emancipatory purpose, which acknowledges the centrality of gender, race and
class in its construction and practice. Here I focus only on gender, still a highly
sensitive subject requiring careful handling if it is to convince both men and
women of the need to question masculinities and their impact on leadership
and management in all sectors of education.

The constitution of a seminar series to redefine educational management
provides an appropriate stage for giving gender not only a speaking part but
also a central role in understanding and developing educational management.
Elsewhere (Hall, 1997) I talk of the need for all involved in leading and managing schools and colleges to challenge others' profound convictions and
biases, where gender is concerned. All of us engaged in redefining educational
management, both men and women, have to think ourselves out of the mainstream paradigms that have shaped our lives and thinking and to which we
have contributed as teachers, researchers, authors and managers. This paper
thus constitutes yet another attempt to throw down the gender gauntlet in
order to contribute to the foundations of a modern version of leadership that
does two things. First it confronts the demands of educational change on
leaders and managers whose repertoires need to extend beyond the confines
of their gender. Second, it aims to bring back into the limelight ideas that

challenge the androcentrism of much of the discourse about leadership and management. The ideas themselves are not new, but they continue to remain marginal to the debate. It challenges gender's usual role of ghost at the education management feast, and aims to demonstrate its right to a substantive presence. Arguably, the recognition of the value of its contribution to understanding would be extended to parallel discussions of race, class and other equity issues. However, it is only possible to throw down one gauntlet at a time and even that may not be enough. The real undertaking is to ensure that the gauntlet is accepted and then, through skilful play, the duel is won. In this case, unlike in a real duel, the goal is not the bloody remains of male egos (as many continue to fear gender perspectives represent), but the triumph of the legitimacy of an understanding of educational management that embraces rather than marginalises gender.

## GENDER OR FEMINIST PERSPECTIVES?

How then is our understanding of education management enhanced by using a gender perspective and challenging management's taken-for-granted discourse as a gender-neutral set of activities? I use the word 'gender' advisedly to describe perspectives on education management that take into account the social construction of men's and women's roles and their impact on management practice. Identifying the gauntlet-thrower as a feminist and the gauntlet as feminist theorising leads most in education management, women as well as men, to flee rather than fight. In some cases, men have entered the gender arena by focusing particularly on management and masculinities (for example, Collinson and Hearn, 1996). Doughty seconds though they are, their presence provides a two-edged sword. In the same way as some occupations rely on the presence of men for their status, so men's preoccupation with gender and power issues legitimates the enquiry, particularly in the eyes of other men. Sinclair, in her study of men and women leading differently, also notes the seductive quality 'of a masculinity which softens itself at the edges, which learns the language of care and consultation' only in order to 'entrench more deeply the subjugation of women and the superiority of a certain kind of masculinity' (Sinclair, 1997, p.74). While discussions such as those by Collinson and Hearn by no means fall into this colonising category, there is a danger that their presence may divert all attention regarding gender to that which pertains almost exclusively to men and masculinity. They may still have to sit at a separate table but they will get the waiter's full attention. The annexation of the gender equity debate in schooling by those concerned with boys' underachievement (as though the provision of equal opportunities for girls was to blame) provides a current example of this trend.

Another potential obstacle to the acknowledgement of gender's legitimacy in the debate about education management is the fight or flight response referred to earlier. In her response to my study of women headteachers (Hall,

1996), Mazda Jenkin (herself a headteacher) suggests that I must have found it unsettling to discover that the women headteachers in the study rejected the feminist perspective. Instead the occasionally challenged whether gender was of any relevance to them and the way they enacted their role (Hall, 1999). This misses the point that a feminist perspective on educational leadership is not the same as feminist educational leadership. My research was influenced by feminist research methods and critical theory but there was no assumption that women headteachers would necessarily be feminist. If a feminist leader is defined as someone who is committed to identifying all kinds of injustice in education and working towards eradicating them, then men as well as women are just as likely to be feminist leaders. Similarly men researchers may choose to draw on feminist perspectives to study gender issues in education and leadership. As we have seen, this occurs most frequently when they are talking specifically of men rather than as part of the general discourse on educational management.

Situating ourselves means recognising the values that permeate the perspectives we take on issues. Unlike many perspectives on management, feminist perspectives start with values about equity, particularly as they relate to men and women in society. All perspectives, whether feminist or not, incorporate value judgements that are influenced by the gender of the value holder. Therefore, whether and how we choose to incorporate gender perspectives into our redefinition of education management will depend on the values we hold about men and women, ourselves and others, organisational life and education. It will also depend on our willingness to articulate these values as part of our theorising and actions. Stoll and Fink (1996, p.111) suggest that effective school leaders need to 'invite themselves physically, intellectually, social, emotionally, spiritually' as a prelude to inviting others to working successfully for their school or college. I would suggest that researchers too need to invite themselves in these ways before they try to understand how others situate themselves in relation to their own practice. It is a necessary step in seeking a deeper understanding of education management, which until relatively recently has been considered a relatively unproblematic phenomenon. The primary challenge is no longer to persuade teachers and lecturers that they must also be managers. Now the issue is what management in education could and should mean.

Other writers, such as Blackmore (1993) have debated how gender or feminist perspectives can contribute to a redefinition of educational management. My concern here is more with what we and others in the field need to recognise as constraints on practice and theory arising from the blinkers imposed by our taken-for-granted attitudes to management as a gender- (as well as class- and race-) neutral process. A theoretical perspective that includes these dimensions transforms the shadows of our understanding and brings new issues into the limelight. Based on a view of gender relations as socially constructed and historically and culturally variable, it has the potential to combine macro- and micro-analyses of the part gender, together with class, culture, hierarchy and sexuality, plays in the reality of education management.

## MOVING ON FROM THE STATISTICS

The usual starting point for discussing gender and education management is the statistical picture. It has become part of our taken-for-granted under-standing that men dominate numerically in senior positions in all phases of education with the exception of nursery and infant schools. Analysts of edu-cation management acknowledge the disparity between women's numbers in the teaching profession and their representation at senior levels. We have all become sophisticated in interpreting and explaining these figures. We are less proactive in rigorously thinking through the consequences of this disparity for the educational and employment opportunities of girls and boys, men and women. Again, the problem only wins official recognition when it appears to have a detrimental effect on boys. The current focus in the UK on the dearth of men entering primary school teaching is implicitly a manifestation of a concern that boys will suffer if they do not have male teachers as role models. Yet primary school teaching continues to be a fast track to headship for those few men willing to enter what is seen as a female enclave, with the lower status that attaches to such occupations.

For other commentators, the statistical reality is a backcloth to the more important discussion, in their view, of the extent to which management is mas-culine. The argument is most trenchantly posited in Blackmore's critique of the historical construction of educational administration as a 'masculinist' enterprise (Blackmore, 1993). Collinson and Hearn, as male feminists, trace a similar path in challenging the ways in which the masculine imagery of man-agement and managers seems to be taken for granted and thereby reproduced and reinforced. Like Blackmore and others, they question men's persistent domination of management, though their purpose is primarily to liberate management rather than liberate women. They remind us that the etymology of the verb 'to manage' is in the Italian word *menagerie* which meant han-dling things, particularly horses (Collinson and Hearn, 1996, p.2). This mili-tary connection becomes domesticated in management's alternative derivation in the French *menager* with its associations of careful housekeep-ing. These derivations show, in their view, that 'management as a function, profession and practice, need not inevitably be dominated by masculine styles, discourses or processes generally or by men in particular' (p.5). Some in edu-cation consider this equation of management and masculinity only to be rel-evant to the harsh realities of corporate life beyond schools and colleges. Others within education have little doubt that the imposed reforms of recent years, combined with gender relations developed over centuries, create work-place cultures in which male hegemony is dominant (Al-Khalifa, 1989; Evetts, 1990; Pritchard, 1996). Even Jenkin, who questions the relevance of gender for understanding school leadership, suggests she is working in 'an intensely political and masculine world' (in Hall, 1999, p.109).

It is important however to challenge the too ready association of management and masculinity as well as recognise its accuracy. It can deter women from applying for promoted posts, to which they might otherwise be attracted. It obscures the possibilities of alternative interpretations of the leader and manager's role, whether enacted by a woman or a man. Elsewhere (Hall, 1997) I have argued the case for reviewing our notion of entrepreneurship in education as just another form of managerial subservience. Looking at women who have leadership positions reveals possibilities of alternative leadership styles, which derive from their integration of their femininity into their sense of identity and their ability to combine individual power with structural constraints. They emerged as education managers (who happened to be women) welcoming reforms to use them for the benefit of the school, thereby demonstrating an ethical entrepreneurship that does not sit easily alongside views of management acquiescence as inevitably unethical.

A further limitation of the 'management is masculine' argument is that management is defined in terms of 'control over', whether over self or others. As well as studying women managers to see if they offer alternative possibilities for managing effectively, we need to look at the ways in which men are socialised into an acceptance as men of the desirability of self and other mastery as a basis for action. By situating ourselves in relation to the 'management is masculine argument' and recognising its strengths and weakness, we can challenge the dominant male discourse of educational organisations in which personal power and the ability to control others and self are desirable characteristics.

Management's emergence as a central activity in education has been accompanied, as Gunter (1997) has forcefully argued, by endless prescriptions for 'taming the dinosaurs'. Yet even critiques of the nature of managerial power and the elitist character of most decision making have only rarely challenged the influence on that discourse of the social construction of male managers as men. The critiques focus on managerial power, control and ideology whether located with men or women. Feminists, whose stance is pre-eminently critical (prescriptions only sometimes follow later), have looked at men's power, control and ideology in order to illuminate women's subordination. They have problematised men and masculinity but rarely examined systematically through research the power and practice of men as managers. A more integrated analysis of gender and management is clearly needed that recognises, as essentialist hegemonic critiques do not, the diversity of masculinities and femininities that characterise managers' behaviour. Returning to the statistical picture referred to earlier, if men dominate management positions in education numerically, and represent in their presence a diversity of masculinities, then these are an indisputable part of management discourse, process and practice. Any attempt at redefining educational management that fails to recognise their influence on both the definers as well as the phenomenon under scrutiny are doomed to fail.

## IMPLICATIONS OF TAKING GENDER INTO ACCOUNT

What then are the implications of including a gender perspective in our attempts to redefine educational management, and what does it involve for us as managers, researchers and teachers? It obviously means taking into account in our considerations findings from research into gender and management issues at all levels of management and in all sectors. There is a tendency for those concerned with educational management only to read in the field with which they have most contact, whether it be schools, colleges or universities. Research tends to be sector specific. Yet the findings from research such as Evetts (1990) in schools, Stott and Lawson (1997) in further education and Deem and Ozga (1997) in higher education together constitute a powerful body of knowledge about management and leadership in all sectors of education, with a common focus on gender. Drake and Owen's (1998) collection of international perspectives on gender and management issues in education examines a wide-ranging set of issues relating to women educators and their work in developing and developed countries. The result is a book which is as much about the purposes of education and management as it is about women. It is also a book, as Davies (*ibid.*, p.13) dispiritedly remarks, which few men will read. The problem lies, she claims, in the assumption that books about gender are exclusively about women. Her own long experience of examining women and educational management in an international context leads her to the conclusion that, 'the "women problem" is a problem of democracy . . . a solution to gender and indeed any other forms of inequity or injustice is to strive for more democratic educational institutions' (p.14). From this perspective, the leaders of such institutions may be women or men holding in common a commitment to equity and a willingness and ability to put in place the structures to achieve it.

Our questions about women as educational managers need to be extended to the connections between men as managers and managers as men. We need to know more about the relationships between home and work, family and career, early socialisation for both men and women. The natural histories of educational leadership, as Gronn (1996) has pointed out, help us understand the genesis of values and how these become embedded in later professional behaviour. They show how agency and structure are integrated in a leadership career framework. Gronn's own work and that of a few other writers (e.g. Ribbins and Marland, 1994) are charting the way for the required natural histories although even these are more reticent about raising gender-specific issues with their subjects. If, as Hodgkinson (1991) claims, two of the megamaxims of effective educational leadership are 'know the followership' and 'know oneself', then men need to confront their quest for self-mastery and the obstacles it may create to self-knowledge. Men and women in education manage other men and women and their interactions are riddled with, for example, the sexual mores for males and females in different cultures. Both seek in different ways to 'manage' any negative effects these may have on their claims to authority and power as managers and leaders, but research suggests that women are much more sensitive than men to the impact of this and other dimensions of their behaviour on others than men. Sinclair (*op. cit.*, p.160), in her research-based account of leadership, goes so far as to claim that, 'Effective leadership is not devoid of sexuality but is partially established by subtle yet powerful expressions of sexualities.' Within her model of leadership behaviour, sexuality is closely entwined with self-esteem, which in turn influences followers' perceptions. Her approach constitutes just one example of challenging taken-for-granted assumptions about the behaviour of leaders and followers from a gender perspective, in a way which forces actors to confront what is really happening in any interaction. Kanter's (1977) discussion (in Men and Women of the Organisation) of men managers' 'homosexual' and 'homosocial' selection practices (i.e. they exclude women and prefer to appoint in their own image) may seem dated now. Yet recent research into selection for headship in Northern Ireland found a mismatch between governors' reported attitudes to gender and school leadership and their practice when selecting a new headteacher. It was clear that the governors, who play a key role in selection decisions, continue to construct authority as gendered, relating it particularly to physical strength and the father role (Rees *et al.*, 1998). Denials of the manifest impact of gender are again undermined by evidence of its latent effects. Selection as a key management task becomes a tool for sustaining management as a masculine enterprise. In contrast my own research showed women in powerful positions as reluctant to be either homosocial or homosexual.

Exploring the relationship between structure and agency in leadership performance from a gender perspective may help us understand more fully the requirements of managing change successfully. Collinson and Hearn (*op. cit.*, p.14) associate men's search for 'identity work' and different forms of male bonding with their need to manage unpredictability and uncertainty. They cite the mutual identification through old school, university or professional association connections, kinship or religious ties, shared sporting interests and heterosexist joking relations as examples of the ways masculine identities in organisations are achieved. The result for women members of the organisations, as Cockburn (1991) has shown, is exclusion and reinforced subordination. They constitute uncreative and rigid responses to environments in which change is continuous and, it might be hypothesised, are more likely to lead to stress and early retirement from work.

A third reason for incorporating a gender perspective into our deliberations has already been touched upon: to identify and explain men's and women's performance in their jobs particularly as it relates to their interactions with the same and opposite sex. Gender will by no means be a sole explanatory factor but it may be contributory in ways that have not hitherto been acknowledged. The reality of schools and colleges as workplaces is constructed from the daily interactions of men and women, boys and girls. To ignore the part that gender plays in those shaping interactions would be to ignore a whole body of sociological and psychological research developed over this century that points to its importance. There is less reluctance to address these issues where the performance of young people is concerned. Although studies of gender, race, class and pupil performance are still likely to be categorised as specialist 'equal opportunities' concerns, they are more likely to become part of the mainstream dialogue than parallel studies of gender, race and class and teacher or manager performance. Yet the goal of managing and leading in education is to create learning environments that successfully support the learning of all students, whatever their age, race, gender or ability.

Opportunities for training and development are part of any leadership framework for both women and men as they seek to take on (or are required to undertake) new responsibilities. Government-funded training programmes in particular derive from beliefs about the kind of managers and leaders schools and colleges will need in the next ten years. To what extent are they programmes that encourage confidence and control of self and others within a framework of unambiguous competencies derived mainly from observation of men at work? Collinson and Hearn (*op. cit.*, p.16) quote research showing MBA cultures as often deeply imbued with masculine values and practices, thereby reflecting and reinforcing the masculinity of management in theory and in practice. As a result, women who actually get as far as attending an MBA programme may experience it as exclusionary and disempowering. Asking similar questions of government-funded leadership and management training programmes for educators is neither popular nor seen as relevant. Yet there are at least three ways in which they need to be audited from an equity perspective. First, what is the model of leadership underpinning the training programme? On what is it based and how far does it take account of alternative ways of leading and managing? Second, how far do the training methods used take account of men's and women's different ways of knowing and learning? Third, what space do the programmes allow for men and women to address and explore personally the ways gender, race and class may influence their own performance as leaders and managers? What opportunities are there to examine the ways in which their own beliefs and their enactment about gender, race and class impact on their colleagues and the students, with positive or detrimental effects for different constituencies? Such an audit may reveal how the learning experience is biased in ways which influence recruitment to the programme, performance on it and subsequent performance in the workplace.

## SHARING THE MENU

This discussion has focused on the need to examine the genderedness of those in positions of hierarchical power in educational organisations. We know enough now about why women and men are differentially represented in these positions in schools and colleges. Accounts abound from women about their experiences of leading and managing in education, which do little to confirm claims that gender is no longer relevant. Missing are the proper research-based accounts of educational management and leadership that take for granted but do not focus exclusively on gender as a factor in the accounts. We know a lot about the practices of people in education management. We know a lot about the practices of women in education management, as the result of a feminist focus on women who manage. We know almost nothing about men in educational management and how their performance and people's perceptions of them are influenced by the fact they are men. This is partly because women interested in gender have chosen to study women rather than women and men. There is minimal evidence of men fore-grounding gender by choosing to study men as managers and how they both create and are constrained by the organisational context. Women researchers have been as slow to focus on men as managers as men have been to examine women as managers. Both remain at their separate tables. The only difference is that they are more likely nowadays to be consulting the same menu. In that respect, the time is ripe for a new taken-for-grantedness in defining, researching and practising educational management – one that includes how organisations reproduce and reinforce masculinities and femininities and the consequences of this for the educational experiences and opportunities of those the organisations are there to serve: the learners, whether children or adults.

## EPILOGUE

I began by representing the theme of gender as the lonely woman guest at a separate table. The image is not novel but it continues to ring true. I have argued the need to analyse more systematically the place of masculine discourse in the definitions and practices of education management. This discourse is itself a barrier to more effective schools and a proper confrontation of all the equity issues that act as barriers to learning. As a manager, researcher and teacher who is also a woman, I want to know what happens when men as well as women challenge this dominant discourse. This chapter has, in part, been a plea to men to throw down the gender gauntlet and issue a challenge through their own coming to consciousness of the ways they contribute to it. Let women for once become the seconds in the gender duel, while men fight it out, not with arms but with enlightened, soul-searching as well as intellectual debate.

# REFERENCES

Al-Khalifa, E. (1989) Management by halves: Women teachers and school management, in H. Lyon and F. Migniuolo, *Women Teachers*, Milton Keynes: Open University Press.

Blackmore, J. (1993) In the shadow of men: The historical construction of educational administration as a 'masculinist' enterprise, in J. Blackmore and J. Kenny (eds.) *Gender Matters in Educational Administration and Policy: A feminist introduction*, London: The Falmer Press.

Cockburn, C. (1991) *In the Way of Women: Men's resistance to sex equality in organisations*, Basingtoke: Macmillan.

Collinson, D. and Hearn, J. (eds.) (1996) *Men as Managers, Managers as Men: Critical Perspectives on Men, Masculinities and Management*, London: Sage Publications.

Davies, L. (1998) Democratic Practice, Gender and School Management, in P. Drake and P. Owen, *op. cit.*

Deem, R. and Ozga, J. (1997) Women managing for diversity in a post-modern world, in C. Marshall (ed.) *Feminist Critical Policy Analysis: A perspective from post-secondary education*, London: Falmer Press.

Drake, P. and Owen, P. (eds.) (1998) *Gender and Management Issues in Education: An international perspective*, Stoke-on Trent: Trentham Books.

Evetts, J. (1990) *Women in Primary Teaching: Career, contexts and strategies*, London: Unwin Hyman.

Freire, P. (1972) *Cultural Action For Freedom*, Harmondsworth: Penguin.

Gronn, P. (1996) From transactions to transformations – A new world order in the study of leadership?, *Educational Administration Quarterly* 24 (1) 7–30.

Gunter, H. (1997) *Rethinking Education. The consequences of Jurassic management*, London: Cassell.

Hall, V. (1996) *Dancing on the Ceiling: A study of women managers in education*, London: Paul Chapman Publishing.

Hall, V. (1997) Dusting off the phoenix: Gender and educational leadership revisited, *Educational Management and Administration*, 25 (3) 309–324.

Hall, V. (1998) Reinterpreting entrepreneurship in education: A gender perspective, paper given at the American Educational Research Association Meeting, San Diego, California, April.

Hall, V. (1999) Dancing on the ceiling: A review symposium, *Educational Management and Administration* 27 (1) 99–116.

Hodgkinson, C. (1991) *Educational Leadership: The moral art*, Albany, N.Y.: State University of New York Press.

Kanter, R. (1977) *Men and Women of the Corporation*, London: Unwin Hyman.

Pritchard, C. (1996) Managing universities: Is it men's work?, in D. Collinson and J. Hearn (eds.) *op. cit.*

Ribbins, P. and Marland, M. (1994) *Headship Matters*, Harlow: Longman.

Rees, T., Heaton, P. and McBriar, L. (1998) Women headteachers in Northern Ireland, in J. Salisbury and S. Riddell (eds.) *Gender Policy and Educational Change*, London: Routledge.

Sinclair, A. (1997) *Doing Leadership Differently: Gender, power and sexuality in a changing business culture*, Melbourne: Melbourne University Press.

Stoll, L. and Fink, D. (1996) *Changing Our Schools*, Buckingham: Open University Press.

Stott, C. and Lawson, L. (1997) *Women at the top in further education*, London: Further Education Development Agency (FEDA).

# 13

## School Effectiveness and School Improvement: Critique of a Movement

### JANET OUSTON

### INTRODUCTION

This paper is a work in progress, in fact it has been in progress for about 15 years since I started to worry about the validity and impact of the body of work called School Effectiveness and School Improvement (SESI). It is deliberately not a research review, although it will draw on some research to illustrate the argument. It is a personal reflection on why I have spent so long being concerned about something that nearly everyone else in education seems to have taken for granted as self-evidently true. It feels a bit like being that small boy in the Hans Anderson story – what sort of clothes is this emperor actually wearing? Rather than getting pulled too deeply into the nitty-gritty of research findings I want to take a more distanced perspective, to look at this remarkable 20-year-old forest rather than at the individual trees.

It should also be kept in mind that this paper was written from outside SESI, not from within. SESI is often called a 'movement' which seems to indicate that it has progressed from being a 'field of study' which Vaill (1991, 64) defines as having divergent views and debates to a 'cult' where 'one either buys the approach or one doesn't'. This is one of my concerns about its impact, and one I will return to later. I am very aware that many of the reservations set out in this paper have been made elsewhere by, for example, Silver (1994), White and Barber (1997) and Slee, Weiner and Tomlinson (1998) among many others, and that I have not done justice to others' work, nor adequately acknowledged their influence on my thinking.

Critiques of SESI can be seen as falling into three categories: the first concerns the validity of research on differential school effectiveness, the second its implications for 'school improvement' and the third its impact on education more widely. They are sometimes run together in an unhelpful way. Here they will be treated separately.

## SCHOOL EFFECTIVENESS

During the 1970s I was a member of a research team which undertook a study of students attending 12 secondary schools in south London, following their progress from the last year in primary school to the end of compulsory schooling (Rutter, Maughan, Mortimore, Ouston and Smith, 1979). Using the best analytic techniques available at the time, we concluded that schools differed from one another both in their 'raw' outcomes (of attendance, in-school behaviour, examination results and delinquency) and after they had been 'adjusted' for attainment and behaviour at the end of primary school. We then related these differences to aspects of the internal life of the schools and created one of those now familiar lists of 'features of effective schools'. (It should be noted in passing that there is a PhD in analysing those lists and the operational definitions used to create them. I returned to *Fifteen Thousand Hours* for the first time for many years recently, to check what we had written about leadership. I was amazed that leadership is not discussed and headteachers are only mentioned in passing: 'obviously the influence of the headteacher is very considerable' (203). But since then leaders have been exhorted to be 'strong', 'firm', 'professional', 'purposeful', 'participative' – in fact almost anything except 'invisible'.)

None of the *Fifteen Thousand Hours* team were school management specialists – did such people exist in the 1970s? Methodologically, we were influenced by Brown's (1966) research on the relationships between ward practice in psychiatric hospitals and patients' recovery, and by Newman's (1972) study of crime and the design of public housing estates in the US. Far from being managerial, which was a criticism made at the time, it was an attempt to encapsulate school life from the perspective of teachers and students using a quantitative methodology. But it was used in an increasingly managerialist political context to support a managerial approach.

The research was published in 1979, a year which was an important turning point in the wider political scene. The election of the Conservative government led to the massive changes in society, in particular in the public sector. Our study of schools in south London created a surprising amount of interest nationally and internationally. While it had been out of tune with the 1970s, it fitted, and helped to create the educational *zeitgeist* of the early 1980s. The message of the research, and of other school effectiveness studies, seemed simple, and fitted – and still fits – the political climate.

Very early on I had two serious doubts about the interpretation of the findings. Did these features of effective schools really relate to all schools or just to the inner city? I have since commented on this (Ouston, 1993) and others have also raised the same question (see for example Brown, Duffield and Riddell, 1995). The second concern was about cause and effect, which in real organisations are inextricably entwined. As all undergraduate psychology students know, one cannot argue causation from correlation. Were the features of what became known as 'effective' schools the result of being effective or the cause of effectiveness? As Stoll and Fink (1996, 29) say 'This is a continuing challenge for researchers'.

A trivial example to illustrate this issue is that of the house-plants. The effective schools were pleasant places to be in. They were clean and cared for and had plants in classrooms. If one had cleaned the classrooms of the less effective schools and given each teacher a house-plant would the exam results have improved? I doubt it: the house-plants would probably have died. But this question raised much more serious questions in its wake. Being good social scientists we set out to try to disentangle causes from effects by working intensively with schools committed to improvement and recording what happened. The results were very disappointing, although we learned a lot along the way (Maughan, Ouston, Pickles and Rutter, 1990; Ouston, Maughan and Rutter, 1991).

Looking back I can see that we were very naïve. The problem with the research was that the schools were so complex, and nothing happened rationally in the way that we thought it might. Even given goodwill and hard work, change didn't happen as we hoped and planned. And it was almost impossible to track. We were asking a question that I think no one has cracked in the rigorous way we sought, and it may actually be uncrackable: how do changes in the management of a school lead to changes in student outcomes, and how can you see that happening in real time? We then did the next best thing, which was to do a retrospective case study of schools that had changed over the previous ten years. Here the task is so much simpler because you start from known 'starting' and 'end' points and the historical perspective allows you to ignore all the clutter and noise of real institutions at work. I learned from this that schools are extremely difficult to conceptualise, and that one has to have theory – both personal theory and public theory – to guide interpretation. I realised too that there could be many theories that might be useful for this purpose, but that all of them were enormously more complex than our simple, rational, model of organisational change.

So professionally I moved away from school effectiveness to school management where at least one could think in higher-order concepts such as organisational systems, authority, power and values. But this is running ahead of the argument. To sum up:

Researchers in school effectiveness have proposed that:

- schools differ from each other in their achievements
- it is possible to 'adjust for' prior attainment, or social factors, and rank schools according to how successful they are in promoting students' progress
- it is possible to relate these rankings to internal features of the schools.

If these conclusions are not valid, either conceptually or technically, then the whole of SESI is in difficulties. If schools don't differ, or we can't measure these differences reliably, then the lists of the features of effective schools have little justification. Much of recent work in this area (e.g. Gray and Wilcox, 1995; Goldstein and Spiegelhalter, 1996; and Croxford and Cowie, 1996) has argued that adjusted differences between schools are very small, that the majority of schools cannot be distinguished from one another. Croxford and Cowie, in their study of 38 Grampian secondary schools, estimated a difference of one grade between the average leaver in the most effective school compared to the least effective after adjusting for social factors. Only three schools were significantly above average, and four significantly below. The remaining 31 schools were indistinguishable. Goldstein and Spiegelhalter similarly conclude from their data that:

> two thirds of all possible comparisons (between schools) do not allow separation. Thus, even with the input adjustment, the use of rankings to judge differences between institutions may have a limited utility. A ranking ... may allow us to isolate some institutions, at the extremes, as candidates for further study. In other words we can use such rankings as screening instruments, but not as definitive judgements on individual institutions.
>
> (397)

Gray and Wilcox (1995) reported that, in their study, school factors might be seen to account for four grade points between the average student in the 'best' and 'worst' schools. They also argue that most schools are indistinguishable from each other.

In all these studies differences between schools were reduced considerably when adjustments were made for differences in intake: these might be in prior attainment, in social class, or in family poverty. In the analysis of exam results from 32 schools Sammons, Thomas and Mortimore (1997) showed that making such adjustments reduced differences, but shifted only six 'middling' schools from below to above average or vice versa. Gray and Wilcox made a similar point:

> in 20 years of reading research on the characteristics of effective schools ... they had not come across effective schools where the environment was poor, where the roof needed repair, or where the school had serious staffing difficulties.
>
> (21)

Reviewing several studies Stoll and Fink estimate that 8–14 per cent of the variance in pupils' achievement is attributable to school factors. They concede that these are not very large, 'but it may turn out to be the crucial difference between success and failure' (Stoll and Fink, 1996, 37). Should such small effects have had such a major impact on educational thinking?

## ECOLOGICAL CORRELATIONS

There is an apparent contradiction in much of the published research on school effectiveness. Some researchers claim that the differences between schools is rather small once prior attainment and/or social factors have been taken into account. Others – mainly policy-makers – argue that differences between 'similar' schools in attainment can be quite large. So it is frequently argued by policy-makers (for example, DfEE, 1997a) that schools with similar percentages of students claiming free school meals (a measure of family poverty) have very different outcomes. Can both of these findings be correct? Policy-makers seem unaware of the misleading results that may arise from correlating averages with averages which were first pointed out by Robinson (1950) – a current example in education would be relating the proportion of students taking free meals with the proportion attaining particular exam or test scores. Researchers have increasingly moved to using individual level data and multi-level modelling (Goldstein and Spiegelhalter, 1996) while policy-makers have continued to use potentially misleading school level data. Fitz-Gibbon (1996) provides several interesting illustrations of the consequences of these different approaches.

At this point we are probably justified in concluding that:

- Differences between schools in their raw scores can be considerable, and that these relate in the main to social factors and prior achievement.
- Adjustments reduce the size of differences between schools but may not change their outcome positions relative to other schools.
- The adjusted differences between the most effective and the least effective schools are relatively small. It should be noted that most writers on SESI accept this point, but go ahead as if they were much larger!

Decisions on what should be seen as appropriate measures to use to 'adjust' exam scores are critical. Girls do better than boys, just as the socially advantaged do better than the disadvantaged. Should we, for example, use gender as one of the individual 'measures' we use to adjust exam scores? Or are we happy to accept that girls do better than boys? If we adjust for gender, gender differences may become invisible. Would this matter? This is a serious issue because the current notion of 'adjusting for social factors' has led some to the misunderstanding that social factors don't matter: any school can achieve anything and 'poverty is no excuse'. Paradoxically it may also have led to a lowering of expectations of schools serving socially disadvantaged communities. Some inner city schools receive two conflicting messages: that they are failing to achieve national averages, and that they are doing really well on 'value-added' measures. While both may be true, neither help schools do as well as they can for their students.

## FEATURES OF EFFECTIVE SCHOOLS

Given that the differences between schools in their adjusted outcomes are small, and that most schools cannot be distinguished from each other, how does it come about that many different research groups come up with similar lists of features? There are two possible explanations for this: first the dominance of 'SESI thinking' has led researchers to look for similar factors. It is worth bearing in mind that most school effectiveness studies in the UK were undertaken before the introduction of LMS and open enrolment. A recent study by Sammons, Thomas and Mortimore (1997), however, comes up with some similar features to those identified in the Rutter *et al.* (1979) study almost 20 years earlier. But they overstated the similarities: we didn't refer to shared vision, clear leadership, or parental involvement. It is not surprising that they didn't identify any items concerned with LMS and open enrolment as they do not appear to have included these items in their questionnaires.

But the more likely explanation of this finding is that these small differences between schools will only be partly explained by the 'features of school effectiveness'. We have, therefore, a very relatively weak explanation of small differences. So what is it that researchers keep picking up? Because differences between schools are attenuated, but not otherwise changed, the effects recorded may in fact be those that relate to absolute differences between schools in outcomes rather than adjusted differences.

A typical list of 'features of effective schools' includes:

- professional leadership: strong, purposeful, involved
- shared vision and goals
- a learning environment
- concentration on teaching and learning
- explicit high expectations
- positive reinforcement
- monitoring progress
- pupil rights and responsibilities
- purposeful teaching
- a learning organisation
- home-school partnerships.

(from Barber *et al.*, 1995)

These bring to mind a similar list published by Peters and Waterman (1982):

- managing ambiguity and paradox
- a bias for action*
- close to the customer*
- autonomy and entrepreneurship
- productivity through people*
- hands on, value driven*
- stick to the knitting*
- simple form, lean staff
- simultaneous loose-tight properties.

The asterisks indicate possible overlaps between the Barber *et al.* list, and Peters and Waterman's list. In fact Peters and Waterman's list might be more appropriate to schools in the current political context, in particular 'managing ambiguity and paradox', 'autonomy and entrepreneurship' and 'simultaneous loose-tight properties'.

To conclude this section, it has been argued that social factors are such powerful influences that they are the main determinants of the individual achievement. When exam outcomes are adjusted for social factors many of the differences between schools are reduced but their general pattern (e.g. above average, below average) is not changed. It was then suggested that the lists of 'features of effective schools' were very similar to that reported by Peters and Waterman in their study of effective companies. This may reflect the fact that what is being evaluated is not the value-added effectiveness of the school, but its unadjusted performance. However, if these are not very different, it will make little difference to features identified. The features themselves are also rather unsurprising: a school with 'academic emphasis' seems very likely to have better average attainment than one without; and that 'good' leadership is better than 'bad' leadership even if the definitions are a bit slippery.

## SCHOOL IMPROVEMENT

There is no reason for the theory and practice of improving schools to be related to research of school effectiveness. Indeed, many theories of the management of change are built on quite different foundations. But school improvers have claimed that the links are important, and even that they should be stronger than they are.

Returning to reconsider our early school improvement project, we assumed – like others – that schools were rational organisations, that their processes were linear, and their feedback loops were negative. Given these assumptions the implementation of change should have been straightforward. All that had to be done was to get less successful schools to look like successful schools and all would be well. The SESI movement has progressed since then, with researchers (e.g. Stoll and Fink, 1996) appreciating that studying features of effective schools may not help. To use a medical metaphor: telling a person with bronchitis that fit people can breathe easily and run up and down stairs doesn't help in their current situation. There has to be a theory about how the sick person might regain health. But the popular presentation of SESI, in for example *Governing Bodies and Effective Schools* (Barber *et al.*, 1995) presents lists of features of effective schools under the heading 'what makes an effective school'. Perhaps the section should have been called what *describes* an effective school.

The school improvement literature includes discussions of the importance of school culture, vision, leadership, pedagogy and so on. Great emphasis is placed on school development planning, and more recently on target setting and self-evaluation. But there is rarely any attempt at developing a dynamic model of school processes although it is frequently mentioned as being desirable. It is my increasingly strongly held belief that one should not attempt to change an organisation without some prior understanding of how it functions, of the key parts of the system and how they inter-relate. One can, of course, change organisations without this understanding, and the outcomes may be positive, but this is accidental rather than intentional. They will also be very vulnerable to adverse outcomes which no one predicted. (Sharp-eyed readers will notice the beginning of the influence of Deming's (1993) ideas at this point!)

Guides to school improvement have a conceptual hole at their centre. They never seem to offer help in answering three key questions, *what will you do to improve? how?* and *why?* Two recent publications are taken as examples. A recent TES article by Myers (1998) offers guidelines on all aspects of running an improvement project: the administration and management of the project, selecting schools, appointing staff, publications, training and many other important tasks are covered. But not these key questions. The gap is also seen in *Setting Targets for Pupil Achievement* (DfEE, 1997b) where stage four of the 'five-phase cycle for school improvement' is 'what must we do to make it happen?' (5). But when one turns to the detail of this phase it is expanded to:

'What will be done?
Who will be responsible for ensuring the action takes place?
What resources and support will be needed?
What will the timetable be?'

(9)

Governors are offered no help about how to decide 'what will be done?'.

It is difficult to resolve these issues because they require answers which build on a theory of schools as organisations, on individual and social psychology, and on the causal links between school management, classroom practice and learning. Effective change is very context dependent. Teachers need to develop their own theory, to understand why certain practices are successful. A data-base of this kind certainly might help by suggesting some alternatives for action. Using small scale innovations which are reviewed and modified, appropriate initiatives can be developed. Deming (1993) called this the plan-do-study-act cycle. He was not proposing end-of-programme evaluation, but *very* frequent formative review: plan it, do it, review and study it, and change it. Then do it again, and again. The 'study' phase is of critical importance as it is here that personal theory and understandings are developed. As Mary Marsh (in Ouston, 1997) explained:

So what it is that you are trying to do often is much less important than how you're trying to do it, and that's the bit you need to get right. Yes, you've got to set clear targets and objectives, but you shouldn't spend weeks developing elaborate ones. Keep it snappy, short, focused, and get on with it. Do it and review it. 'Is it working? No, it isn't. What do we do next?' So it's much more immediate and not so large scale.

(143)

Deming proposed that the management of continuous improvement requires four sets of underpinning concepts:

- That organisations are interlinked systems, where actions in one area will have consequences elsewhere.
- That all systems have outcomes which fluctuate over time. Improvement must be interpreted against this background variation.
- That one has to develop and test out a theory of how and why innovations will lead to particular outcomes.
- That one has to have a knowledge of psychology, which will lead to an understanding of how all the people in the system will respond to the innovation.

School improvement writing assumes that schools are rational organisations and that rational planning models – such as school development planning – are appropriate. But many writers have argued that chaos theory (Stacey, 1992) or the idea of the learning organisation (Senge, 1990), may provide more useful insights. Surprisingly, Fullan's challenging book *Change Forces* (Fullan, 1993) has made little impact on mainstream school improvement writing. Fullan argues that a new approach is needed to educational change which takes account of the rapidly changing context. He argues against the current emphasis on vision and strategic planning, and against strong top-down leadership, rationality and accountability. He proposes that in the current context teachers need a personal moral purpose and to themselves be change agents. He quotes Block (1987, 97–8):

> Cultures get changed in a thousand small ways, not by dramatic announcements from the boardroom. If we wait until top management gives leadership to the change we want to see, we miss the point. For us to have any hope that our own preferred future will come to pass, we provide the leadership.

(14)

Stacey (1992) also argues that decision-making should be devolved, and diversity encouraged. The extent to which these less-rational approaches are appropriate to schools has been discussed in Ouston, 1998a.


## IMPACT OF SESI ON EDUCATION MORE WIDELY

SESI has had a huge influence on national education policy. It has become part of 'what everybody knows' about education and it is very difficult to discuss or argue against – there is no alternative valid language for debate outside the academic world and not much within. The SESI discourse runs throughout the education policies of both the previous and the present government and seems to have been adopted without hesitation by teachers, governors, parents and academics.

Ball (1990) wrote about the 'discourse of derision' in education in the late

1980s. The school improvement movement can be seen as a contributor to this discourse. Does 'school improvement' mean that all schools need improving, is the message that all schools are weak? It was often said that LMS centralised decision-making and devolved blame. LMS and the discourse of derision have created a blame culture, and SESI has enhanced this by creating the impression that schools and, in particular, headteachers are entirely responsible for their educational outcomes.

The SESI movement has over-emphasised the role of the head (or leader) and top-down management. This too has meshed with the current political climate. The shift to a managerialist view of schools has led to an increasing gap between the managers and the managed (Clarke and Newman, 1997; Whitty, Power and Halpin, 1998). In NPQH (TTA, 1997), for example, headteachers are required to 'lead, motivate, support, challenge and develop staff to secure improvement' (7). The headteacher 'creates an ethos' and 'provides educational vision' (6). There is little space for collaboration or for encouraging the diverse and self-motivated body of teachers Fullan (1993) argues are needed for the future. Ten years ago Torrington and Weightman (1989) commented that the emphasis on the headteacher-as-leader in their research schools was far in excess of that found in organisations outside education. They questioned 'this dangerous dependence on one person' (230).

A major outcome of the school effectiveness movement and its interpretation by policy-makers has been the emphasis on using examination and test results as the major performance indicators for schools – a good school has become one with good exam results. Nuttall once distinguished between high and low stakes measures of performance. League tables are high stakes, and, as Deming (1993) pointed out, such performance indicators will lead to a distortion of educational processes. Their impact is discussed in Ouston, Fidler and Earley (1998).

Definitions of school effectiveness reflect the political and cultural frameworks within which policy-makers set priorities. They are open to examination, evaluation and change. As an example, we can consider the contrasts between English and Japanese educational priorities. The Japanese are trying to move away from an examination driven system because of its narrowing and inflexible impact on education while we are moving towards it in order to increase literacy and numeracy. Currently each country's policy-makers seem intent on revisiting the educational history of the other (Ouston, 1998b) in order to promote their current, different, definitions of 'educational effectiveness'. The time has come to examine critically our taken-for-granted definitions. Are the research findings as firmly based as we think? What are the costs and benefits of current approaches to school effectiveness and school improvement? What are the opportunity costs? What values underpin current practice? How will these influence the lives of the young people currently in school? There are important and difficult questions to be asked about 'good' education and how it is to be achieved.

There is a serious question to be confronted. How much improvement can schools reasonably expect in the attainment of their pupils? It seems likely that any particular school's examination results will be constrained by its intake; and it seems realistic to assume a band of performance within which the majority of schools will lie.

Students must be given the opportunity for high achievement, but many years ago Jencks (1972) argued that even if schools had little long-term impact on students' lives their immediate effects are important:

> Some schools are dull, depressing, even terrifying places, while others are lively, comfortable, and reassuring. If we think of school life as an end in itself rather than as a means to some other end, such differences become enormously important. Eliminating these differences would not do much to make adults more equal, but it would do a great deal to make the quality of children's (and teachers') lives more equal.
>
> (256)

Schools – particularly those serving disadvantaged families – need to be respectful, values-based, exciting environments for children to grow up in. These may offer all kinds of positive outcomes in addition to the acquisition of examination results. This is an important challenge for all teachers including those with management responsibilities, and one that requires a high quality of management knowledge, understanding and skills.

## REFERENCES

Ball, S. J. (1990) *Politics and Policy Making in Education*, London: Routledge.

Barber, M., Stoll, L., Mortimore, P. and Hillman, J. (1995) *Governing Bodies and Effective Schools*, London: DfEE.

Block, P. (1987) *The Empowered Manager*, San Francisco: Jossey Bass.

Brown, G. W. (1966) *Schizophrenia and Social Care*, Oxford: Oxford University Press.

Brown, S., Duffield, J. and Riddell, S. (1995) School effectiveness research: the policy makers' tool for school improvement? *European Educational Research Association Bulletin*, 1, 1, 6–15.

Clarke, J. and Newman, J. (1997) *The Managerial State*, London: Sage.

Croxford, L. and Cowie, M. (1996) *The Effectiveness of Grampian Secondary Schools*. Report of a research programme undertaken by Grampian Regional Council and the Centre for Educational Sociology, Edinburgh. Edinburgh: CES.

Deming, W. E. (1993) *The New Economics for Industry, Government and Education*, Cambridge, Mass: MIT.

DfEE (1997a) *Excellence in Schools*, London: DfEE.

DfEE (1997b) *Setting Targets for Pupil Achievement: Guidance for governors*, London: DfEE.

Fitz-Gibbon, C. (1996) *Monitoring Education: Indicators, quality and effectiveness*, London: Cassell.

Fullan, M. (1993) *Change Forces: Probing the depths of educational reform*, London: Falmer.

Goldstein, H and Spiegelhalter, D. J. (1996) League tables and their limitations: statistical issues in comparisons of institutional performance, *Journal of the Royal Statistical Society, Series A*, 159, 3, 385–443.

Gray, J. and Wilcox, B. (1995) *Good School, Bad School*, Buckingham: Open University Press.

Jencks, C. (1972) *Inequality: A reassessment of family and schooling in America*, London: Penguin Books.

Maughan, B., Ouston, J., Pickles, A. and Rutter, M. (1990) Can schools change? I: Changes in outcomes, *Journal for School Effectiveness and Improvement*, 1, 3, 188–210.

Myers, K. (1998) Improve and feel no pain, *Times Educational Supplement*, 15 May 1998, 28.

Newman, O. (1972) *Defensible Space*, New York: Macmillan.

Ouston, J. (1993) Management competences, school effectiveness and education management, *Educational Management and Administration*, 21, 4, 212–221.

Ouston, J. (1997) Chapter 8: Mary Marsh in conversation with Janet Ouston, in P. Ribbins (ed.) *Leaders and Leadership in the School, College and University*, London: Cassell.

Ouston, J. (1998a) Managing in turbulent times, in A. Gold and J. Evans (1998) *Reflecting on School Management*, Lewes: Falmer.

Ouston, J. (1998b) Educational reform in Japan: Some reflections from England, *Management in Education*, 12, 5, 15–19.

Ouston, J., Fidler, B. and Earley, P. (1998) The educational accountability of schools in England and Wales, *Education Policy*, 12, 1–2, 111–123.

Ouston, J., Maughan, B. and Rutter, M. (1991) Can schools change? II: Changes in practice, *Journal of School Effectiveness and Improvement* 2, 1, 3–13.

Peters, T. J. and Waterman, R.H. (1982) *In Search of Excellence*, New York: Harper and Row.

Robinson, W. S. (1950) Ecological correlations and the behavior of individuals, *American Sociological Review*, 15, 351–357.

Rutter, M., Maughan, B., Mortimore, P., Ouston, J. and Smith, A. (1979) *Fifteen Thousand Hours*, London: Open Books.

Sammons, P., Thomas, S., and Mortimore, P. (1997) *Forging links: effective schools and effective departments*, London: Paul Chapman Publishing.

Senge, P. (1990) *The Fifth Discipline*, New York: Doubleday.

Silver, H. (1994) *Good Schools, Effective Schools: Judgements and their histories*, London: Cassell.

Slee, R., Weiner, G. with Tomlinson, S. (1998) *School Effectiveness for Whom? Challenges to the school effectiveness and school improvement movements*, London: Falmer.

Stacey, R. (1992) *Managing Chaos*, London: Kogan.

Stoll, L. and Fink, L. (1996) *Changing our Schools: Linking school effectiveness and school improvement*, Buckingham: Open University Press.

Torrington, D. and Weightman, J. (1989) *The Reality of School Management*, Oxford: Blackwell.

Teacher Training Agency (TTA) (1997) *National Professional Qualification for Headteachers*, London: TTA.

Teacher Training Agency (1998) *National Standards for Headteachers*, London: TTA.

Vaill, P. B. (1991) *Managing as a Performing Art: New ideas for a world of chaotic change*, San Francisco: Jossey Bass.

Whitty, G., Power, S. and Halpin, D. (1998) *Devolution and Choice in Education: The school, the state and the market*, Buckingham: Open University Press.

White, J. and Barber, M. (eds.) (1997) *Perspectives on School Effectiveness and School Improvement*, London: Institute of Education.

# 14

## Can Leadership Enhance School Effectiveness?

### PHILIP HALLINGER AND RONALD HECK

Since the emergence of research focusing on school effectiveness in the late 1970s, educators internationally joined the leadership bandwagon. Despite the admonition of respected scholars (e.g., Bossert, Dwyer, Rowan and Lee, 1982; Bridges, 1982; Miskel, 1982; Rowan, Dwyer and Bossert, 1982; Cuban, 1988; van de Grift, 1989, 1990) the assumption of positive leadership effects in schooling prevailed in research and practice. In fact, since 1980 leadership became a newly influential domain of educational management despite the fact that the *empirical knowledge base* was mired in a sea of ambiguity.

In this chapter, we discuss findings drawn from a review of empirical literature on principal effects disseminated internationally between 1980 and 1998. We seek to understand what scholars have learned about the substance of claims that principal leadership makes a difference in school effectiveness. The body of the chapter is devoted to a discussion of findings drawn from a series of related papers that have investigated state-of-the-art perspectives on school leadership (Hallinger, 1995; Hallinger and Heck, 1996a, 1996b, 1997; Heck and Hallinger, 1999). This paper builds on the earlier efforts by synthesising and extending our findings on school leadership as it operates in an international context.

### CAN LEADERSHIP ENHANCE SCHOOL EFFECTIVENESS?

The studies included in our review were conducted between 1980 and 1998 in 11 countries. Common criteria for inclusion of studies in the review included a focus on school leadership and its relationship to quantitative measures of *school effectiveness and/or student achievement*. In the first phase of the review, we examined 42 studies published between 1990 and 1995 (see Hallinger and Heck, 1996a, 1996b, 1997). We then expanded the review to include qualitative and quantitative research published on principal leadership and *school improvement* (see Heck and Hallinger, 1999) and extended the dates of the overall review to 1998. We organise the presentation of findings into two sections: avenues of leader influence, the context of school leadership.

## AVENUES OF LEADER INFLUENCE

We constructed our findings from the review around a framework that proposes leadership as a construct that influences the attitudes and behaviour of individuals and also the organisational system in which people work (see also Leithwood, 1994; Ogawa and Bossert, 1995). We found evidence for the proposition that leadership influences the organisational system through three primary avenues: 1) purposes, 2) structure and social networks, 3) people.

### Purposes

The past 20 years in organisational leadership could be termed the era of vision. The literature exhorts leaders in all sectors to articulate their vision, set clear goals for their organisations, and create a sense of shared mission. Our review supports the belief that formulating the school's purposes represents an important leadership function. In fact, the research suggests that mission-building is the strongest and most consistent avenue of influence school leaders use to influence student achievement.

Despite this conclusion, lack of theoretical clarity has hindered our understanding of how school leaders shape organisational purposes to influence school effectiveness. Researchers have included a wide variety of operational measures under the heading of *goal-setting*: teachers' educational expectations, the framing of educational purposes, principal's clarity in articulating a vision, the substance of the school's mission, consensus on goals, and the principal's role in goal-setting processes (e.g., Hallinger and Murphy, 1986; Andrews and Soder, 1987; Scott and Teddlie, 1987; Bamburg and Andrews, 1990; Heck et al., 1990; Brewer, 1993; Cheng, 1994; Goldring and Pasternak, 1994; Leithwood, 1994; Silins, 1994). Researchers often use terms such as vision, mission, and goals synonymously in discussions of leadership while operationalising them quite differently in empirical investigations. This lack of conceptual clarity is problematic in that the terms have different theoretical foundations and point towards alternate conceptualisations of how leaders influence school outcomes.

The notion of a *personal vision* articulated by the school leader draws its influence from its impact on the leader's own behaviour and also from its potential to energise others and invest work with meaning. For example scholars such as Barth, Duke, Greenfield, Sergiovanni, Caldwell, and Deal have argued that *meaning-making* is a central role of the school leader. A personal vision is the starting point of finding meaning in one's work.

An *organisational mission* exists when the personal visions of a critical mass of people cohere in common sense of purpose within a community. Like 'vision' the word 'mission' often connotes a moral purpose. The moral or spiritual character of a shared mission reaches into the hearts of people and engages them to act on behalf of something beyond their own immediate self-interest. Note also that a vision or mission is a *quest* in the sense that success does not necessarily depend upon its achievement. Their power lies in the motivational force of a *shared quest* to work towards the accomplishment of something special.

In contrast to vision and mission, a *goal* is a functional target. An educational goal might describe the state that a school wishes to achieve by the end of the year in relation to student learning, attendance, graduation rates, or school climate. We often define success by whether or not the school's functional goal(s) has been achieved. Unlike a vision or mission, the power of a goal or management objective lies not in its inspirational or motivational force, but in its ability to focus the attention of people on a limited frame of activity. Goals derive their motivational power from from reward and sanction.

Vision, goal-framing and mission-building take on different emphases in the practice of school leadership. By way of illustration, we are reminded of Roland Barth's (1986) observation that educators do not jump eagerly out of bed at 6:00 a.m. and rush off to school because they wish to raise scores on achievement tests. Engaging in a shared quest to accomplish something special motivates educators. Yet, school improvement policy frequently mandates that principals engage in goal-setting exercises in the belief that research supports this prescription (Barth, 1986; Cuban, 1988).

Despite the *potential impact* of this leadership function, there remains considerable ambiguity in how leaders shape the school's purposes to foster student learning. At this point in time, we are confident that this avenue is important. However, scholars should view this conclusion as a solid starting point for further elaboration rather than a practical prescription.

### Structure and social networks

A second avenue of leadership influence involves the interplay between organisational structures and social networks in and around the school. Ogawa and Bossert (1995) define social structures and networks as the regularised aspects of relationships existing among participants in an organisation.

Empirical evidence from our review supports this view of leadership. For example, Leithwood found that the principal's leadership shapes three distinct psychological dispositions of teachers: their perceptions of various school characteristics, their commitment to school change, and their capacity for professional development. Weil and colleagues (Weil, Marshalek, Mitman, Murphy, Hallinger and Pruyn, 1984) found that principal support of teachers and a proactive stance on problem-solving differentiated leadership in effective *vs.* typical elementary schools. Leithwood and colleagues (1993, 1994) and also Silins (1994) determined that leadership which provides individualised support and challenging work, and which fosters a shared mission in the school contributes to successful school improvement.

Studies across several national contexts found that greater involvement from stakeholders in decision-making is characteristic of higher-producing schools. For example, Heck (1993) found that collaborative decision-making and more flexible rule structures were associated with higher-achieving secondary schools in Singapore. Cheng (1994) concluded that strong primary school principal leaders in Hong Kong schools tended to promote participation in decision-making. This resulted in stronger and more cohesive social interactions, greater staff commitment, and higher morale. In a Canadian study, Leithwood (1994) reported greater implementation of school improvement outcomes where there was greater collaboration in decision-making.

A recent trend towards viewing the school as a learning organisation represents a noteworthy approach to invigorating structure and social networks with educational content. The principal's role in a learning organisation involves creating structures that facilitate communication and collaboration among staff around the school's valued purposes. This conceptualisation suggests a different set of intervening variables linking leadership to school effectiveness than predominated during the *effective schools era*. These include but are not limited to shared mission, teacher participation in decision-making, scheduling, use of teaming, principal stimulation of staff learning, patterns of collaboration, and team learning (see Leithwood, Leonard and Sharratt, 1997).

## People

Several frameworks (e.g., Bridges, 1977; Bossert *et al.*, 1982; Leithwood, 1994; Ogawa and Bossert, 1995) propose that administrative activity is largely directed at influencing people in the school organisation. Evidence accumulated from the past 20 years of research on educational leadership provides considerable support concerning this domain of principal leadership.

For example, Leithwood (1994) highlights 'people effects' as a cornerstone of the transformational leadership model. More specifically, Leithwood's (1994) empirical investigation found that principal effects are achieved through fostering group goals, modelling desired behaviour for others, providing intellectual stimulation, and individualised support (e.g., towards personal and staff development). With respect to outcomes, leadership had an influence on teachers' perceptions of progress with implementing reform initiatives and teachers' perceptions of increases in student outcomes.

Other studies using an instructional leadership model also provide support for principal effects on people as a means to affect outcomes. Heck, Larson and Marcoulides (1990) found that teachers in higher-producing schools spent more time in direct classroom supervision and support of teachers. At both the primary and secondary levels, they also gave greater attention to working with teachers to coordinate the school's instructional programme, solving instructional problems collaboratively, helping teachers secure resources, and creating opportunities for in-service and staff development.

These conclusions reinforce the image of school leadership as a *people-oriented* activity. Strategy, planning, and resource management are important facets of the educational manager's role. Yet, in the end leadership involves working with and through people (Bridges, 1977; Cuban, 1988). Researchers have begun to identify the means by which school leaders put this into practice to foster quality learning environments.

## THE CONTEXT OF SCHOOL LEADERSHIP

The assumption that leadership makes a difference is supported by our review. Yet scholars have also noted that leaders operate in different contexts and that these contexts place constraints on leadership behaviour (see, for example, Bridges, 1977, 1982; Rowan et al., 1982; Cuban, 1988). While researchers have only begun to include context variables in their empirical models, this is an area that demands greater attention. Initial findings reinforce the hypothesis that a variety of school context factors shape the particular needs for leadership that may exist within a school. Moreover, it appears that the ability to provide leadership that is suited to a particular school context carries over to effects on students.

### The school as a context for leadership

Despite a range of conceptual and methodological problems in incorporating context variables into studies of leadership effects, we discerned an interesting trend among the studies. Socio-economic factors in the school and community appear to influence principal leadership and its impact on school effectiveness (e.g., Rowan and Denk, 1984; Hallinger and Murphy, 1986; Andrews and Soder, 1987). For example, Andrews and Soder (1987) reported that principal leadership affected reading and maths outcomes in elementary schools. When controlling for SES and ethnicity, however, the effects of principal leadership on reading and maths outcomes tended to disappear in high SES or predominately Caucasian elementary schools. They remained significant in predominately African-American or low SES schools. This supported their hypothesis of context effects on principal leadership.

Hallinger and Murphy (1986) found that community SES affected how elementary school principals perceive their work. For example, they worked quite differently in defining the school mission in low and high SES effective schools. In low SES schools, principals stressed the mastery of basic skills and did appear to define clear school-wide goal-targets for instruction. They allocated more time to basic skills instruction and built fairly elaborate systems of rewards and recognition for student success. Moreover, principals in low SES schools tended to define their leadership role more narrowly in terms of curriculum coordination, control of instruction, and task orientation.

Similarly, Scott and Teddlie (1987) identified a link between SES and elementary school principals' expectations. Principals' expectations, in turn, affected their sense of responsibility; however, Scott and Teddlie determined that principal responsibility was not directly related to outcomes. Although untested by Scott and Teddlie, we noted a possible *indirect* effect (likely statistically significant) of principal expectations on school outcomes through principal responsibility.

Context influences were also found to impact upon principal behaviour with respect to structures and social networks. Hallinger and Murphy (1986) found that school linkages to the home and parent involvement were weaker in low SES effective schools. In contrast, linkages to the home and parent involvement were strong and pervasive in high SES schools. In the lower SES schools, principals acted as buffers, controlling access to the school and protecting the school's programme from outside influences that might dilute its effectiveness. In higher SES schools, the principal acted as a boundary spanner, constantly seeking ways to involve community members who had great interest and stake in the school's operation. These findings hint at the relationship between wider community context, the corresponding school culture and the role of the principal. The different extent of contact between school staff and community is important because teacher and administrator attitudes appear to be shaped by expectations and beliefs of the wider community (e.g., Hallinger and Murphy, 1986; Ogawa and Bossert, 1995).

Cheng (1994) noted that other contextual factors (e.g., school size, teacher background) were not generally found to exert any important influence over principal leadership in secondary school settings. Heck (1992) found differences in principal discussion of instructional issues and problems and discussion about how instructional techniques impact student achievement to be similar across school level, with principals in both effective elementary and high school schools more involved with these variables than their counterparts at low-achieving schools. There is an interaction with level, however, with principals in effective elementary schools more heavily involved than principals in effective high schools. Heck (1992) also noted that principals in elementary schools (controlling for effectiveness) spend more time attempting to communicate goals to teachers and others than principals in secondary schools.

Again, research in this domain has only begun to identify patterns of effective leadership. It is only with the recent advent of better statistical tools that researchers are able to empirically study comprehensive models that incorporate context variables along with leadership and school outcomes

(Hallinger and Heck, 1996b). We would encourage the conduct of mixed-methods studies as qualitative data have the potential to tease out important patterns identified in quantitative research (Heck and Hallinger,1999).

## Cultural context

Another feature of context that begs systematic investigation is the cultural context in which leaders act. It is possible – even likely – that differences in the social construction of the leadership role enacted in organisations differs across societies (Hofstede, 1980). As Getzels and colleagues (Getzels, Lipham and Campbell, 1968) theorised and researchers outside educational adminis-tration have empirically investigated, organisational culture is only a portion of a broader social culture (Hofstede, 1980; Brislin, 1993; Ralston, Elissa, Gustafson and Cheung, 1991). The broader societal culture exerts an influ-ence on administrators beyond the influence exerted by a specific organisa-tion's culture (Getzels *et al.*, 1968; Hofstede, 1976, 1980; Gerstner and Day, 1994). Surprisingly, scholars in educational administration have devoted little effort towards uncovering the cultural foundations of leadership when used in this broader sense (Cheng, 1995; Hallinger, 1995; Bajunid, 1996; Hallinger and Heck, 1996b; Heck and Hallinger, 1999).

Gerstner and O'Day (1994) assert:

> Because leadership is a cultural phenomenon, inextricably linked to the values and customs of a group of people, we do not expect differences in leadership proto-types to be completely random. Rather they should be linked to dimensions of national culture.
>
> (123)

Their own cross-cultural research in the business sector found significant dif-ferences in how different nationalities perceive the traits of leaders. Additional analyses found that these perceptual differences were also signif-icant when countries were grouped as being an Eastern or Western culture. Unfortunately, less empirical data is available concerning the impact of culture on the behaviour, as opposed to the perceptions of leaders.

Culture is the source of values that people share in a society. As such culture can be viewed as having effects on multiple features of the school and its environment. Culture shapes the institutional and community context within which the school is situated by defining predominant value orienta-tions and norms of behaviour (Getzels *et al.*, 1968). It influences the predilec-tions of individual leaders as well as the nature of interactions with others in the school and its community. Moreover, it determines the particular educa-tional emphasis or goals that prevail within a cultures system of schooling. Since cultural values vary across nations, we would expect cross-cultural variation in the educational goals of societies as well as the normative practices aimed towards their achievement (Getzels *et al.*, 1968).

Current conceptualisations of administrative practice represent a useful point of departure for better understanding the relationships between leadership and societal culture. Frameworks such as those proposed by Bossert and colleagues (Bossert, Dwyer, Rowan, and Lee, 1982) point to important antecedents of leadership – variables that shape the needs and requirements of leadership within the organisation – as well as paths by which leaders may achieve an impact on the organisation. What remains is to make the social culture explicit in such frameworks in order to explore its impact on the social and institutional system in which leadership is exercised. Theoretical work in educational administration (e.g., Getzels *et al.*, 1968; Cheng, 1995; Cheng and Wong, 1996) and research in the general leadership literature provide useful direction in this quest (e.g., Hofstede, 1976, 1980; Brislin, 1993).

Given the general trends of globalisation and broader, faster access to information, we expect that investigations of the nature of leadership across cultures will assume a central place in the research community in the coming decade. Investigations of the cultural context of schooling and the subsequent roles played by leaders at different organisational levels (e.g., district administrators, principals, senior teachers) represents a rich vein for future exploration (Cheng, 1995; Hallinger, 1995; Bajunid, 1996; Cheng and Wong, 1996; Heck, 1996; Wong, 1996; Hallinger and Leithwood, 1998).

## FUTURE DIRECTIONS FOR RESEARCH IN EDUCATIONAL MANAGEMENT AND LEADERSHIP

Research conducted over the past two decades answers the question 'can leadership enhance school effectiveness?' in the affirmative. In the two decades since the advent of the school effectiveness research, scholarship has benefited from improvements in the application of both theory and methodology. Consequently, we have increasing confidence in the belief that school leaders – especially principals – do make a difference in schooling outcomes.

While our review supports the belief that principal leadership influences school effectiveness, we temper this conclusion in two important respects. First, school leaders achieve effects on their schools *indirectly*. Skilful school leaders influence school and classroom processes that have a *direct* impact on student learning. Second, school leaders themselves are subject to considerable influence via the norms and characteristics of the school and its environment.

Thus, although the findings reinforce the notion that leadership makes a difference in school effectiveness, they do not support the image of the heroic school leader. School leaders do not *make* effective schools. Rather the image we draw from this review is that of leaders who are able to work with and through the staff to shape a school culture that is focused yet adaptable. They work with staff to foster development of a school culture in which staff find meaning in their work and are motivated to learn and solve problems with a greater degree of collaboration than typifies many schools.

Our satisfaction in seeing significant progress towards answering a potentially important question for policy and practice is moderated, however, by continuing limitations in this knowledge base. Persisting blind spots and blank spots (Heck and Hallinger, 1999) in the research base form the basis for our identification of priorities in this field.

1. Untangle the conceptual confusion concerning how school leaders employ vision, mission and goals to influence school effectiveness. Both the frequency with which vision/mission/goals appeared as a significant intervening variable and the general popularity of this construct among scholars and practitioners suggest that it ought to receive high priority in the next phase of investigation. Attacking this problem will require researchers to link their conceptual and operational definitions of variables more clearly. For example, researchers have at times operationalised vision and mission as functional goal targets. The absence of clarity in language has led to confusion in interpretation of results.

Scholars must also extend this research by clearly explicating *in advance* of investigation the theoretical rationale for relationships among variables. We found a tendency among researchers to offer a framework of commonly used variables (e.g., mission, teacher expectations, principal supervision), without fully elaborating on how and why these variables would interact to result in the proposed effects (see Rowan and Denk, 1984 and Weil *et al.*, 1984 as worthy exceptions to this tendency). For example, if vision is part of a model of leadership effects, *how* would the researcher expect leaders to employ vision and *why* would this interaction likely influence other variables in the model?

2. Broaden investigation of school leadership and its effects beyond the principalship. The notion of distributed leadership is not only theoretically attractive, but also potentially powerful in practice. The past decade witnessed a normative shift away from the dominant leader and towards an egalitarian model of leadership. Yet the fact remains that school principals occupy a position of significance in the structural hierarchy of schools.

In the year 2,000 it is as foolish to think that *only* principals provide leadership for school improvement as to believe that principals *do not* influence school effectiveness. Unfortunately, whether out of inconvenience or conceptual ambiguity, few researchers have undertaken empirical investigation of alternate sources of leadership in educational management. With some notable exceptions, rhetoric, prescription and advocacy continue to dominate discussions of distributed leadership in schools (see Leithwood, Jantzi, Ryan and Steinbach, 1998). Concerted effort is needed to define and investigate leadership more broadly while simultaneously maintaining a focus on leadership that emanates from the principal's office.

3. Incorporate the construct of the school as a learning organisation into

explorations of school leadership and its effects. The bulk of published research in our review was theoretically grounded in the school effectiveness research (e.g., Andrews and Soder, 1987; Heck *et al.*, 1991; Cheng, 1994). This reflects the general popularity of this framework during the 1980s and 1990s. Although this remains a useful heuristic, scholars in educational management would benefit from expanding their approach to conceptualising and studying school leadership effects.

We believe in the potential efficacy of the learning organisation construct for research in this domain. It is notable that the main avenues of leader influence identified in this review – shared mission, structure and social networks, people – are hallmark components of the learning organisation (Senge, 1990). These represent a complementary perspective for viewing the manner by which leaders contribute to school effectiveness. Use of this construct in empirical research is already evident in the work of Leithwood and colleagues (1997) and appears worthy of a wider effort.

4.   Study leadership in its cultural context with an intention to explicate the influence of cultural norms on the conceptualisation and exercise of leadership. While the studies included in our review were conducted in numerous different countries, none was conducted with a specific eye towards the influence of that nation's culture. In each case, culture was an assumed background variable; in effect, it was 'held constant'.

There is much to learn through explicit attention to the exploration of leadership within its *cultural* context. Theoretical and practical advances in the field will derive from two sources. First, the ready dissemination of knowledge and educational policies internationally makes it imperative to understand how local culture reshapes globally popularised policies and practices (Cheng, 1995; Hallinger, 1995; Heck, 1996; Hallinger and Leithwood, 1998). For example, the means by which leaders share decision-making, provide instructional leadership, articulate a vision and set goals may well differ across cultures. These differences have practical implications for achieving school effectiveness (e.g., see Cheng and Wong, 1996).

Second, differences in cultural construction of leadership that researchers may identify in practice will have acute implications for theory. To date, the international knowledge base in educational management reflects a severely limited set of conceptions grounded in Judeo-Christian notions of human motivation (Cheng, 1994; Bajunid, 1996). The field will benefit from further development of this perspective via exploration of this potentially rich vein.

These directions by no means represent the only ones suggested by this research. They do, however, represent priority directions by virtue of their theoretical and practical significance. It is this intersection of theoretical and practical concerns that will continue to make research in this domain exciting in the coming decade.

# REFERENCES

Andrews, R. and Soder, R. (1987) Principal instructional leadership and school achievement, *Educational Leadership*, 44, 9–11.

Bajunid, I. A. (1996) Preliminary explorations of indigenous perspectives of educational management: The evolving Malaysian experience, *Journal of Educational Administration*, 34(5), 50–73.

Bamburg, J. and Andrews, R. (1990) School goals, principals and achievement, *School Effectiveness and School Improvement,* 2(3), 175–191.

Barth, R. (1986) On sheep and goats and school reform, Phi Delta Kappan, 68(4), 293–6.

Brewer, D. (1993) Principals and student outcomes: Evidence from US high schools, *Economics of Education Review*, 12(4), 281–292.

Bridges, E. (1982) Research on the school administrator: The state-of-the-art, 1967-1980', *Educational Administration Quarterly*, 18(3), 12–33.

Bridges, E. (1977) The nature of leadership, in L. Cunningham and R. Nystrand (eds.), *Educational Administration: The developing decades* (pp. 203–230). Berkeley: McCutchan.

Bossert, S., Dwyer, D., Rowan, B. and Lee, G. (1982) The instructional management role of the principal, *Educational Administration Quarterly*, 18(3), 34–64.

Brislin, R. (1993) *Understanding Culture's Influence on Behavior*, New York: Harcourt Brace.

Cheng, K. M. (1995) The neglected dimension: Cultural comparison in educational administration, in K. C. Wong and K. M. Cheng (eds.), *Educational Leadership and Change: An international perspective*, Hong Kong: Hong Kong University Press.

Cheng, K. M. and Wong, K. C. (1996) School effectiveness in East Asia: Concepts, origins and implications, *Journal of Educational Administration*, 34(5), 32–49.

Cheng, Y. C. (1994) Principal's leadership as a critical factor for school performance: Evidence from multilevels of primary schools, *School Effectiveness and School Improvement*, 5(3), 299–317.

Cuban, L. (1988) *The Managerial Imperative and the Practice of Leadership in Schools*, Albany, NY: SUNY Press.

Eberts, R. and Stone, J. (1988) Student achievement in public schools: Do principals make a difference? *Economics of Education Review*, 7(3), 291–299.

Gerstner, C. and O'Day, D. (1994) *Leadership Quarterly*, 5(2), 121–134.

Getzels, J., Lipham, J. and Campbell, R. (1968) *Educational Administration as a Social Process*, New York: Harper & Row.

Goldring, E. and Pasternak, R. (1994) Principals' coordinating strategies and school effectiveness, *School Effectiveness and School Improvement*, 5(3), 239–253.

Hallinger, P. (1995) Culture and leadership: Developing an international perspective in educational administration, *UCEA Review*, 36(1), 3–7.

Hallinger, P. and Heck, R. (1997) Exploring the principal's contribution to school effectiveness, *School Effectiveness and School Improvement*, 8(4), 1–35.

Hallinger, P. and Heck, R. (1996a) Reassessing the principal's role in school effectiveness: A review of empirical research, 1980–1995, *Educational Administration Quarterly*, 32(1), 5–44.

Hallinger, P. and Heck, R. (1996b) The principal's role in school effectiveness: A review of methodological issues, 1980-95, in K. Leithwood *et al.* (eds.), *The International Handbook of Research in Educational Administration*(723–784), New York: Kluwer.

Hallinger, P. and Leithwood, K. (1994) Exploring the impact of principal leadership, *School Effectiveness and School Improvement*, 5(3), 206–218.

Hallinger, P. and Leithwood, K. (1998) Unseen forces: The impact of social culture on leadership, *Peabody Journal of Education*, 73(2), 126–151.

Hallinger, P. and Murphy, J. (1986) The social context of effective schools, *American Journal of Education*, 94(3), 328–355.

Heck, R. (1996) Leadership and culture: Conceptual and methodological issues in comparing models across cultural settings, *Journal of Educational Administration*, 30(3), 35–48.

Heck, R. (1992) Principal instructional leadership and the identification of high- and low-achieving schools: The application of discriminant techniques, *Administrator's Notebook*, 34(7), 1–4.

Heck, R. (1993) School context, principal leadership, and achievement: The case of secondary schools in Singapore, *The Urban Review*, 25(2), 151–166.

Heck, R. and Hallinger, P. (1999) Conceptual models, methodology, and methods to study school leadership, in J. Murphy and K.S. Louis (eds.), *The Second Handbook of Research on Educational Administration*, New York: Longman.

Heck, R., Larson, T. and Marcoulides, G. (1990) Principal instructional leadership and school achievement: Validation of a causal model, *Educational Administration Quarterly*, 26, 94–125.

Heck, R. and Marcoulides, G. (1996a) School culture and performance: Testing the invariance of an organizational model, *School Effectiveness and School Improvement*, 7(1), 76–95.

Heck, R. and Marcoulides, G. (1996b) The assessment of principal performance: A multilevel approach, *Journal of Personnel Evaluation in Education*, 10(1), 11–28.

Heck, R., Marcoulides, G. and Lang, P. (1991) Principal instructional leadership and school achievement: The application of discriminant techniques, *School Effectiveness and School Improvement*, 2(2), 115–135.

Hofstede, G. (1980) *Culture's Consequences: International differences in work-related values*, Newbury Park, CA: Sage.

Hofstede, G. (1976) Nationality and espoused values of managers, *Journal of Applied Psychology*, 61(2), 148–155.

Leithwood, K. (1994) Leadership for school restructuring, *Educational Administration Quarterly*, 30(4), 498–518.

Leithwood, K., Begley, P. and Cousins, B. (1992) *Expert Leadership for Future Schools*, London: Falmer Press.

Leithwood, K. and Jantzi, D. (1990) Transformational leadership: How principals can help reform school cultures, *School Effectiveness and School Improvement*, 1 (1), 249–280.

Leithwood, K., Jantzi, D., Ryan, S. and Steinbach, R. (1998) Distributed leadership and student engagement in school. Paper presented at the annual meeting of the American Educational Research Association, San Diego, CA.

Leithwood, K., Jantzi, D., Silins, H. and Dart, B. (1993) Using the appraisal of school leaders as an instrument for school restructuring, *Peabody Journal of Education*, 68(1), 85–109.

Leithwood, K., Leonard, L. and Sharratt, L. (1997) Conditions fostering organizational learning in schools. Paper presented at the annual meeting of the International Congress on School Effectiveness and Improvement, Memphis, TN.

Miskel, C. (1982, April). An analysis of principal effects. Unpublished speech to the

National Graduate Student Seminar in Educational Administration, Princeton, New Jersey.

Ogawa, R. and Bossert, S. (1995) Leadership as an organizational quality, *Educational Administration Quarterly*, 31(2), 224–243.

Ralston, D., Elissa, P., Gustafson, D. and Cheung, F. (1991) Eastern values: A comparison of managers in the United States, Hong Kong, and the People's Republic of China, *Journal of Applied Psychology*, 77(5), 664–671.

Rowan, B. and Denk, C. (1984) Management succession, school socioeconomic context and basic skills achievement, *American Educational Research Journal*, 21(3), 17–537.

Rowan, B., Dwyer, D. and Bossert, S. (1982, March) Methodological considerations in the study of effective principals. Paper presented at the Annual Meeting of the American Educational Research Association, New York.

Schein, E. (1996) Culture: The missing concept in organization studies, *Administrative Science Quarterly*, 41, 229–240.

Scott, C. and Teddlie, C. (1987, April) Student, teacher, and principal academic expectations and attributed responsibility as predictors of student achievement: A causal modeling approach. Paper presented at the Annual Meeting of the American Educational Research Association, Washington D.C.

Senge, P. (1990) *The fifth discipline*, New York: Doubleday.

Silins, H. (1994) The relationship between transformational and transactional leadership and school improvement outcomes, *School Effectiveness and School Improvement*, 5(3), 272–298.

van de Grift, W. (1990) Educational leadership and academic achievement in elementary education, *School Effectiveness and School Improvement*, 1(3), 26–40.

van de Grift, W. (1989) Self perceptions of educational leadership and mean pupil achievements, in D. Reynolds, B.P.M. Creemers and T. Peters (eds.), *School Effectiveness and Improvement*, Cardiff/Groningen: School of Education/RION (227–242).

van de Grift, W. (1987) Zelfpercepties van onderwijskundig leiderschap, in F.J. Van der Krogt (ed.), *Schoolleiding en management* (33–42), Lisse: Swets & Zeitlinger.

Weil, M., Marshalek, B., Mitman, A., Murphy, J., Hallinger, P. and Pruyn, J. (1984, April) Effective and typical schools: How different are they? Paper presented at the annual meeting of the American Educational Research Association, Chicago.

Wong, K.C. (1996, December) Developing the moral dimensions of school leaders. Invited paper presented at the meeting of the APEC Educational Leadership Centers, Chiang Mai, Thailand.

## ACKNOWLEDGEMENT

The authors acknowledge the helpful comments of Edwin Bridges, Larry Cuban, Ken Leithwood, Joseph Murphy and George Marcoulides to earlier versions of this paper.

## SECTION 4

# RESEARCH IN EDUCATIONAL MANAGEMENT

Edited by Les Bell

# 15

---

# Educational Administration, Leadership and Management: Towards a Research Agenda

RAY BOLAM

## 1. INTRODUCTION

The tasks of re-thinking and reviewing research in this field from a British perspective have been carried out at roughly ten year intervals since the 1960s when Baron and Taylor (1969) edited what proved to be a seminal text on educational administration and the social sciences. Subsequently, Baron (1980) produced a major survey of research for the first BEMAS research conference and Saran and Trafford (1990) edited the first book on British research in education management and policy following the 1988 BEMAS research conference. Now, ten years on, the papers from the 1997–98 ESRC Seminar Series, many of which are in the present book or the special issue of the journal *Educational Management and Administration*, confirmed that, although we have undoubtedly moved on a great deal, we continue to wrestle with several important issues which have been of concern from the outset.

The next part of this chapter attempts to deal with, if not resolve, some of these apparently intractable dilemmas by offering a series of propositions about the broad field of educational administration together with some proposals for the theoretical part of a research agenda. It should also be read as an attempt at ground-clearing for the third part which proposes a thematic framework for a research agenda and priorities on school leadership with particular reference to teaching and learning. The conclusion outlines some strategic ideas about how this agenda should be carried forward. Contributions to the ESRC Seminar Series are used to illustrate the argument.

## 2. TOWARDS A CONCEPTUAL MAP

The tasks of building a research agenda and identifying priorities would be greatly facilitated by easy access to a conceptual map. Unfortunately no such map exists at present, in part because its potential scope is so broad. What follows is a contribution to the important meta-task of developing this map, a task which will have to be ongoing to take account of contextual changes.

### i  What's in a Name?

First, we should recognise and act upon the fact that three terms – educational management, leadership and administration – are in common usage and that the differences between them are far from clear, still less agreed. My own view is that the case for defining administration as the superordinate category continues to have considerable pragmatic force: it is consistent with the conceptualisation and terminology which are widely accepted internationally; it enables us to adopt a broader concept of the field, and thus to embrace policy studies as well as institutional management; and it enables us to be inclusive rather than exclusive in building a research agenda. In adopting this approach, however, we ought always to make clear which aspect of the field is under scrutiny at any one time by offering a stipulative definition from the outset.

So, in this paper I use 'educational administration' in a broad, generic sense to cover educational policy, leadership and management activities at all levels; I take 'educational leadership' to have at its core the responsibility for policy formulation and, where appropriate, organisational transformation; I take 'educational management' to refer to an executive function for carrying out agreed policy; finally, I assume that leaders normally also have some management responsibilities and that both leaders and managers must take due account of their governing body and wider context.

### ii  What Is It?

Second, I regard educational administration as a field of study and not a discipline. Like teaching and teacher education, it is essentially a practical activity and, in deciding how it should be studied and researched, we may profitably adapt the approach used by Hirst (1966) who argued convincingly that education does not have the logical characteristics of a discipline; rather, it is a field of study which draws upon several forms of knowledge and a range of disciplines. Thus, I take educational administration to be a field of study which draws upon several disciplines, mainly but not exclusively in the social sciences (e.g. sociology, political science, philosophy, history, law and psychology), and forms of knowledge (e.g. economics, general management studies, education and training and andragogy).

A second ongoing meta-task is to evaluate the usefulness of each of these disciplines and forms of knowledge for researching and understanding specific problems in educational administration.

### iii   Why Do It?

Third, we need to address some of the dilemmas and tensions around the question: what are the fundamental purposes of study and research in educational administration? Some of these have arisen because, in discussion, we often conflate and confuse our own roles and activities as members of a scholarly community whose purposes include, but are not confined to, research. I suggest that we engage in four separate projects, each with its distinctive rationale, mode of working and target audiences.

#### a.   The 'knowledge for understanding' project

The immediate aim of this project is to understand the nature and processes of educational administration, via theory building and basic research. Researchers, and lecturers, in this tradition use mainly social science-based, theory and research methodology to describe, analyse, explain and criticise. Researchers are usually funded by a research council or their own university. Typical questions are: what happens and why; and what are the most appropriate theories and methodologies for answering such questions? The outcomes are targeted mainly at peers, i.e. other theoretical researchers, applied researchers and lecturers, and outcomes are communicated mainly in reports for the funding agency and via articles in international, refereed journals, academic books and also, to a lesser extent, in professional journals and books. Although the ultimate aim may be to improve educational administration, this aim is not always 'up front' and, in any case could only be achieved indirectly by working through other people via the other projects. Lecturers engaged in this project design and teach on 'traditional', social science-based Masters and Doctoral programmes. The aim of a distinctive sub-group is to offer a critique of practice and policy:

> The point of theory and of intellectual endeavour in the social sciences should be, in Foucault's words, 'to sap power', to engage in struggle, to reveal and undermine what is most invisible and insidious in prevailing practices.
>
> (Ball, 1995, p. 267)

#### b.   The 'knowledge for action' project

The immediate aim here is to inform policy-makers and practitioners about the nature, processes and effectiveness of educational administration in order to promote its improvement. Researchers in this tradition are often funded by a government agency, may be based in a university and pursue various forms of applied research including survey, development, and evaluation research. They, too, describe, analyse and explain for understanding but, in addition, make evaluative judgements and recommendations for action. Typical questions are: how effective are various interventions and which one is most appropriate to the problem in hand?. Their proximate aim is usually to improve educational administration by working through others. Hence, the outcomes are targeted mainly at policy-makers and educational administrators, at other 'knowledge for action' researchers and lecturers and at 'instrumentalists'. Lecturers engaged in this project design and teach on 'traditional' and 'new' Masters and Doctoral programmes and on some continuing professional development (CPD) courses. Written outcomes are communicated in technical and evaluation reports and via articles in professional journals and books.

### c. The 'instrumentalist' project

The immediate aim of this project is to improve the practice and effectiveness of education managers via training and consultancy, often by providing structured schemes and practical instruments or methods. Examples include preparatory and training schemes for headteachers, often competency-based; individual-focused methods like mentoring and coaching; organisation-focused consultancies (e.g. Total Quality Management and Investors in People); and some 'new' Masters programmes, especially those with a work-based component. These training and consultancy activities are usually funded by the participants or clients themselves or by their employers. They are directly aimed at change for improvement, often utilise practitioners' experience, possibly supplemented by, but not usually rooted in, theory and research which is selected from a range of sources (e.g. social science, industrial management training, occupational psychology, adult learning), and concentrate on activities for the development and enhancement of participants' skills. A typical question is: how can this be improved? But, equally typically, it is often implicitly assumed that the trainers and consultants already have an acceptable answer to this question and so they offer prescriptive solutions, instruments or methods from the outset. The activities are targeted directly at practitioners although some outcomes, including 'training trainers' courses and published accounts in professional journals and books, may be targeted at other trainers and consultants.

### d. The 'reflexive action' project

The immediate aim of those engaged in this project is to improve their own, their team's or their organisation's, performance and effectiveness via action research, survey feedback, self-evaluation for school improvement, team building and other variants on experiential learning, reflective practice, organisation development and evidence-based practice. It is, in many ways, similar to the 'instrumentalist' project with which it shares several characteristics. Its distinctive status derives from the fact that it is self-directed and that it has now developed its own body of theories and procedures, not always entirely compatible one with another (e.g. Kolb, 1975; Schon, 1987; Schmuck and Runkel, 1985; Argyris et al., 1985; Elliott, 1991), although many of its exponents operate atheoretically and without incorporating systematic research in their action processes. Moreover, it is seen as being consistent with current initiatives to promote evidence-based practice in classroom teaching and, by extension, in school management (Cordingley, Chapter 17) although not by everyone (*vide* Eraut, Chapter 9).

These distinctions and labels are unavoidably arbitrary but the four ideal-typical projects and the typology should be judged on the basis of their utility as a heuristic. Most members of the educational administration academic community probably engage in more than one of the projects. However, each project has its own rationale and involves different activities and role requirements. The first two projects clearly involve basic and applied research, mainly social science-based, whereas the third does not. The fourth project is more problematic. Where it is implemented in an instrumentalist fashion, then it does not constitute a research activity; where it is theory-based, rigorous and open to peer scrutiny, then it does. Moreover, it also offers considerable potential for innovative research.

I suggest that research in educational administration is mainly located within the 'knowledge for understanding' (or basic) and 'knowledge for action' (or applied) projects. I propose, further, that we should continue to work on critical studies of a policy sociology kind but that, in addition, greater emphasis should be given to 'knowledge for action' research which focuses on activities within the instrumentalist and reflexive action projects and that we should explore the potential of research within the reflexive action project itself. These proposed priorities are unexceptionable if, as researchers, we are content to seek funding from a range of agencies. However, a great deal of work will be needed if proposals in the 'knowledge for action' and the 'reflexive action' projects are to be funded by the, hitherto unreceptive, Economic and Social Research Council, and thus to carry weight in the Research Assessment Exercise as it is currently structured.

### iv  Theory for Practice or Theory for Research?

We ought also to be clearer about the different purposes of theory in the practice of educational administration on the one hand, and in research into educational administration on the other. Following Aristotle, Hodgkinson (1991) distinguished between three modes of action: *theoria*, theory which abstracts and generalises by induction, deduction and hypothesis; *techne*, technique or technology which applies and interacts with theory; *praxis*, purposeful, ethical action in a political context. He went on:

> Praxis . . . clearly applies to all administration . . . [and] . . . suggests the conscious, reflective intentional action of man as opposed to mere reflex or mechanical responses to stimuli.

(p. 43)

and concluded that praxis is at the core of educational administration.

Researchers engaged in the first two 'projects' are clearly concerned with *theoria*. They see theory as an essential foundation for, and as integral to, the research process. Those engaged in the instrumentalist project are concerned with *techne* and so, too, are practitioners like heads, inspectors and key decision-makers. They take an essentially pragmatic view of theory: they want it to inform, and preferably to underpin, practice and, by extension, they want research findings to fulfil the same purposes. Those engaged in the reflexive action project are involved in *praxis* and, like the instrumentalists, take a pragmatic view of theory.

Thus, it is unsurprising that, although organisation and leadership theories designed for *theoria* or research purposes have deepened our understanding, they have provided little practical help either for school managers or their trainers (*vide* Hoyle, 1986). A research agenda should, therefore, address these two parallel problems regarding the role of theory by:

- dealing with the continuing fall-out from the presumed failure of the so-called 'New Movement' which sought to use positivist social science as the basis for research and practice in educational administration (*vide* Griffiths, 1988; Strain, 1998). This would require more explicit consideration of the appropriateness for research in educational administration of particular paradigms (e.g. positivist or interpretive) and their implications for research design and methodology, using, I suggest, 'fitness for purpose' as the main criterion;
- exploring the role of different types of theory in the instrumentalist and reflexive action projects, particularly in relation to evidence-based practice.


### v  Levels and Topics

A conceptual map of educational administration would also explicate two further components:

- Potential levels or units of analysis, for example: individual roles (e.g. teacher/lecturer, head of department, headteacher/principal/vice-chancellor); organisations (e.g. pre-school, nursery, primary, secondary and special schools, independent schools, adult and community education, youth and careers services, tertiary and FE colleges, universities); organisational sub-units (e.g. departments and teams); local education authorities and agencies; unions and professional associations; consultants and private agencies; national agencies (e.g. DfEE/WO/DENI, OFSTED/ OHMCI/ NII); political parties and politicians; international organisations and agencies (e.g. OECD; World Bank, EU).
- Major topics, topic areas and research questions, for example: the impact on educational leadership and management of personal factors (e.g. values; gender; training); major policy changes (e.g. the national curriculum, assessment, inspection, LMS, centralisation and 'new managerialism'); contextual developments (e.g. work and labour markets; governance and

accountability within a democratic context; social exclusion, inclusion and justice); changing strategic tasks (e.g. the management of induction, CPD, performance management and the use of value-added data).

### vi   Comparative Studies and Alternative Futures

Finally, the map would highlight the possibilities for informing research and practice in educational administration via comparative studies across countries, sectors and alternative futures. Thus, McEwen (1997) reported that because of administrative tasks generated by marketisation and other Northern Ireland reforms, secondary headteachers had difficulty in exercising their professional knowledge and skills, were often reluctant to delegate major leadership tasks and concentrated on low and middle order priority tasks. Crowther *et al.* (1997) reviewed research on educational leadership and site-based management in Australia, concluding that efforts to re-conceptualise leadership must take account of the complexity of site-based management and the maturity of the teaching profession in any one country. Karstanje (see Chapter 3) pointed to increasing de-centralisation in many European countries, especially those in the former Soviet bloc, as the major influence on the role and training needs of school leaders and outlined a comparative analytic framework, based on three degrees of centralisation and regulation, for researching the national and local contexts within which school headteachers in various European countries operate. Hart (1999) reviewed changes in the USA in the nature of the knowledge base and the preparation of educational leaders, concluding that we could learn from each other in clarifying and re-defining theory and re-assessing its utility for research and practice. The Seminars also included contributions focused on experience in other sectors, notably further education (FE) colleges, higher education institutions (HEIs) and private sector business which, albeit incidentally, illuminated issues in school management. Wallace (see Chapter 10) combined two theoretical perspectives – cultural and political – to analyse and explain the management strategies used by an LEA in a major reorganisation of its schools, together with the associated staff re-deployment, across the authority. Bottery (1999) argued that research should aim to help us understand and deal with future global challenges to educational management.

## 3.   A FRAMEWORK FOR RESEARCH IN EDUCATIONAL LEADERSHIP

It is against the background of this embryonic conceptual map that the following framework for a research agenda is proposed. It deals with only one part of the field, focusing exclusively on educational leadership and management in primary and secondary schools and, more specifically, on the management of teaching and learning, or pedagogy. It is organised under three thematic headings.

### i  The Management of Teaching and Learning

The management of school improvement and, more directly, of teaching and learning, emerged as key themes in the Seminars. Ouston (1999) was doubtful as to whether the emphasis on the role of the headteacher in school effectiveness and school improvement was warranted whereas Hallinger and Heck (see Chapter 14) argued that principals do contribute to student achievement, that the effect is indirect and small, though statistically significant, concluding that future research should concentrate on explaining the means whereby principals exert such influence.

Turner and Bolam (1998) used a provisional model, based on contingency theory, to analyse the role of heads of subject departments in improving teaching and learning in secondary schools, together with the factors which influence them. Cordingley (see Chapter 17) used her central concept of 'teaching as evidence-based practice' to pose a series of research questions about the role of education managers in promoting it, and proposed that education managers, too, ought to engage in evidence-based practice. She summarised her arguments thus:

> current priorities for the education management research agenda should be shaped by and accede priority to work which takes pedagogy as the starting point and which explores the capacity of education management and leadership to contribute to the improvement of teaching and learning.
>
> (p. 228)

As a priority, the research agenda should focus on the distinctive core processes of educational leadership, i.e. its linkages with, and its effects on, teaching and learning, and should explore directly the extent to which research in educational leadership can and should be carried out by practitioners and have evidence-based leadership as a desirable goal. In so doing, account should be taken of the ESRC's 'Teaching and Learning' programme (BERA, 1999) and the policy outcomes of the Green Paper proposals (Secretary of State for Education and Employment, 1998) on performance management.

### ii  Individual Characteristics and Contextual Pressures

Several papers dealt with the influence of individual characteristics and contextual pressures on heads' tasks and performance. Hall (see Chapter 12) argued that we should recognise the centrality of gender. Levačić et al. (see Chapter 2) analysed the impact of external requirements that heads should adopt a rational-technicist style. Four common themes emerged from

Southworth's study of the impact of recent policy and legislation on primary headteachers: intensification of work; increased accountability; an emphasis on school development; a range of feelings of satisfaction and dissatisfaction (see Chapter 4). Bell (see Chapter 5) concluded that, in spite of the pressures, an educational market has not fully evolved in primary schools. McMahon found that much CPD now took the form of short workshops and courses aimed at the national agenda and that, as a result, it was now extremely difficult for headteachers to use CPD to promote sustained professional learning and growth (see Chapter 8). Simkins (1999) argued that the impact of recent and current policy changes on educational management should be researched using managerialist and bureau-professional models of organisations.

It is essential that the biographies and characteristics of individual heads should continue to be researched. In a dynamic and changing national context, it is also essential that the impact of policy changes on educational management tasks and roles should be studied and that such research should recognise the interdependence of policy and practice in the provision of a public, democratically accountable service. As an illustration, strategic research questions are generated from the ways in which four sets of external change processes – the increasing centralisation of power to government and its appointed agencies, the redistribution of power amongst organisations which influence schools, the widespread adoption of 'new managerialism' style techniques and a quasi-market model of schools – impact on, for example:

- the values, vision and behaviours of educational leaders;
- organisation design, stuctures and procedures;
- professionalism, teachers' work and how these are managed;
- accountability and boundary management;
- leadership and management strategies and methods.

In addressing these questions, account should be taken of Glatter's (1999) arguments against the selective and uncritical adoption from industry of certain 'new managerialist' methods (e.g. performance management) and rejection of others (e.g. human resource development).

### iii   Training and Development for Educational Leadership

A third priority theme relates to questions about how school leaders and managers learn and how they are and might be trained and developed in general and, specifically, to promote evidence-based practice. Bolam (1997) presented an analytic and semi-historical account of recent developments in the organisation of school management training, its content and teaching methods, its underlying theory and its use of research into the professional knowledge base. Weindling (see Chapter 7) re-examined data from a series of studies of secondary headteachers over a ten year period using socialisation theory while Ribbins (see Chapter 6) explored the concept of 'leadership as a career', applying it to the development of headteachers via the NPQH. Hall (see Chapter 12) argued that adult learning theory should be central to management development. Eraut (see Chapter 9) analysed the nature of headteachers' knowledge, learning, cognition and practice, presented a critique of the national standards approach, exemplified in the National Professional Qualification for Headship (NPQH) and posed fundamental questions about the feasibility of the evidence-based practice model. Glatter (1999) proposed that CPD for educational leadership should focus on the whole job, warning against the atomisation implicit in the standards approach, that a national strategy should be pluralist not centralist, that HEIs should be given a bigger role in leadership training and that the complex issues raised by Eraut (see Chapter 9) about the learning and use of propositional and procedural knowledge are of central importance.

The research issues generated by these ideas should be pursued. In addition:

- the implications of evidence-based leadership for training and development, including studies, should be explored;
- so, too, should the potential of cognitive and problem-based approaches (Hart, 1999);
- finally, the contributions of the NPQH and related TTA programmes, including the projected National Leadership Centre and the implications of the projected introduction of performance management, should be studied and evaluated as a high priority.


## 4.  CONCLUSION

This chapter presents a preliminary conceptual map of educational administration and an outline research agenda for educational leadership in the light of the ESRC Seminar Series and other related literature. The underlying rationale for the research agenda and priorities is, in summary, that they should:

- be both reactive and proactive and, therefore, be responsive to funding initiatives as well as pursuing carefully argued priorities based on a refined conceptual map;
- aim to improve the quality and relevance of research by building on earlier work through the accumulation and replication of empirical findings and by aiming to promote school improvement, thus taking account of the issues (*vide* Hargreaves, 1997; Hammersley, 1997; Tooley and Darby, 1998; Hillage *et al.*, 1998) and policy initiatives (Sebba, 1999) generated by the wider debate on educational research;

- aim to inform policy and practice by publishing evidence-based critiques, for instance on the nature, scope and impact of 'new managerialism' and by developing and testing middle range theories;
- be grounded in a strategy based on greater collaboration and consultation with practitioners when planning and undertaking research, in improved collaboration, coordination and communication between ourselves as researchers, and in more systematic dissemination to targeted audiences, for example by using commissioned reviews of an aspect of the field.

Three caveats are offered by way of conclusion. First, it was beyond the scope of this paper to consider issues of design and methodology which, of course, are of critical importance and should be seen as integral to the development of a conceptual map. Second, the proposals are illustrative, not exhaustive and the thematic framework aims to assist researchers, practitioners and policy-makers in setting specific operational priorities in the context of available funding opportunities. Third, I have deliberately adopted a limited, even restricted, definition of educational leadership and management, locating it firmly as a sub-set of educational administration. This is essentially a technical distinction adopted primarily as a necessary, sensible step towards the production of a conceptual map of the wider field. Yet even this limited definition generates a host of important and difficult research topics and questions. Moreover, it enables us to be critical, to be explicit about our value positions and to collaborate with policy sociologists and others in the 'knowledge for understanding' project in order to 'speak truth to power' (Fitz, 1999). Equally important, as we collectively seek to improve education within the 'knowledge for action', 'instrumentalist' and 'reflexive action' projects, it also enables, and arguably requires, us to offer truthful empowerment to practitioners and policy-makers.

## REFERENCES

Argyris, C., Putnam R. and McLain Smith, D. (1985) *Action Science*, London: Jossey Bass.

Ball, S. (1995) Intellectuals or technicians? The urgent role of theory in educational studies, *British Journal of Educational Studies* 43, 255–271.

Baron, G. and Taylor W. (eds.) (1969) *Educational Administration and the Social Sciences*, London: Athlone.

Baron, G. (1980) Research in educational administration in Britain, *Educational Administration 8.1*.1–33.

Bolam, R. (1997) Management development for headteachers: retrospect and prospect, *Educational Management and Administration* 25(3), 265–283.

Bottery, M. (1999) 'Rowing the boat' and 'Riding the bicycle' – metaphors for school management and policy in the late 1990s?, *Educational Management and Administration*, forthcoming.

British Educational Research Association (1999) News of the ESRC Teaching and

Learning research programme, *Research Intelligence* 67, 21.

Crowther, F., Gronn, P. and Townsend, T. (1997) Leadership and site-based management: underlying assumptions. Paper presented at the ESRC Seminar Series 'Redefining Educational Management: Leicester June 1997.

Elliott, J. (1991) Competency-based training and the education of the professions: is a happy marriage possible? in Elliott, J. *Action Research for Educational Change*, Buckingham: Open University Press.

Fitz, J. (1999) Researching restructuring – problems and prospects for educational management studies, *Educational Management and Administration*, forthcoming.

Glatter, R. (1999) Reconceptualising educational management, *Educational Management and Administration*, forthcoming.

Griffiths, D. (1988) Administrative theory, in N. J. Boyan (ed.) *Handbook of Research on Educational Administration*, London: Longman.

Hammersley, M. (1997) Educational research and teaching: a response to David Hargreaves' TTA lecture, *British Educational Research Journal 23.2*, 141–62.

Hargreaves, D. H. (1997) In defence of research for evidence-based teaching: a rejoinder to Martyn Hammersley, *British Educational Research Journal 23.4*, 405–19.

Hart, A. (1999) The state of the field in the USA, *Educational Management and Administration*, forthcoming.

Hillage, J., Pearson, R., Anderson, A., Tamkin, P. (1998) *Excellence in Research on Schools,* Suffolk: DFEE Publications.

Hirst, P. (1966) The logical and psychological aspects of teaching a subject, in R. S. Peters (ed.) *The Concept of Education*, London: Routledge & Kegan Paul.

Hodgkinson, C. (1991) *Educational Leadership: The moral art*, Albany NY: State University of New York Press.

Hoyle, E. (1986) *The Politics of School Management*, London: Routledge.

Kolb, D. A. (1975) *Experimental Learning*, London: Prentice Hall.

McEwen, A. (1997) Management and values: the changing role of the secondary headteacher. Paper presented at the ESRC Seminar Series 'Redefining Educational Management', Cardiff, October.

Saran, R. and Trafford, V. (eds.) (1990) *Research in Education Management and Policy: Retrospect and prospect*, Lewes: The Falmer Press.

Schmuck, R. and Runkel, P. (1985) *The Handbook of Organisation Development in Schools*, Palo Alto and London: Mayfield.

Schon, D. A. (1987) *Educating the Reflective Practitioner: Towards a new design for teaching and learning in the professions*, London: Jossey Bass.

Sebba, J. (1999) Educational research: developing and implementing the Government's action plan, *Research Intelligence* 67, 19–20.

Secretary of State for Education and Employment (1998) *Teachers: Meeting the challenge of change*, Sudbury, Suffolk: Department for Education and Employment, Publications Centre.

Simkins, T. (1999) Values, power and instrumentality: Theory and research in educational management, *Educational Management and Administration*, forthcoming..

Strain, M. (1998) Educational managers' knowledge: The quest for useful theory, in M. Strain, B. Dennison, J. Ouston and V. Hall (eds) *Policy Leadership and Professional Knowledge in Education*, London: Paul Chapman Publishing Ltd.

Tooley, J. and Darby, D. (1998) *Education Research: An OFSTED critique*, London: OFSTED.

Turner, C. and Bolam, R. (1998) Analysing the role of the subject head of department in secondary schools in England and Wales: Towards a theoretical framework, *School Leadership and Management 18.3*, 373–88.

# 16

# Overview of a Group of Research Projects with Relevance to School Management

## MIKE WALLACE AND DICK WEINDLING

Managing schools is not what it used to be. Central government reforms over the past decade or so have given rise to many new management tasks alongside significant changes in those that existed before, and the pace of reform shows no sign of abating as the present British government delivers the Prime Minister's pre-election promise to prioritise 'education, education, education'. Global forces place unrelenting pressure on central government politicians to drive up standards in the interest of increasing competitiveness in the world economy. The 'new modernisers' (Bottery, 1999) dominating the present British government have eschewed reliance on their predecessors' reforms which brought in market forces to steer education loosely from a distance. 'Power-assisted steering' through a combination of mandate, target, surveillance and corrective action is now the name of the education game. Though whether education is being steered in a 'profitable' direction remains deeply contentious.

The business of researching, conceptualising, and informing practice in education management is not what it used to be either. For many researchers concerned with whose ideologies win out in the refashioning of education policy, applying principles of the 'new public management' (Foster and Plowden, 1996) to education, where more must be delivered for less in the new market to win parental favour, amounts to unwarranted 'managerialism' (e.g. Grace, 1995; Menter *et al.*, 1997; Whitty *et al.*, 1998). The increase in school autonomy and diversity much trumpeted by the past government is regarded as a sleight of hand, belying the centralising tendency of reforms which actually expand the ability of central government ministers to 'steer at a distance'. (The present government has, arguably, exchanged sleight of hand for the heavy hand of overt centralisation.) For some academics more concerned with how to manage schools in the new policy context, education reforms have been viewed as a source of managerial liberation, enhancing the ability of headteachers and governors to shape provision offered in their 'self-managing' school (e.g. Davies and Ellison, 1997; Davies and West-Burnham, 1997). Yet many researchers reject an explictly evaluative stance, whether concentrating on patterns in the policy process at national level, patterns in teaching, learning and management at the institution level, or linkage between policy making and what happens on the ground.

Evidently, changing practice in schools is contributing to the academic market in ideas about what is or should be happening in educational management. To inform the ongoing debate which is redefining this field, we consider what may be learned from our recent review of research projects designed to disseminate practical implications of their findings for leadership and management in schools. Our purposes in this chapter are: first, to highlight emergent cross-project themes about the impact of national reforms and promising directions for efforts to improve management practice; and second, to reflect on implications of the content and conceptual orientations of these projects for a new research agenda and theoretical development in the field.

## SCOPE OF THE REVIEW

In April 1996 the Research Grants Board of the Economic and Social Research Council (ESRC) – the British central government agency which funds social science research – commissioned us to review completed projects with relevance to school management. We were asked to produce a booklet summarising key findings of the projects to disseminate this ESRC work to a 'non-academic user' audience. The Board funds research in a responsive and incremental, rather than programmatic, manner: individuals put forward unsolicited proposals based on their research interests and about one in five are supported. The theme of 'school management' identified by Board members therefore necessitated a selection being made from projects addressing disparate topics. ESRC officials made an initial choice of 20 awards and furnished us with the final report for each. We selected 15 projects (two entailing two awards) which appeared to have most relevance to school management practice. Award holders were invited to send us copies of publications arising from the projects and to comment on our draft summary of their project findings and management implications which we had based on their publications and final project report.

The booklet (Wallace and Weindling, 1997) was disseminated by the ESRC in spring 1997. Table 16.1 summarises the titles and dates of the 15 projects, and gives bibliographic information to which reference may be made for further details of each project. They are grouped according to the management implications of their focus: six projects were relevant to managing teaching and learning, of which three investigated aspects of the curriculum and its assessment and three examined issues connected with educational needs of particular groups of pupils. The other nine projects were more relevant to managing conditions necessary to promote teaching and learning: two

**Table 16.1** *The 15 research projects reviewed which had relevance to school management*

| Management relevance | Management task area | Project title/focus | Period of funding | A key publication (names of award holders are highlighted in bold) |
|---|---|---|---|---|
| **Managing teaching and learning** | *Curriculum and assessment* | National assessment in primary schools | 1990–93 | **Gipps, C, Brown, M**, McCallum, B and McAlister, S (1995) *Intuition or Evidence: teachers and national assessment of seven year olds* Buckingham: Open University Press |
| | | The implementation of the National Curriculum in clusters of small rural schools | 1992–94 | **Hargreaves, L**, Comber, C and **Galton, M** (1996) The National Curriculum: can small schools deliver? Confidence and competence levels of teachers in small rural schools *British Educational Research Journal* 22, 1: 89–99 |
| | | Differential school effectiveness: departmental variation in GCSE attainment | 1993–95 | **Sammons, P, Thomas, S and Mortimore, P** (1997) *Forging Links: effective schools and effective departments* London: Paul Chapman |
| | *Pupil needs* | Factors influencing the progress of below average pupils in more and less effective schools | 1992–95 | **Brown, S, Riddell, S** and Duffield, J (1996) Responding to pressures: a study of four secondary schools, in Woods, P (ed) *Contemporary Issues in Teaching and Learning* London: Routledge |
| | | Children excluded from school: policies and practices in England and Wales | 1993–95 | **Hayden, C** (1997) *Children excluded from primary school: the debates, the evidence, the responses* Buckingham: Open University Press |
| | | Local management of schools and provision for special educational needs | 1992–94 | Vincent, C, **Evans, J, Lunt, I and Young, P** (1995) Policy and practice: the changing nature of special educational provision in schools, *British Journal of Special Education*, 22, 1: 4-11 |
| **Promoting conditions for effective teaching and learning** | *Staff and governors* | The role of the senior management team in secondary schools | 1991-92 | **Wallace, M** and Hall, V (1994) *Inside the SMT: team approaches to secondary school management* London: Paul Chapman |
| | | Reforming school governing bodies | 1988-93 | **Deem, R, Brehony, K J** and Heath, S (1995) *Active Citizenship and the Governing of Schools* Buckingham: Open University Press |

| | | | |
|---|---|---|---|
| **The market** | The operation and effects of markets in secondary education | 1991–94 | Gewirtz, S, **Ball, S J and Bowe, R** (1995) *Markets, Choice and Equity in Education* Buckingham: Open University Press |
| | Parents and school choice interaction (two awards) | 1990–95 | **Glatter, R,** Woods, P and Bagley, C (1997) *Choice and Diversity in Schooling: perspectives on secondary schooling* London: Routledge |
| **Resources** | The effects of the Education Reform Act's formula funding on the resourcing of schools | 1989–92 | **Levačić, R** (1995) *Local Management of Schools: analysis and practice* Buckingham: Open University Press |
| | Innovatory staffing practices in city technology colleges | 1993–95 | **Mortimore, J and Mortimore, P** (1996) Policy into practice: staffing innovations in CTCs, in Bernstein, B and Brannen, J (eds) *Children, Research and Policy* London: Taylor and Francis |
| **School development** | The impact of school development planning in primary schools | 1992–94 | **MacGilchrist, B, Mortimore, P,** Savage, J and Beresford, C (1995) *Planning Matters: the impact of development planning in primary schools* London: Paul Chapman |
| | Grant maintained schools policy (two awards) | 1989–94 | **Fitz, J, Halpin, D** and Power, S (1993) *Grant Maintained Schools: education in the marketplace* London: Kogan Page |
| | Programmes to assess the quality of schools | 1992–94 | Wilcox, B and **Gray, J** (1996) *Inspecting Schools: holding schools to account and helping schools to improve* Buckingham: Open University Press |

concerned staff or governors; two looked at the nature of the new education market; two related to management of resources; and three dealt with aspects of institutional development.

Limitations following from the timing, span and purpose of the review should be borne in mind. First, findings inevitably relate to the stage of implementation of reforms reached when fieldwork was completed. Events since 1995 – not least the arrival of a new central government aiming to build on its predecessor's reforms with its own education agenda – mean that they may have variable applicability to the current context. Second, the review excludes ESRC funded projects for which no final report was available by mid-1996. Third, it does not encompass the range of concurrent research not sponsored by the ESRC, much of which was more directly focused on school management. The review should not, therefore, be taken to represent all substantial projects of the time. Finally, its practical thrust precluded more academic concerns being addressed.

In the remainder of the chapter we first present practical school management themes featuring in the booklet, indicating how national reforms had impacted on school leadership and management and suggesting ways of improving managerial effectiveness. Next we consider the content of the projects as a group, including their range of focus, researchers' value orientation, and gaps in coverage, leading to suggestions for further research. Finally, we examine the diversity of approaches towards theorising the investigations and the variety of their conceptual content, and speculate on their implications for development and testing of theory.

## PRACTICAL MESSAGES OF THE RESEARCH

The search for patterns across the 15 projects yielded six themes indicating how central government reforms had affected school leadership and management during the first half of the 1990s.

1. *Headteachers continue to play a pivotal role in leadership and management.*

All projects indicated that headteachers' authority for day-to-day running of the school meant they shouldered unique responsibility for orchestrating changes in response to reforms and harnessing support of other staff and governors.

2. *There have been changes in almost every management task area.*

These changes entailed either the requirement to carry out new tasks (like managing a budget and appraising staff) or to make changes in familiar ones (such as managing the curriculum and catering for pupils with special educational needs).

3. *A new and varied range of stakeholders is centrally involved in managing schools, with consequent changes in working relationships between them.*

The reforms had altered the balance of authority between school staff, governing bodies, local education authorities (LEAs) and central government. It had become imperative to forge new ways of working through a variety of partnerships: within schools, as with senior management teams; between school staff and governors; among neighbouring schools, as in cluster arrangements; between the various agencies associated with exclusion of pupils from schools; and with OFSTED inspectors and central government officials.

4. *There is greater mutual dependence between those responsible for and affected by management, requiring a substantial degree of participation.*

The various partners must not only make an input but also develop their ability to collaborate in making and implementing decisions.

5. *There is a positive role for LEAs in supporting school leadership and management.*

Services which LEA staff were well placed to provide ranged from offering training and information support to LEA and grant maintained schools, through participation of LEA teams in OFSTED inspections, to facilitating management tasks like development planning and school improvement.

6. *School leaders face a widening range of ethical dilemmas.*

Many reforms increased the number of choices which school leaders have to make with implications for social justice, whether relating to educational values (such as under what circumstances to exclude pupils) or political values (like how far to seek a competitive edge by attracting pupils from neighbouring schools). Others affected their managerial values (for example how closely to involve governors in oversight of teaching and learning in the school).

Conversely, the impact of reforms was bounded. Despite evidence of widespread implementation, they had not necessarily achieved stated central government aims. The way schools were managed in responding to these reforms also influenced their impact: there had been limited development of market research and marketing in schools, even in urban areas where a quasi-market had been established; and the potential of grant maintained schools to increase the diversity of educational opportunities had not been fully realised.

That said, the overall impact of reforms on school management had been profound by 1995: multiple changes had projected headteachers into building a new network of relationships. The declining significance of LEAs, apart from their role in implementating reforms in schools, was offset by the increasing importance of other local stakeholders. Management activity was dominated by the over-riding task of coping with reform overload. It was compounded by frequent updating of central government reform policies which precipitated extensive interaction within the new configuration of partners in schooling.

A second set of themes consisted of prescriptions suggested by the project findings for improving the effectiveness of school leadership and management. The first four concerned potentially constraining factors that should be taken into account:

1. *Local and school contexts, including the recent history of management practice, have a highly significant effect on school management and improvement activity.*

Headteachers should reflect on any general recommendations in the light of local circumstances and avoid advocating universal 'quick-fix' solutions.

2. *Managing change is a long, difficult and often unpredictable process.*

Sufficient time must be allowed, whether implementing recommendations of an OFSTED inspection, developing voluntary school clusters, or promoting teamwork.

3. *Effective school management implies addressing ethical dilemmas in the attempt to justify managerial actions.*

Examples of value laden issues include whether to encourage wide participation among school staff in decision-making, or remove educational injustice (as in the case of discrimination against pupils from certain ethnic backgrounds or with special educational needs).

4. *Inequity of LMS funding between phases and types of school imposes constraints on managers of those that are least well resourced.*

Primary sector LEA maintained schools had less flexibility over staffing and releasing managers during the school day than their secondary or grant maintained school counterparts.

The remaining themes suggested fruitful avenues to be explored:

5. *Managers should focus simultaneously on improving management procedures and improving teaching and learning.*

Priority must be given both to developing the ability of school staff and other partners to work together towards shared goals, and to identifying and meeting needs of all pupils.

6. *The task of monitoring the performance of the school may benefit both from capitalising on the requirement to gather a variety of information and from collecting additional data.*

Examples included analysing assessment and examination data to inform teaching, tracking implementation of school development plans, or conducting market research to gauge parents' concerns.

7. *Where LMS allows flexibility over deployment of teaching and associate staff, a greater diversity of appointments should be made.*

Priorities for new types of appointment might include staff, like bursars, who can support school managers.

8. *External support, especially in the form of training, is particularly significant for those carrying out new tasks including collaborating in teams or partnerships.*

Key groups included heads of department to whom more was now delegated under LMS, governors whose awareness might need raising about the importance of avoiding sexism and racism, or senior staff managing implementation of an action plan following inspection.

Project findings implied that improving leadership and management in a context of continual but disjointed multiple change requires present and future school leaders to be geared up for career-long professional learning. Their management development can be facilitated both by formal training and informal support. Headteachers are not only centrally responsible for school leadership and management, but they are also uniquely placed to foster other partners' learning. Their aim should be to create a 'learning partnership' among staff, parents, pupils, governors, and representatives of other agencies with a stake in school management. Policy-makers must therefore continue to prioritise identifying and meeting the learning needs of headteachers – especially those who are new to the job – in their role as both managers and facilitators of others' learning.

## SUBSTANTIVE COVERAGE OF PROJECTS: INFORMING CONSIDERATION OF A RESEARCH AGENDA

The spread of topics addressed across the projects gives rise to several issues which may inform consideration of directions for future research on school management. First, as a group they tell us demonstrably more about the early implementation of reforms of the past Conservative central government than they do about school leadership and management tasks either then or now. Management structures and tasks were the central focus for one project alone: a study of secondary school senior management teams. In the remaining 14, the main concern was to trace the impact of particular reforms introduced between 1986 and 1995 – rather than how to manage them – or to identify factors impinging on effectiveness of pupil learning in secondary schools. Given that most projects were never designed as management studies, it is not surprising that their focus on relevant management activity was limited. Coverage excluded reforms like managing staff appraisal and development, and managing support for pupils from minority ethnic groups under changed central government funding arrangements.

Gaps in our research knowledge of management practice by the mid-1990s have since widened further with the new wave of national reforms, especially in primary schools which are being so heavily targeted. Arguably other research, whether ESRC sponsored or not, has done relatively little to bridge this gap. Priorities for future research into education management (in whatever sector) should include a focus on managing change: implementation of individual reforms; subsequently managing institutions in the context of these reforms if and when they become institutionalised; and, perennially, managing an evolving profile of multiple reforms. Other changes, like the integration of new information and communications technology into school management practice, should also be high on the priority list. By implication, there is a need for a related focus on the socialisation and development of school leaders and middle managers who have to develop the capacity to work in such an environment.

A second and related issue concerns the variability of gaps in our research knowledge of institutional management practice in different phases of schooling. While the group of projects addressed both primary and secondary schools, more attention (including the one management study) was given to the latter. There has yet to be a major funded study of primary school headship (Hall and Southworth, 1997); management in 'minority' sectors such as institutions for pre-school provision, special schools and independent schools remains to be thoroughly researched.

The third issue concerns how far project researchers expressed their values about reforms and management, with consequences for the claims they made. In eight projects, investigators took an explicit value stance towards management practice related to the reforms they explored. The researchers for four of these investigations apparently held a negative stance towards the reforms which was reflected in the findings and their critical interpretation, while researchers for the other four appeared to adopt a more positive attitude towards the reforms and evaluated findings positively and negatively according to their assumptions about good practice. In the remaining seven projects, the researchers did not adopt an explicit value orientation (in accord with the value of impartiality) towards either reforms or associated management practice, but in five cases they highlighted and explored the value laden nature of management. This diversity reflects the researchers' different methodological and political allegiances. While it is widely accepted that no researcher can be value neutral in an absolute sense, there are differences in degrees of impartiality or value commitment with direct consequences for selection of priorities for the focus of enquiry and the audience to whom interpretations will be addressed. Part of the process of identifying a research agenda must be to account for researchers' educational, managerial and political values and how far they should have a place in prioritising research topics, focusing investigation, evaluating findings, and communicating to the intended audience.

Fourth, there was a dearth of studies focusing on development of individual or group managerial competence and associated learning support. A priority for future research should be the socialisation and professional learning of headteachers, since they were singled out as key figures in most projects. Others might fruitfully include impact of governor training; forms of external support from LEA staff and consultants; development of middle managers; managing emergent partnerships between schools; and evaluation of LEA supported improvement projects.

Fifth, the sense that these projects are already dated because policy and practice have moved on underlines the need for longitudinal studies that are capable of tracking the interpenetration of changes in management practice and related policy over the five-year lifespan of a single government at least. Fieldwork for most projects was completed in less than three years, exceptions being where two awards were made. There is a case for designing more 'long thin' projects, given likely funding restrictions, which sample evolving management activity in a small number of sites over a lengthy period.

## THEORETICAL ORIENTATIONS: THE NEED FOR CONCEPTUAL DEVELOPMENT

As might be expected with independently conceived projects grouped after the event, there was striking diversity both in approaches to adoption and development of explanatory frameworks and in their content. An important consideration for the attempt to redefine the field is the degree to which it is feasible and desirable to work towards more coherent conceptual development. We identified four heuristic categories of conceptualisation occurring before and after data collection and analysed their application to the projects, suggesting patterns with implications for theory development and testing:

1. initial conceptualisation that guides data collection

a) adopting an existing explanatory theory or broad perspective
b) adopting one or more existing descriptive typologies or models

2. conceptualisation after data collection

a) developing a descriptive or analytic typology, model or set of factors into which findings are grouped
b) developing explanatory theory to interpret findings and relate them to a broad theoretical perspective.

The categories are not mutually exclusive, and the studies varied between two extremes: in one case no conceptualisation was either adopted or developed; on the other hand two projects took existing theory as a starting point and, in the light of data collection, developed related typologies and incorporated them in working towards a refined explanatory theory. There was a strong correlation between one quite widely employed approach to conceptualisation and the adoption of an explicit negative value stance towards particular reforms and related management practice. Amongst six projects where a positive or negative value stance was articulated, an existing theory or typology was adopted at the outset. Yet no conceptualisation was developed in the light of the findings in five cases and, in the sixth, such conceptualisation was limited to the development of a simple typology. It appears that the aim of this approach was more to support an evaluative interpretation of findings according to a pre-specified conceptual framework and value stance than to test or refine theory.

In three projects, data collection was undertaken without prior conceptualisation, and the typology, list of factors or theory developed was subsequently linked with existing research and theoretical literature. In the remainder, there was a variable degree of conceptualisation both before and after data collection. Two projects entailed adoption of a typology which was later refined. Three were more ambitious, adopting a perspective and developing a typology which in two cases were linked to, and served to refine, this theoretical orientation. None of the projects was designed primarily to test an existing theory or typology.

The diversity of approaches to conceptualisation was matched by diversity in the content of theories and typologies employed or developed. While the different orientations are not necessarily incompatible, they do not appear to have mutually informed the different investigations. There was, for example, varying emphasis on power, professional culture, marketisation and the management of single innovations, yet only a few researchers attempted to combine concepts drawn from different traditions (as in the the the dual cultural and political perspective adopted in the study of secondary school senior management teams). The diverse orientations of the studies may also reflect underdevelopment of middle range theories in the field of educational management, there being limited coherence between those that exist.

The conceptual fragmentation of these projects suggests that the attempt to redefine the field of educational management gives rise to urgent conceptual issues: first, there is an obvious need for conceptual mapping and synthesis amongst the diverse conceptualisations which exist in this field, insofar as they can be rendered compatible. Second, the policy focus of several projects, with links made to wider public policy and management, belied some conceptual myopia – little use was made of concepts developed in such cognate fields. There is a need for deeper consideration of the applicability of theories in related areas including other public sector domains and private sector management.

## A CASE FOR MORE PROGRAMMATIC DEVELOPMENT OF THE FIELD?

The group of projects clearly indicates that educational management in the schools sector has changed as a result of central government reforms. It falls short, however, of providing a comprehensive picture of management in the present context where implementation of most of the reforms investigated has continued for several years since particular projects ended and new reforms have been unleashed. Divergence among researchers over whether to adopt an explicit positive or negative value stance towards reforms and management practice suggests that different researchers investigating similar phenomena will give prominence to different findings and give them a different conceptual spin.

Incremental funding of independent projects appears here to have militated against convergence of approaches leading to development of a coherent theory of educational management, let alone its potential link with general management theory. A rather disjointed picture emerges which mirrors the divide mentioned at the beginning of this chapter between researchers seeking to inform policy-makers but little concerned with implications of their often highly critical analyses for management on the ground; researchers into institutional management who wish to speak to practitioners but are little concerned with policy and economic conditions lying behind changes in practice; and those who focus on the mediation between practice and policy. Certainly, there is a good case for more policy aware management studies and policy focused research which speaks to practitioners as well as policy-makers – no manager is an island, nor any policy more than a bunch of policy texts without managers.

A promising alternative to incremental support for individual projects would be to mount a more programmatic strategy (see the chapter by Bolam in this volume), developing conceptually linked projects with a similar approach towards conceptualisation and concern with the interrelationship between practice and policy. It might seem a tall order in a field marked by incompatible educational, methodological and political value commitments among researchers to expect them to share in the same enterprise. Yet with constructively critical dialogue and mutual compromise a programmatic strategy might bring about real improvement to the field and so, let us hope, to the way education is steered and the direction in which it is pointed.

## REFERENCES

Bottery, M. (1999) 'Rowing the boat' or 'riding the bicycle' – metaphors for school management and policy in the late 1990s?, *Educational Management and Administration* (forthcoming).

Davies, B. and Ellison, L. (1997) *School Leadership for the 21st Century: A competency and knowledge approach*, London: Routledge.

Davies, B. and West-Burnham, J. (eds.) (1997) *Reengineering and Total Quality in Schools*, London: Pitman.

Foster, C. and Plowden, F. (1996) *The State under Stress*, Buckingham: Open University Press.

Grace, G. (1995) *School Leadership: Beyond educational management*, London: Falmer Press.

Hall, V. and Southworth, G. (1997) Headship: State of the art review, *School Leadership and Management*, 12, 2: 151–70.

Menter, I., Muschamp, Y., Nicholls, P. and Ozga, J. with Pollard, A. (1997) *Work and Identity in the Primary School: A post-Fordist analysis*, Buckingham: Open University Press.

Wallace, M. and Weindling, D. (1997) *Managing Schools in the Post-Reform Era: Messages of recent research*, Cardiff: Cardiff University for the Economic and Social Research Council.

Whitty, G., Power, S. and Halpin, D. (1998) *Devolution and Choice in Education: The school, the state and the market*, Buckingham: Open University Press.

# 17

## Pedagogy, Educational Management and the TTA Research Agenda

### PHILIPPA CORDINGLEY

### THE TTA STARTING POINT

The TTA's focus is pedagogy. TTA's core priority in relation to school management is helping teachers to improve teaching and learning so that pupils achieve more. These values drive all of TTA's work including its research work and its views of the research agenda.

In the research context the TTA focus on pedagogy has sometimes been challenged and sometimes been welcomed. The most intense challenge comes from those who feel that a focus on pedagogy ignores learning. For TTA, focusing on teaching simply does not make sense if it takes learning out of the equation. Research which can help us to improve the quality of teaching must focus on both the quality of the teachers' work and the quality of pupils' learning experience and outcomes. The polarisation of teaching and learning may well have started from a legitimate desire to move away from transmission models of teaching which failed to focus on learning but, in too much educational research, the pendulum has swung too far. The detailed knowledge, understanding, skills and beliefs which govern teachers' actions in classrooms too often remain invisible in research reports. It is as though many researchers have looked out of teachers' eyes and fastened on to the complexities of the curriculum and pupils' learning processes and achievements but failed to record, analyse, communicate or in research terms, problematise, the teachers' contribution. This is particularly true of much teacher research and some TTA reflections on this are explored in more detail in the consultation paper, *Off the Shelf* (TTA, 1998b), about its attempts to provide small grants for the dissemination of MA and PhD work done by teachers.

Of course, the TTA recognise there are other fields of enquiry which can and should shape the education management research agenda. For example, the school improvement movement has focused upon management and leadership, although in pursuing whole school effects and improvement programmes it has only recently begun to reach into classrooms to explore the complexities of what managers and leaders in schools can do to improve the quality of teaching and learning. There is also a good deal of evidence and literature from the direct study of school management and leadership.

The TTA's view is that the systematic study of school management and leadership has been significantly greater in volume than the study of pedagogy, in response, for example, to the school management reforms of the late 1980s and to the literature and empirical evidence about management and leadership in other fields. But, as was perhaps inevitable, the response to a sudden and rapid increase in administrative and management tasks in the late 1980s was to focus upon policies, continuing professional development and research activities geared to support school managers and leaders with their new responsibilities. But managing budgets, school plant and staffing structures are a means to an end rather than an end in themselves. In the context of an infrastructure of headteachers and senior managers well able to understand, undertake and even conceptualise such tasks there is now a need to refocus attention on their purpose. Managing budgets and bidding for and attracting resources skillfully means managing them so that they provide a springboard for the development of teaching and learning. Managing quality assurance processes and even attaining external validation for these, as in the case of IIP or Charter marks, is only useful in so far as the processes are bent to the core goals and values of the school; to improve teaching and learning. Headteachers and their senior colleagues turning to research in this context may well be served with literature and evidence about the internal logic of the management processes. They seem to be much less well supported in connecting such processes to pedagogy. Here again, too much of the research stops short at the classroom door. Just as the term pedagogy should not separate teaching and learning, effective thinking about school management and leadership should not be separated from the core work of leading, challenging, monitoring and developing the classroom work of teachers.

It is the imbalance and disconnection between pedagogic and other research which has led TTA to try to place a spotlight on pedagogic research and evidence. There is now a ground swell of interest in what research and evidence can contribute to teaching and learning. The Department for Education and Employment (DfEE) funded Review of Education Research (1998), the establishment of the ESRC Teaching and Learning Programme and the coverage of education research issues in the popular press all suggest that there has never been a time when more attention has been paid to education research. The climate for education management research for the first five years of the new millennium is likely to be favourable – provided that it genuinely responds to the needs of school leaders and managers who are focused on improving teaching and learning in order to raise standards. In the following section I summarise the kinds of research issues and questions relevant to managing and leading pedagogy which teachers and headteachers have raised with TTA as priorities for research over the next ten years.

## AN EARLY PICTURE OF TEACHER PERCEPTIONS OF
## RESEARCH PRIORITIES

First of all the teachers we have worked with want research which focuses on the detailed characteristics of effective teachers and teaching. This is not to say they want detailed solutions to detailed problems; they know there are no single bullets and that they will have to interpret complex findings for their own settings. But they do believe that the finer grained the data, the easier it is for them to understand it, use it and connect it with their own experiences. Questioning skills, in particular probing and open questioning are very common examples of the detailed focus these teachers are seeking.

Those with leadership responsibilities similarly express a keen interest in understanding the kinds of knowledge and experience which shape teachers' choices of teaching strategies and their effectiveness in using them. They seek detailed examples of the characteristics of programmes which impact observably on teaching and learning. They don't just want to know about teaching but also about teachers.

In seeking detailed findings teachers and their leaders are not opposed to theory. Rather they want theory which is linked to practice and they want to see this illustrated in concrete ways with vivid and annotated examples of classroom practice so that they can unpack what lies beneath the surface.

Finally, in generic terms, they want research which is credible. If teachers are to embark on the process of reviewing and increasing existing knowledge and skills in order to take on board new ideas they need to be convinced it will be worth the labour, uncertainty and discomfort. For those we have worked with, this means relating qualitative findings and case studies to empirical evidence about learning gain, because helping pupils to achieve more is what they believe teachers are all about.

These research priorities are of course to do with the genre of research and key types of data to be collected, as much as its focus. It is much harder to discern clear patterns amongst those we consult in terms of priority curriculum areas, not least because of the small numbers consulted so far (only 500 or so) and the wide range of phases, subjects and responsibilities they support. Nonetheless, there is a clear and particular desire for research of the type described above in relation to: literacy, special educational needs, effective models of professional development, numeracy, technology and overcoming disaffection.

## THE POTENTIAL CONTRIBUTION OF RESEARCH TO
## MANAGING SCHOOLS

The job of making use of such work, even when it is funded and reported in teacher-friendly ways remains a challenging task. TTA takes a very particular stance to teacher use of research and evidence in promoting teaching as a research and evidence based profession. Its aim is highly focused on what research can do to help teachers improve their teaching and so help pupils attain more. Its basis is an analysis and interpretation of the research literature. In the next section of this chapter I shall illustrate this, show how this informs the TTA research agenda and try to show how the education management research agenda can contribute to and be informed by this approach. The context for this analysis is an emphasis on both management and leadership which interprets leadership as focusing on the values of headteachers and management as focusing on their day-to-day tasks. The key questions relate to the ways in which these values and tasks support and contribute to a passionate concern for classrooms standards and pupil achievement.

Teaching in any context is a complex business. It includes fast-paced interactions between teacher, learner, content, environment and teaching strategies. School teaching adds to such complexities the need to teach large numbers of pupils with wide-ranging social, cultural, economic, educational and intellectual starting points within the framework of a common and sustained curriculum. Multiple variables interact dynamically and at a quite startling pace. Charles Desforges (1995) has shown that, in the face of such complexity, teachers attempt to return classrooms to the status quo. In other words they try to hold some of these variables constant. This can be interpreted as resistance to change or, as a creative strategy which frees teachers to concentrate upon those aspects of teaching and learning most likely to meet the needs of the pupils in that particular class at that particular point in time. In all its research work TTA is seeking to ensure that teachers are able to work within the latter framework, with the support of high quality research evidence which enables them to make such judgements as objectively as possible. But we recognise that there is much to do to achieve this in terms of developing both the supply of research and in developing discerning demand for and use of it.

Another research model which informs our work is David Hargreaves' (1991) work on a practical, common sense model of teaching. This develops the notion of teachers controlling variables as a coping strategy, by identifying the ways in which they gradually widen their conception of their roles. It suggests teachers move from working as beginning teachers controlling as many variables as possible in order, for example, to maintain control, to becoming expert teachers able and willing to introduce, respond to and interpret variables relating to other pupils, other areas of the curriculum, whole school policies, local community needs and so on. This model raises interesting questions about how teachers, and especially teachers who manage and lead other teachers, can sharpen up the process of recognising, responding to and managing the variables in the ways which most effectively promote learning. There may be two routes to exploring these issues. It is certainly possible to explore the management questions involved. The TTA Research Committee chooses, rather, to give priority to answering the pedagogic questions involved. This is not to say that the pedagogic questions are or can be divorced from their management counterparts. It is to propose that the best approach to the management question is through the pedagogic problems managers must address.

For example, the Kings College, Effective Teachers of Numeracy Project (Askew *et al.*, 1998) funded by TTA provided vivid examples of teachers deliberately introducing wide-ranging pupil starting points in whole class teaching about numeracy. The report shows how the teachers were able to take the risk that the class discussion would roam freely – away from their learning goal – because their knowledge of the number system was so secure that they knew they could make connections between the pupils' mathematical ideas and experiences and continually connect these to lesson goals. In exploring how the teachers came to be able to work this way, the project also explored in some detail the roles of subject co-ordinators, joint planning and teacher development, thus illuminating management issues from a pedagogic starting point. This is just one example of a contribution to the body of knowledge about education management which flows directly from a focus on pedagogy and enables connections between the two, over-separated, fields.

There is one particular aspect of the Kings Study (Askew *et al.*, 1998) highlighted here which lies at the heart of TTA's research work, that of the need for in-depth, internalised knowledge. The effective teachers of numeracy needed not just deep understanding of the number system in order to encourage and work with pupils from their own starting points, they needed to internalise such knowledge in order to deploy it freely and responsively whilst maintaining their pedagogic purpose.

The significance of effective teachers' internalised knowledge, for this paper, lies in:

- its implications for what is needed to develop such knowledge;
- the role which research can and should play in developing teachers' knowledge and understanding;
- the tasks of managers who support teachers in developing their knowledge and understanding.


## DEVELOPING PEDAGOGIC KNOWLEDGE

The implications for developing teachers' internalised knowledge can be illustrated by reference to another TTA-funded research project, *The Effective Teachers of Literacy* project carried out by Exeter University (Medwell *et al.*, 1998). In this study, many of the teachers known to be effective through a range of measures, including assessment of learning outcomes, demonstrated only a partial awareness of the full complexity of their classroom practice. In describing their teaching in a questionnaire these teachers said that they did not give much emphasis to word and sentence level work but were in fact observed teaching such material systematically and with considerable skill. Similarly, in response to a quiz about literacy, out of the context of the classroom the teachers were only able to talk about some aspects of literacy in rather limited ways even though they had just been observed teaching this effectively. Their knowledge and teaching seemed internalised to the point where they took for granted and were unaware of important aspects of what they did. They knew what they taught deeply, but very specifically, in the form in which they taught it.

The degree of internalisation of knowledge demonstrated by effective teachers has significant implications for teacher development and for the creation of knowledge about how to support this. New knowledge must be related to existing knowledge if it is to be retained or put to work. If existing knowledge is implicit it must be made explicit before its relationship with new knowledge can properly be explored. Learning using new knowledge also calls for a range of other conditions. A period of elapsed time, study, exposure to expertise and reflection to enable teachers to identify implications and to test and then internalise new approaches are all highlighted as important factors in seeing effective development within both the Kings (Askew *et al.*, 1998) and Exeter (Medwell *et al.*, 1998) studies and in other research relating to professional development and use of research. This is, of course, a complex and challenging process. As Rich (1993) notes, whilst assimilating new teaching concepts, strategies or curricula expert teachers behave in very similar ways to beginning teachers and experience similar patterns of uncertainty and discomfort, albeit for shorter periods.

## THE TASKS OF MANAGERS AND LEADERS

This raises interesting questions about the role of managers and leaders in teacher development. How do managers encourage in teachers the energy and skills to work through such challenging processes in order to ensure their practice is shaped by up-to-date knowledge and information? How do they enable teachers to review existing practices or to evaluate new evidence and debate objectively? The TTA standards (1997 and 1998a) set out a framework of requirements in this context. Research which reveals detailed key factors to be taken into account in the process of developing practice which meets these standards would no doubt contribute to increasingly research- and evidence-based management and leadership in school.

## THE ROLE WHICH RESEARCH CAN PLAY

The business of making the implicit explicit or of probing the gap between common sense accounts of classroom practice and the complex interactions which lie beneath the surface is, of course, the very fabric of high quality education research. Triangulated and detailed data about teachers, teaching and learning can, in expert hands, reveal important and distinctive patterns. If such patterns can then be communicated to teachers and teacher managers and leaders vividly and effectively, then research accounts have the capacity not only to acquaint them with new knowledge, ideas and approaches but also help them to recognise and evaluate objectively their existing practice.

For many teachers and researchers the capacity of research techniques to reveal existing practice has fuelled an interest in undertaking action research, in order to probe even more deeply their internalised skills and knowledge. This has created a good deal of effective continuing professional development and, from time to time, small-scale but cumulative case study work with the capacity reliably to inform the practices of colleagues. But TTA believes that not all teachers need to do research to be able to use it to reflect on and develop their own practice. Teachers working in School Based Research Consortia or alongside teacher researchers, for example in Study Groups like the one developed over two years by Jim Hines (1997) at John Mason School, have become interested in engaging with research done by others, as much as in engaging in research themselves. Nonetheless some will need to do research in order to increase teacher interest in research and raise demand and enthusiasm for it.

The TTA professional standards (1997 and 1998a) set out in some detail what teachers, including teacher managers, need to know and do about research and evidence at various points in their development. Similarly efforts are being made to build the potential contribution of research and evidence to improving pedagogy into the training programmes for headship both in terms of rooting the training programmes in research and, increasingly, in explicitly drawing to candidates' attention the potential contribution of research and evidence to school leadership.

## IMPLICATIONS FOR THE RESEARCH AGENDA

As will be clear, TTA's view of the Research Agenda, pedagogy and management challenges both researchers and teachers to develop more interactive and proactive models of the relationship between research and practice. For teachers, TTA proposes a model of effective research and evidence-based practice which involves:

- Seeing all forms of professional development, including research, as a means of improving teaching and raising standards rather than as an end in itself.
- Seeking out high quality research and evidence and developing skills in evaluating such material. This means abandoning the notion that teachers have to invent solutions to pedagogic problems on their own – or only

with the help of other teachers and seek and use help from a wide range of sources.

- Accepting that understanding and talking about teaching is a challenging but crucial component of continuing professional development – and a key to raising the esteem in which the profession is held. This means moving beyond the view that practice can only be understood or communicated in common sense terms.
- Interpreting research and evidence confidently in the light of good information about the needs of their own potential pupils, subjects, schools and communities. This means abandoning the victim mentality which treats external evidence, debate and critique as a threat to be resisted.
- convincing academic colleagues that teachers are equal but distinctive partners in the complex process of creating knowledge about teaching and using it to raise standards – and that the two processes are or can be related.

This analysis suggests that the tasks of managers and leaders who support teachers in developing knowledge, understanding and practice need themselves to be involved in demonstrating effective research and evidence-based practice, and in becoming skilled mediators of research. Those who teach and support school leaders and managers must also match deeds and words. For this to happen there is an urgent need for more, relevant pedagogic research communicated in ways which are accessible to classroom teachers and their leaders.

## THE TTA RESEARCH AGENDA

It is with regard to providing such material and re-forming teacher/researcher relationships and conceptions that TTA frames its understanding of the research agenda. In this context there are firm views about research priorities.

The TTA believes that first and foremost the research agenda needs to give greater priority to pedagogy. NFER calculated that under 30 per cent of the research submitted to the last RAE related to pedagogy. It seems to TTA highly likely that a significant element of this will have failed to probe deeply the knowledge, skills and beliefs which govern teachers' classroom practice, not least because of the difficulties in doing so. More significant still, as the DfEE Review (1998) notes, only a small proportion of this work will provide teacher-friendly accounts of research findings which contain extensive, vivid classroom exemplifications of findings.

The research agenda must also address issues of the credibility, relevance or accessibility of research outputs and the appropriate involvement of teachers and those who lead and manage them in research processes. Doing more research in traditional forms, on even the most pressing problems, will not resolve our current difficulties no matter how good the quality. The research agenda must address the demand for research as well as its supply. New ways of consulting teachers about the persistent problems they face in classrooms must be found and these results must feed into deliberations about which pedagogic research questions are both most urgent and most capable of being illuminated by research. The earlier analysis in this paper about the links between pedagogic research and management research would suggest that the outcomes of such processes should also be key factors in the development of the education management research agenda.

The very detailed consultation and advice taking which has gone into the different headship programmes does cast some light upon potential education management research priorities. In understanding needs and developing programmes in consultation with teacher trainers, teachers and academics, TTA has been able to draw directly upon a good deal of material relating to the content of the headship task. Education managers and leaders seeking to address strategic management issues, management structures, the context for school improvement and some of the key levers have been able to draw on extensive research findings and scholarship from within and beyond education research. The analysis of the differences, connections and similarities between leadership, headship and management has also been fully developed. But those wishing to address the all-important question of how to translate the resulting 'content' or the 'what' of the professional knowledge and understanding required for headship into activities which impact on teaching and learning, for example, are felt to be much less well served by existing research. Those who are working on the skills and attributes section of the National Standards for Head Teachers and the characteristics of highly effective headteachers used in the Leadership Programme for Serving Head Teachers turn for rigorous, detailed empirical research findings about the processes and beliefs which enable leaders and managers to help their teaching colleagues to develop their practice and raise standards.

Some evidence, as I indicated below, exists but more is needed. An important aim of these training and development programmes for headship is rediscovering the pedagogic leadership role of headteachers. The characteristics of highly effective headteachers who have seen a step change in standards of pupil achievement in their schools, suggests that the best heads are pedagogic leaders (TTA, 1999) who focus on questions such as 'how do education managers and leaders challenge and support average teachers to develop into effective ones?' How do they develop an accurate assessment of their personal effectiveness in providing effective teaching and learning? How do they help their colleagues do the same? Effective leaders are those who are continually looking for ways to improve. They need evidence to do so; evidence about their own practice, and tools for collecting and interpreting this and evidence about what is possible, what works and what does not work in a range of contexts. Of course researching what are in effect the details of human processes, their relationship with the personal learning styles of individuals and groups is difficult. Doing this in the context of schools where the link with teaching and learning in classrooms is paramount is doubly challenging. But developing effective models of how teachers and leaders develop is a line of enquiry which could lead to significant progress. Importantly it is one where researchers can be confident of a lively interest from potential users and where there is the potential for active and reflective engagement by users in the research process. The scale of investment proposed by the Government in the profession as a whole and in headship in particular provides the motor for this.

## STEPS IN THIS DIRECTION

TTA sees its own research agenda as focusing very directly upon creating informed demands for research in ensuring that the education research agenda responds to burning teaching and learning problems. To this end it has:

- Established four pilot School Based Research Consortia to enable schools, HEIs and LEAs to work together to develop and understand research and evidence-based practice and, increasingly, leadership. For example, the evolving roles of School Research Co-ordinators, teacher coaches and senior management teams all provide important insights into the contributions which insightful and self-aware leaders and managers can make to raising standards through research and evidence-based practice.
- Awarded grants to teachers to create debate about teachers' role in research and to promote teacher experiments in research dissemination and use. These include headteachers and senior managers directly as researchers and, explicitly but less directly, in setting the climate for other teachers conducting and disseminating their work.
- Commissioned larger scale pedagogic research projects and set in place experiments in dissemination and interpretation of this work.
- Built research- and evidence-based practice into its professional standards at all levels, including headship and into its continuing professional development activities.
- Mounted a major national conference for teachers on research and followed this up with questionnaires and a partnership programme of local conferences aimed at raising teacher expectations about what research can do for them and what they can do for research. TTA has also considered a questionnaire survey of teacher views of research to be followed up with further questionnaire work at the partnership conferences.
- Established a National Advisory Panel of Teachers for Research to offer government agencies, and others who seek it, a teacher perspective on research priorities, the implications of research for practice and the promotion of teaching as a research and evidence-based profession.

## SUMMARY

This paper has argued that current priorities for the education management research agenda should be shaped by and accede priority to work which takes pedagogy as the starting point and which explores the capacity of education management and leadership to contribute to the improvement of teaching and learning. It has suggested that the TTA professional standards offer an important context in which the connections between management and pedagogy can be understood and provides explicit support in exploring the responsibilities of teachers and managers with regard to interpreting and using research. It explores the specific importance of the forms of internalised knowledge required by classroom teaching. At its heart lies an exploration of the kinds of research topics and forms of research outputs which teachers who are experimenting with research and evidence-based practice see as being most likely to be credible and relevant to teachers and therefore to those who manage and lead them.

## REFERENCES

Askew, M., Brown, M., Rhodes, V., Johnson, D. and Wiliam, D. (1998) *Effective Teachers of Numeracy*, London: Kings College.

Desforges, C. (1995) How does experience affect theoretical knowledge for teaching, in *Learning and Instruction*, Vol. 5, 385–400. Great Britain: Elsevier Science Ltd.

Hargreaves, D. (1991) A common sense model of the professional development of teachers, in *Reconstructing Teacher Education: Teacher development*, Elliott, J. (ed.), London, Falmer Press.

Hillage, J., Pearson, R., Anderson, A. and Tamkin, P. (1998) *Excellence in Research on Schools*, DfEE (Department of Education and Employment).

Hines, J. (1997) Raising students' performance in relation to NFER CAT scores, in *Teaching as a Research Based Profession*, Teacher Training Agency.

Huberman, A.M. (1983) Improving social practice through the utilization of university-based knowledge, *Higher Education*, Vol. 12, No. 3, 257–272.

Joyce, D. and Showers, D. (1998) *Student Achievement through Staff Development*, New York and London: Longman.

Medwell, J., Wray, D., Poulson, L. and Fox, D. (1998) *Effective Teachers of Literacy*, Department of Education: University of Exeter.

Rich, I. (1993) Stability and change in teacher expertise, *Teachers and Teaching in Education*, Vol. 9, No. 2, 137–146.

TTA (1999) *Models of Excellence for Senior Head Teachers*, London: Teacher Training Agency.

TTA (1997 and 1998) *The Professional Standards for Teachers*, London: Teacher Training Agency.

TTA (1998b) *Off the Shelf*, a consultation paper, London: Teacher Training Agency.

TTA *The Report of the Proceedings Prepared for the Participants in the TTA Teachers and Research Conference held in December 1997*, London: Teacher Training Agency.

TTA (forthcoming) *Models of Excellence for Senior Headteachers*, London: Teacher Training Agency.

# 18

## Researching and Constructing Histories of the Field of Education Management

### HELEN GUNTER

### INTRODUCTION

The purpose of this chapter is to present, use, and problematise historical research within and about the field of education management in England and Wales. Writing histories of a field is demanding, partly because of the scope and complexity of the task, and also because it seeks to uncover, and no doubt challenge, the privileging of practice which is evident in the current education policy context. There is no policy imperative to undertake historical analysis in education. It is not one of the national standards, and NPQH/LPSH candidates are not required to know or understand the historical setting for the current training structure and curriculum. However, in pursuing an historical agenda I could be experiencing what Ladwig (1996) describes as the 'academic delusion that our debates matter to anyone other than ourselves' (p. 10), and I am also aware that I am on dangerous territory because seeking to raise questions about knowledge claims has been labelled as 'anti-management' (Caldwell and Spinks, 1998). The position taken is that these debates do matter to and for the practitioner, and to argue otherwise is to collude with the anti-intellectual climate in which the practitioner works (Hargreaves and Evans, 1997). I am under no illusions that the task I have set is huge, it is more about identifying possibilities than about providing answers. The chapter begins by raising questions which might start to open up the professional practice of field members to historical analysis. The chapter then goes on to present a conceptual analysis to support the investigation of those questions, before concluding with the presentation of a research agenda.

### FIELDS, TERRITORIES AND PRACTICE

Fitz (1997) argues that there are three types of knowledge worker who position themselves within the field: the academic in Higher Education Institutions (HEIs), the practitioner in a wide range of educational institutions, and the entrepreneur who generates income through the provision of courses and consultancy. The field is concerned with both practice and the study of practice (Bush, 1995), and so there is a complex network of participants who both 'do' it and study it at the same time. There is a plurality of professional scenarios for field participants, for example, a teacher may be a practising manager but at the same time undertaking a postgraduate course in education management; or a consultant may have previously been a headteacher and is currently involved in professional development; or a lecturer in an HEI is undertaking OFSTED inspections as a part of his/her income generation role at the same time as working on a piece of scholarly research. The balance within an individual's portfolio may be a product of personal discretion and/or the product of employer determination through contract compliance.

What this suggests is that a field is a metaphor for understanding the intellectual territory which members inhabit, there are spaces where field members locate themselves and their work, and there are boundaries which demarcate those who are within the field from those outside. In mapping and understanding the dynamics of this terrain it is useful to begin with the professional practice of field members. For example, the emphasis on practice is based on action and experience within the work place as a site of knowledge production, in which the practitioner can and does engage in the processes of description, theorising, and understanding. Another site of knowledge production could be the interaction between the HEI lecturer and the practitioner in a research supervision, in which descriptions, theories, and understandings developed in alternative settings to that currently inhabited by the practitioner are used and critically evaluated.

The traces of this professional practice can be found in the working lives of field members and is often documented in events, and papers, from institutional development plans, dissertations lodged in HEI libraries, through to a journal article. Examining these traces raises a wide range of options for understanding the knowledge claims of the field, how membership is understood, how boundaries are drawn, and where field members are and are not prepared to go.

The following are some suggested questions which could begin such an enquiry for individual and clusters of field members:

- **Practice:** what professional tasks do I perform and why? How might I describe and understand those tasks: teaching, administration, management, leadership, research? Is professional employment within a school or an HEI significant for the type of practice engaged in? Do the terms and conditions of employment make a difference? Is my professional identity separate from, or an intrinsic part of my life in general?
- **Knowledge:** what is my disciplinary background, and how does this impact on values and epistemology? What is controversial within the field and how are disputes aired and resolved within the field? What is agreed within the field and how is this revisited and confirmed?

- **Networks:** who do I associate formally and informally with, both external and internal, to the organisation which employs me? In what ways are those networks open or closed, and how is membership determined? What brings professional recognition and rewards: client satisfaction, credentials, publishing?
- **Context:** how has the growth in the management imperative through legislation and funding processes impacted on my professional practice? How is this shaping my practice?

These questions are not about improving field leadership and management, but about approaching the field because it is an interesting site to investigate the professional practice and epistemological claims of field members, and because it will add to our knowledge about intellectual work.

Distancing ourselves from action is not unusual or unproductive. As Strain (1997) argues in his introduction to an historical analysis of the BEMAS journal from 1972:

> Perhaps we can still learn from that past: not so much from the events themselves, but from a re-examination of the records of earlier research agendas which are preserved in this journal, professional and academic discussions of issues which seemed problematic, urgent, or in need of clarification and wider dissemination. What are the functions of a journal written by and for both teachers and academics? How much of what we record here represents substantive knowledge, with utility beyond the horizon of interests entertained by those who produced it? These questions are not regularly examined but they may be worth considering again now, when the demand for articles seems to outstrip the supply of significant new work and the supply of published material appears to exceed demand from practitioners?
>
> (213)

This leads on to further questions: who are knowledge workers within the field, where are the sites of knowledge production, and how do we understand knowledge work? Connell (1983) argues that intellectual work is undertaken by people who are not structurally defined as intellectuals. Intellectual work is a *labour process* in which we all think, write and talk. What distinguishes the academic is that historically the university has been constructed as a site of knowledge production, and that

> academic activity is no more and no less than a specialised kind of intellectual work, with its own particular milieu, audiences, customs, contradictions and possibilities.
>
> (239)

Conceptualising the school or the LEA as a site of knowledge production opens up the work of the practitioner to the importance of theorising as illustrated in the growth of site-based action research. Nevertheless, Connell (1983) goes on to show how the setting in which intellectual work takes place is important as it affects the relationship with practice, and how this is judged.

This setting is complex and includes the institutional or employment location, and is overlain by legalistic-policy interventions, and the structural context of culture and the economy. This enables the intellectual work of the field member to be understood in relation to the contradictions and dilemmas in their professional practice. For example, bidding for resources and contractual compliance is a growing external discipline on professional practice. If the field member is conceptualised as being in receipt of frameworks which have already decided the answers, and so the field member operationalises rather than challenges, then as Connell (1983) argues there is no intellectual work to be done. It is work but it is not *intellectual* work:

> Intellectual work is not necessarily radical, but it must always be subversive of authority in its own domain. There is nothing exotic about this, it is implicit in the very notion of intellectual *work*.
>
> (250, author's emphasis)

For those who work within professional development, whether in a school, LEA, HEI, or consultancy, this is the context in which what is relevant to the practitioner is being constructed and promoted.

Historical analysis is one aspect of intellectual work which enables the structures and systems in which we are working to be problematised and debated (Halpin and Fitz, 1990). Increasingly biographical work is important, and Deem (1996) provides an interesting account of what it has been like to experience and inhabit the border territories between disciplines. In this sense, historical analysis enables us to understand how our activities are labelled and graded, perhaps given status or even marginalised, and how various agendas and arguments endure while others are lost. As Skeggs (1997) argues:

> Wherever and whoever we are we are always implicated in relations of knowing. These relations have historically produced positions of power for the subjects and objects of knowledge to occupy which they may reproduce and challenge. The traditional distinction made between object and subject highlights the role knowledge plays in the (re)production of power and legitimacy. Certain knowledges are normalized, authorized and legitimated; only certain groups are seen to be respectable, to be worthy objects or subjects of knowledge.
>
> (18)

Opening up possible areas of enquiry into what is and is not respectable in the knowledge claims of the field is an interesting intellectual activity and raises issues about power and dominant interests which shape and structure what should and should not be known. Questions can be raised which extend our interest beyond the utility of theory, to understanding the context in which theory is produced and promoted.

Taking these issues forward through an historical analysis requires a theory of practice in order to describe and explain both the self within the process and the activity being charted and analysed. Theory can enable the historian to construct frameworks in which to understand actions and choices by people. I intend to use Bourdieu's theory of practice (Bourdieu, 1988, 1990) because it is both 'good to think with' (Jenkins, 1992, p. 12), and is dynamic in its development through and within empirical work. Bourdieu is critical of those who engage solely in armchair analysis because: 'they cross borders with empty suitcases – they have nothing to declare' (Harker *et al.*, 1990, p.x). In this sense I see this chapter as a process of unpacking and repacking in which the intellectual territory which is inhabited by field members can be explored.

Bourdieu (1990) uses thinking tools: firstly, *habitus* and its genesis from structured and unstructured dispositions which generate practices; secondly, the structure of the *field* in which agents take up positions in a struggle for legitimacy in both material and symbolic production; and, thirdly, the field of education is related to the dominant power relations in society. Thinking with these concepts facilitates connections between agency and structure, and problematises claims about neutrality. The individual's position can be explored in relation to their habitus, and how they seek to position them-selves: entering and moving within the field, and who s/he has aligned them-selves with. This is connected with status, recognition, and consecration: in other words, '. . . producers do not exist independently of a complex institu-tional framework which authorizes, enables, empowers and legitimizes them' (Johnson, 1993). Furthermore, this can be linked to power structures; and questions can be asked about whether field members are dominated by systems of economic and cultural production.

## RESEARCHING AND CONSTRUCTING HISTORIES OF THE FIELD OF EDUCATION MANAGEMENT

It is 20 years since Glatter (1979) reflected on the development of the field and argued that there is a continuum between micro and macro policy studies within education. However, while much has been written within the field since, little has been produced to describe, analyse and explain the purpose and practice of the field. What does exist is of high quality, detailed in content and analysis, and is helpful to the development of an historiography. There are bibliographies and literature reviews which either aim to give a general picture (Howell, 1978; Harries-Jenkins, 1984, 1985), or focus on a particular aspect (Fidler, 1994; Hall and Southworth, 1997). At different stages in the development of the field individuals have either sought to review changes and continuity (Baron, 1980; Bone, 1982), or have marked an anniversary (Hughes, 1997; Strain, 1997). Important contributions have been made about theory from the pioneering work of Baron and Taylor (1969) through to the devel-opment and application of conceptual pluralism from the 1980s: Bush (1986, 1995), Hoyle (1982, 1986), Hughes *et al.* (1985), Wallace and Hall (1994). Work by Greenfield and Ribbins (1993) in bringing together important papers and conversing about Greenfield's intellectual journey has both contributed to theory development, and an understanding of how habitus interacts with field dynamics. Increasingly, the history of practitioners and their work in schools, colleges and LEAs is being made visible (Preedy, 1989, Tomlinson *et al.*, 1999), and collaborations between field members in different sectors is supporting the productive use of biographical methods to understand the realities of practice (Ribbins, 1997).

What we can learn from all of this activity is that while historiography is important to some field members, overall it is a marginal activity. It seems that those outside the field write more about the knowledge claims, development and purpose than field members do (Ozga, 1987, 1992; Ball, 1990, 1995; Grace, 1995; Hartley, 1997, 1998). This is in contrast with field members in North America and Australia where charting and understanding field development is regarded as an integral part of professional practice (Callahan, 1962; Culbertson, 1988; Evers and Lakomski, 1991; Gronn, 1996; Burlingame and Harris, 1998). The strength of this type of work lies in the focus on understanding knowledge claims as controversial, and located in the often contradictory and stressful working lives of those who promote and challenge them. This stimulates intellectual work which can question what it is that we are being asked to do, why and who by, and so historical analysis can enable us to critically evaluate controversies and concerns about professional activities. Building on this I would like to use a way of thinking which would make the construction of critical histories of the field of education management both possible and open up possibilities. What is presented is not settled or rigid, and should be used to chart our way through the past rather than to measure historical prowess and methodological competence. It is based on a study of the work of those who have developed and used historical approaches to understanding educational change and in particular the relationship between policy and practice (Ozga, 1994). The approach taken is to present questions that a field member can ask themselves to support appropriate disclosure:

> it is . . . a lacework of meanings and significations which shape action and inquiry. Revealing this conceptual lacework involves making not only the products but also the processes of intellectual work visible so that other researchers can see how it is that particular meanings and significations have come to be salient, how they are grounded in empirical experience/data, and their place and relative importance in the researcher's conceptual framework.
>
> (Seddon, 1996, 211–212)

These questions are listed in Figure 18.1, and they are about linking the individual field member with the context in which a project is being constructed and conducted. The aim is to move beyond technicalities common within the research methods literature and instead foreground the choices on which the researcher has to clarify their position.

Seddon (1996) argues that asking the question: *what am I studying?* is not just about choosing a topic, but is about how the topic interconnects with

> What am I studying?
> What is my location within the study?
> What or who am I studying it for?
> What is my position on what I am studying?
> What is the value system underpinning my position?
> How do I intend to undertake the study?

**Figure 18.1**   Research questions

bigger issues. For example, an evaluation of the content, structure, and impact of the NPQH is important, but it will not of itself have sufficient scope to understand how the NPQH relates to professional reformation and development. Perhaps we should ask: why do we want headteachers to be able to write vision statements? Why do we describe parents and children as stakeholders? Why are claims being made that effective headship leads to effective schools? Broadening out questions asked about the present to ask questions about the past, enables the potential for alternative pasts and presents to be revealed, and in particular to understand the language we use.

These types of questions do not come out of mid-air but are linked to the person constructing the study and hence there is a need to ask: *what is my location within the study?* Seddon (1996) building on the work of Ozga (1994) describes this as the orientation of the researcher towards the project, or being explicit about the 'intellectual resources' (Seddon, 1996, p. 200) that are being drawn upon to design and conduct the study. For example, Hoyle (1982) uses concepts of power to describe micropolitics within educational organisations, while Wallace and Hall (1994) use a 'dual metaphor' (p. 23) based on political and cultural concepts to understand senior management teams. How we make these types of choices is not linked into a consumer approach to buying theory 'off the shelf' but is deeply engrained in who we are and how we see the world. Goodson (1997) has recently quoted C. Wright Mills as saying:

> the most admirable thinkers within the scholarly community . . . do not split their work from their lives. They seem to take both too seriously to allow such disassociation and they want to use each for the enrichment of others.
>
> (40)

Making this sort of analysis visible also enables the following question to be asked: *what is the value system underpinning my orientation?* By this I mean the beliefs and attitudes which matter, and in addition, perhaps a more messy analysis of what Ozga (1994) calls 'personal baggage' (p. 231). Developing a research biography is a productive process in which research questions which are of interest can be understood through habitus, and this is why Hargreaves and Evans' (1997) recent work on the anti-intellectual thrust of education policy resonated with me, because it raises questions about how we conceptualise the practitioner. If the field is about practice, then we could ask: is the development of capability about technical competence, or is it also about intellectual rigour in asking questions which may not lead directly to action but does lead to understanding (Hoyle, 1986)? The baggage I bring to this type of issue is whether the practitioner really is the expert as a result of experiential learning, or whether the practitioner is being set up to be accountable for the resourcing of education?

This connects with a further question: *what or who am I studying it for?* Historical studies could very easily be characterised as irrelevant, useless, and unfit for purpose. Nevertheless, not asking historical questions is dangerous, and it seems that unless we chart and analyse the past we are unable to resist unwelcome change in the present or to develop alternatives. It seems pertinent to ask: if historical work is not a central feature of field member activity is this because field members are not interested or is it because it is not fundable? How many postgraduate courses in education management have modules which seek to problematise management concepts by seeking to locate them within an historical framework? How many field members in HEIs are aware of the circumstances which brought about the validation of postgraduate courses in education management and the appointment of individuals and clusters of field members to teach it? How many of us are interested in how the field shifted its name from educational administration to management? Does it matter that it seems that incremental change is taking place with the adoption of educational leadership to describe field activities? Such questions are uncomfortable, and invite challenge that they are not the only questions and may even not be the appropriate ones. However, asking these types of questions enables field members to reflect on their position in the field, and what we regard as distinctive and valid both about and within our professional practice.

This raises questions about research design, and this leads on to: *how do I intend to structure a project?* My own work on the history of the field has been to chart and analyse developments through completing 16 interviews with field members in HEIs who have created and been involved in the development of the field from the 1960s. The prime purpose of the interview was to record the professional biography of the person and as the story unfolded I was able to probe on issues related to values, attitudes and professional location. In addition to this I was kindly given access to the papers from BEAS and BEMAS. These papers have enabled me to trace through professional biographical details and to support the mapping of domestic and international networks and boundaries. Engaging in historical investigation has enabled me to foreground my position and so avoid what Jenkins (1991) identifies as the epistemological and methodological 'fragility' integral to objectivist methods. I am a member of the field of education management and I am a part of its recent history and this is not a problem. The field member is not and cannot be a neutral agent or a conduit through which the past is transmitted.

## ISSUES IN RESEARCHING AND CONSTRUCTING HISTORIES OF THE FIELD OF EDUCATION MANAGEMENT

So far I have argued that the intellectual life of field members is embodied, and that they take up positions and are positioned within the field. However, much of who we are and what we stand for remains invisible, and while important work is being done to develop historical analysis within and about the field, this remains a minority activity. There seem to be some interesting issues which field members could engage with, and at the heart of this is to ask the question: what type of histories do we want to write about ourselves and to have others write about us? The following are some suggested issues with questions for the development of research agendas.

### i  Developing and Using Chronological Maps

When does history begin for field members? Do we allow chronology to be determined by legislation such as the 1988 Education Reform Act? There is the possibility for some interesting work on how field members understand and use significant turning points, and also recognise the continuities. In this sense we can no longer treat history as if it is useful in creating a management imperative, but rather we need to see historical analysis as problematic.

### ii  Making Links with the Policy Context

The field has established the importance of site-based policymaking, but an area of possible development is how we chart and theorise the connections between macro policy interventions and what professionals in schools, LEAs, and HEIs, actually do. This could revitalise the Glatter (1979) continuum and facilitate some productive links to enable the practitioner not just to respond to what is happening to them but to also understand it. This might enable alternative approaches to the TTA model of professional development to be created.

### iii  Institutional Location

An interesting area of research could be to look at how education management entered the curriculum within an HEI. Who supported it and how did the field establish its academic credentials? Within the polytechnic sector it would be interesting to research the role and impact of the CNAA on the early growth and structure of the field. As field members are located in schools, colleges, LEAs, and HEIs, it would be interesting to consider how this pattern of membership has grown and developed, and how field members make choices about their location. It would be interesting to ask questions about professional identity and how a practitioner with a management title and job description sees this type of work compared with other activities. Increasingly, leadership is replacing management, and how and why this label is being used and how it links to knowledge claims requires analysis.

## iv    Knowledge Claims

Analysing the published work of field members, such as books and articles, could enable an historical analysis of theory and research agendas to take place. Possibilities are numerous, but questions could be raised about how we might investigate the epistemological claims underpinning conceptual pluralism. Work could be undertaken into the intellectual resources which field members have been using, and we might ask when and why did we stop citing Baron and Taylor (1969) and start using Peters and Waterman (1982)? When did field members begin to use the language of vision and mission, fitness for purpose, effectiveness, improvement? Field members have used and have usefully transferred theory developed in non-educational settings (Bottery, 1992), but it would be interesting to research how the terminology and the assumptions underpinning 'best practice' in government policy is being engaged with by field members. Furthermore, field members in England and Wales have been given access to education management models developed in different cultural and historical settings, and while important work is being done to critically evaluate this work (Adler *et al.*, 1993; Smyth, 1989, 1993), it would be interesting to develop explanatory comparative approaches so that we can understand the contextual setting in which models are developed and 'whether, and how, international networks have promulgated their ideas from one country to the next' (Gordon and Pierce, 1993, p. 180).

## v    Networks

Field members are a part of networks and it would be interesting to map the formal links both at home and internationally. Why was BEAS formed? Why did it become BEMAS? How is its membership made up and how might this be significant for the aims of the organisation? What are the connections with international organisations such as CCEA/CCEAM, UCEA, and the IIP? Boundaries are interesting here, and as Fitz (1997) shows where we publish is linked to habitus, it is where we invest capital and seek rewards through prestige and recognition.

## SUMMARY

In summary, historical work seems to be telling us that education management is a vibrant field in which members in schools, LEAs, and HEIs have worked collaboratively and productively to develop understanding and practice. However, this work also tells us that this is a field which does not take its history seriously enough, and seems to put more faith in developing visions of the future. McCulloch (1997) argues that those working within educational studies need to be wary about this because:

> these notions of the future present the twenty-first century as a blank canvas upon which may be projected the hopes and fears of the present. They also serve to facilitate a disregarding of the past, since it appears that the problems that afflicted education in the nineteenth and twentieth centuries will somehow cease to exist after the year 2000.

(22)

In this sense using Bourdieu's thinking tools to open up our intellectual suitcase can enable field members to focus on their own practice and purpose. This has a value beyond performance management, and it is about sensitising field members towards their own historical involvement within the field. It seems that unless we know and understand our origins then we will have difficulty in presenting our work as distinctive and based on robust knowledge claims. Any moves towards relabelling our activities as leadership or improvement should not be based on marketing and repackaging strategies, but on understanding what the label means for the nature and type of intellectual work which field members engage in. In this sense the field will evolve and develop, and change will be based on reflexivity about purpose rather than be a reaction to policy interventions. As Bourdieu (1990) argues:

> I think that enlightenment is on the side of those who turn their spotlight on our blinkers. . .

(16)

## ACKNOWLEDGEMENTS

I would like to thank the 16 people who allowed me to interview them about their professional practice and involvement in the field of education management. It has been a privilege to work with them and to be given access to their professional work and lives. I would also like to thank the officers of BEAS/BEMAS for giving me access to formal documents to use in my research.

## REFERENCES

Adler, S., Laney, J. and Packer, M. (1993) *Managing Women*, Buckingham: Open University Press.

Ball, S.J. (1990) Management as moral technology: A Luddite analysis, in S. J. Ball, (ed.) *Foucault and Education*, London: Routledge.

Ball, S.J. (1995) Intellectuals or technicians? The urgent role of theory in educational studies, *British Journal of Educational Studies* Vol. XXXXIII, No. 3, 255–271.

Baron, G. (1980) Research in educational administration in Britain, *Educational Administration* Vol. 8, No. 1, 1–33.

Baron, G. and Taylor, W. (eds.) (1969) *Educational Administration and the Social Sciences*, London: The Athlone Press.

Bone, T.R. (1982) Educational administration, *British Journal of Educational Studies,* Vol. XXX, No. 1, February 32–42.

Bottery, M. (1992) *The Ethics of Educational Management*, London: Cassell.

Bourdieu, P. (1988) *Homo Academicus*, Cambridge: Polity Press in association with Blackwell Publishers, Oxford.

Bourdieu, P. (1990) *In Other Words: Essays towards a reflexive sociology* translated by Matthew Adamson, Cambridge: Polity Press in association with Blackwell Publishers, Oxford.

Burlingame, M., and Harris, E. L. (1998) Changes in the field of educational administration in the United States from 1967 to 1996 as a revitalization movement, *Educational Management and Administration* Vol. 26, No. 1, 21–34.

Bush, T. (1986) *Theories of Educational Management*, London: Paul Chapman.

Bush, T. (1995) *Theories of Educational Management*, second edition, London: Paul Chapman.

Caldwell, B. J. and Spinks, J. M. (1998) *Beyond the Self Managing School*, London: Falmer Press.

Callahan, R. A. (1962) *Education and the Cult of Efficiency*, Chicago: University of Chicago Press.

Connell, R. W. (1983) *Which Way is Up? Essays on sex, class and culture*, Sydney: George Allen and Unwin.

Culbertson, J.A. (1988) A century's quest for a knowledge base, in N. J. Boyan (ed.) *Handbook of Research on Educational Administration*, New York: Longman.

Deem, R. (1996) Border territories: a journey through sociology, education and women's studies, *British Journal of Sociology of Education*, Vol. 17, No. 1, 5–19.

Evers, C. and Lakomski, G. (1991) *Knowing Educational Administration*, Oxford: Pergamon.

Fidler, B. (1994) State of the art review: Staff appraisal, *School Organisation and Management Abstracts*, Vol. 13, No. 2, 61–70.

Fitz, J. (1997) *Research and Restructuring: Problems and Prospects for Educational Management Studies*, paper presented to the ESRC Seminar, Redefining Educational Management, Forte Posthouse Hotel, Cardiff, 9–10 October 1997.

Glatter, R. (1979) Education 'policy' and 'management': one field or two? in T. Bush, R. Glatter, J. Goodey and C. Riches (eds.) (1979) *Approaches to School Management*, London: Harper Educational Series.

Goodson, I. (1997) 'Trendy theory' and teacher professionalism, in A. Hargreaves and R. Evans (1997) *Beyond Educational Reform: Bringing teachers back in*, Buckingham: OUP.

Gordon, L. and Pearce, D. (1993) Why compare? A response to Stephen Lawton, *Journal of Education Policy*, Vol. 8, No. 2, 175–181.

Grace, G. (1995) *School Leadership: Beyond Education Management*, London: Falmer.

Greenfield, T. and Ribbins, P. (eds.) (1993) *Greenfield on Educational Administration*, London: Routledge.

Gronn, P. (1996) From transactions to transformations, *Educational Management and Administration*, Vol. 24, No. 1.

Hall, V. and Southworth, G. (1997) *Headship, School Leadership and Management*, Vol.

17, No. 2, 151–170.

Halpin, D. and Fitz, J. (1990) Researching grant maintained schools, *Journal of Education Policy*, Vol. 5, No. 2, 167–180.

Hargreaves, A. and Evans, R. (1997) Teachers and educational reform, in A. Hargreaves and R. Evans (eds.) (1997) *Beyond Educational Reform: Bringing teachers back in*, Buckingham: Open University Press.

Harker, R., Mahar, C. and Wilkes, C. (eds.) (1990) *An Introduction to the Work of Pierre Bourdieu*, London: Macmillan.

Harries-Jenkins, G. (1984) Education management: Part 1, *School Organisation and Management Abstracts*, Vol. 3, No. 4, 213–233.

Harries-Jenkins, G. (1985) Education management: part 2. A bibliography, *School Organisation and Management Abstracts*, Vol. 4, No. 1, 5–16.

Hartley, D. (1997) The new managerialism in education: A mission impossible? *Cambridge Journal of Education*, Vol. 27, No. 1, 47–58.

Hartley, D. (1998) In search of structure, theory and practice in the management of education, *Journal of Education Policy*, Vol. 12, No. 1, 153–162.

Howell, D. A. (1978) *A Bibliography of Educational Administration in the UK*, Windsor: NFER .

Hoyle, E. (1982) Micropolitics of educational organisations, *Educational Management and Administration*, Vol. 10, 87–98.

Hoyle, E. (1986) The management of schools: theory and practice, in E. Hoyle and A. McMahon, *World Yearbook of Education 1986: The management of schools*, London: Kogan Page.

Hughes, M. (1997) From bulletin to journal, *Educational Management and Administration*, Vol. 25, No. 3, 243–263.

Hughes, M., Ribbins, P. and Thomas, H. (1985) *Managing Education: The system and the institution*, Eastbourne: Holt, Rinehart and Winston.

Jenkins, K. (1991) *Re-Thinking History*, London: Routledge.

Jenkins, R. (1992) *Pierre Bourdieu*, London: Routledge.

Johnson, R. (1993) Pierre Bourdieu on art, literature and culture, editor's introduction in P. Bourdieu, *The Field of Cultural Production*, Cambridge: Polity Press.

Ladwig, J. G. (1996) *Academic Distinctions*, London: Routledge.

McCulloch, G. (1997) Marketing for the millennium: Education for the twenty-first century, in A. Hargreaves and R. Evans (eds.) (1997) *Beyond Educational Reform: Bringing teachers back in*, Buckingham: Open University Press.

Ozga, J. (1987) Studying education policy through the lives of the policymakers: An attempt to close the macro-micro gap, in S. Walker and L. Barton, *Changing Policies, Changing Teachers: New directions for schooling?* Milton Keynes: Open University Press.

Ozga, J. (1992) Review essay: Education management, in *British Journal of Sociology of Education*, Vol. 13, No. 2, 279–280.

Ozga, J. (1994) Frameworks for policy analysis in education, in D. Kallos and S. Lindblad (eds.) *New Policy Contexts for Education: Sweden and the United Kingdom educational reports No. 42/1994*, Sweden: Umea University.

Peters, T. and Waterman, R. (1982) *In Search of Excellence*, Glasgow: Harper/Collins.

Preedy, M. (ed.) (1989) *Teachers' Case Studies in Educational Management*, London: Paul Chapman Publishing Ltd.

Ribbins, P. (ed.) (1997) *Leaders and Leadership in the School, College and University*, London: Cassell.

Seddon, T. (1996) The principal of choice in policy research, *Journal of Education Policy*, Vol. 11, No. 2, 197–214.

Skeggs, B. (1997) *Formations of Class and Gender*, London: Sage.

Smyth, J. (ed.) (1989) *Critical Perspectives on Educational Leadership*, London: The Falmer Press.

Smyth, J. (ed.) (1993) *A Socially Critical View of the Self Managing School*, London: Falmer Press.

Strain, M. (1997) Records of Achievement, *Educational Management and Administration*, Vol. 25, No. 3, 213–242.

Tomlinson, H. Gunter, H. and Smith, P. (1999) *Living Headship: Voices, values and vision,* London: Paul Chapman Publishing.

Wallace, M. and Hall, V. (1994) *Inside the SMT: Teamwork in Secondary School Management*, London: Paul Chapman Publishing.

# Index